I'm STILL a Keeper

Successfully Parent and Partner with Your Teenager

Ray W. Lincoln

ISBN: 978-0-9961208-5-2 (Paperback)
Library of Congress Control Number: 2015959848

Published in the United States of America
Apex Publications
Littleton, CO
January of 2016

Dedication

To all the parents who have done their best,
have struggled and failed at times,
felt the need of forgiveness,
were not perfect,
and yet perceived their parenting as a calling
to raise a new generation
that could make the world a better place.

Other Books by Ray W. Lincoln

I May Frustrate You, But I'm a Keeper
INNERKINETICS
A Journey Through Fear to Confidence
Introduction to Faith and the Temperaments
The InnerKinetics® of Type
Intelligently Emotional
Your Child's Emotional World, Parts 1 and 2
Break Free!
I'm STILL A Keeper!

What This Book Will Do for You

Travel a journey for parent and teen that will:

For the parent:
Help you understand your teen and how he/she is designed
Encourage a path that respects your teen's temperament and design
Create meaningful bonding
Describe what is taking place in teen development
Deal with the teen mind, brain, and temperament
Supply a new-found confidence in parenting your teen
Prepare your teen for adulthood according to their inner blueprint.

For the teen:
Set a path for understanding how you are made
Answer why emotions flare and what to do about it
Give direction for your life
Help with social issues according to your temperament
Explain how you function and develop
Focus on the big important issues of your teenage years
Help you find your way in life early

CONTENTS

Preface

Introduction

A Final Prayer

Preface

Why This book?

Parenting changes with the onset of the teens. The changes — physical, mental, and emotional — in our child's development demand different approaches. The teens' growing understanding of themselves and their mounting desires for social encounters, freedom, and independence (even though they may still want the security blanket of parents) poses the question, "Are the pre-puberty parenting methods still the most effective?" Very little is said about what the changes are or how to make these much needed changes. Therefore, this book has been called for as a follow-up volume to my previous Amazon bestseller, *I'm a Keeper.* If your child is from nine years old through their teens, this book is for you.

Titled *I'm STILL a Keeper* and subtitled *Successfully Parent and Partner with Your Teenager*, it suggests the challenge of these years and the need for sustained hope and encouragement for both parents and teens. However, a knowledge and practical application of temperament is still the most important element in parenting your teen. How is it to be applied in teenage years as opposed to pre-teen parenting? What heartaches will it save? Now that the teen is beginning the journey of self-understanding, how do we lead them with appropriate speed to maturity via the development of their strengths? The pages ahead will attempt to answer these issues and many more.

The degree to which we know and understand our inner design will determine many of our choices in our teens. This plays out with a sense of urgency since how we develop profoundly affects our future and the journey of the teenager is all too short for repeated missteps. Join me in this change of direction for parenting and the introduction of new methods for teenage parenting. May the wisdom of the ages and the confirmation and discoveries of our own age be yours from which to benefit.

As always, I am deeply indebted to more people than I can name or even remember. I am, as we all are, a product of our expanding relationships and continued learning. For the expertise of my editor, Dr. Marian Bland, and my ever-devoted and skilled partner, Mary Jo Lincoln, I express gratitude which is more deeply felt than I can express.

Ray W. Lincoln

Littleton, Colorado, USA

Introduction

Raging hormones, introduction to a world of drugs, pornography, sex, Internet addictions, and street philosophies that shout, "Just follow your heart...The world owes you...If it feels good, do it" — this is the world of the today's teen. Many other misleading guidelines for life add to the growing pains that face the teenagers of today. The gauntlet has been thrown down and parenting faces provocations it has never faced before.

The tendency is to dissect each issue, such as sexual urges, the drug culture, and challenges of an unedited Internet, in search of magic answers. But as helpful as that may be, there is a root cause for much of this behavior and it is found in our basic drives. It's the way we are designed and how we handle or mishandle who we are that holds many answers parents can effectively apply.

Teenagers are humans and that's where we will start. We must understand ourselves, how we function, and how we can best equip ourselves as parents and as teenagers to combat the issues that could derail us for life or leave a scar that we will deeply regret. Am I overstating it? You decide. However, I would suggest to parents that you help your teens discover themselves and, at the same time, that you deepen your understanding of yourself and of how the differences between you and your teen are impacting your relationship and how the teen determines the value of your help. Parenting requires this knowledge in order to succeed.

For teens, I suggest that this understanding of yourself will educate you and help you make your own choices in the face of reliable knowledge about why you think, feel, and act the way you do and why teens are not all the same. You will learn how you can run the teenage race and win so that you will be the best you can be and not miss out on the fun along the way.

We will look at the brain and the mind. The brain is the most complex and sophisticated processing device in this universe. It is the main organ of the body and it serves us well to take care of it and use it efficiently. The mind is the most amazing creative, non-physical instrument in the universe. It is our virtual world. Rocket science is simple in comparison to the complexity of human emotions and the mysterious powers and abilities of the mind.

Where should we begin our understanding of teenagers? Temperament. Although temperament is hard-wired and can only be modified, not changed, environment does its best to change us. Its influence is less important than the development of our temperament's core strengths. People often choose to do the opposite of what the influences of environment are urging them to do.

Here's another issue we must not forget: Should we influence a teen's values? What do you think? Beliefs and values (we can think of values as beliefs) are the mental force behind actions. Want good behavior? Instill good beliefs.

As we have said, most of the help available today for parenting teens and for teens themselves to find their way through teenage focuses on problem behaviors or social issues, such as drugs, sex, gangs, violence, damaging motivations, and anger in the home. We will not lose sight of these, but I want to emphasize a forgotten factor of the greatest importance: the development of your teen's temperament impacts in one way or another their beliefs and all of a teen's challenging issues. When we focus on this, we offset many problems and create a life-direction that will pay off in all of our teen's concerns. Getting the teen machine going in the right direction saves a lot of damaging side trips.

This emphasis on understanding our temperament (core drives) is not new. In fact, I have drawn from the vast literature of the last almost 2,500 years and, in particular, the contributions of Plato, Aristotle, Jesus, Adickes, Carl Jung, Myers-Briggs and their followers' many writings, David Keirsey, Stephen Montgomery (who writes a very readable summery of temperament), and many others who have left a trail of knowledge that none of us can afford to ignore. I am a limited human and am clearly reliant on those who have gone before. To all of them I give credit.

Section One:
Understanding

1: Who Am I? — Identity Is Unfolding!

Parents don't often think of identity as a teenage crisis. More likely, they think of drugs or sex. But the hidden struggles are often causes or triggers for the obvious challenges that a teen faces. Making good decisions looms large in a teen's maturing process. So, as we begin our understanding of teenagers to parent them successfully, the identity crisis and struggle comes to the fore.

The Teen's Search for Personal Identity

"Who am I?" is no purely academic question that is unrelated to life. For the teenager, it unfolds as an unrealized search for the most part. Yet it is basic to all the struggles they will face. When we don't know who we are, we try to be whoever the present circumstance call for us to be. Trouble can then brew.

As their horizons broaden and the need to relate meaningfully to many people becomes more demanding, the puzzle of who they are will tend to become a conscious quest for the teen. The sooner they can be introduced to their core strengths and understand how these will equip them for successful and satisfying interactions with the world, the better. Seldom does the teen ask for help in this personal issue of self-discovery.

Unfortunately, when we are in our teens, we try to understand ourselves based on our experiences and the way we perform or behave. Whenever we are in the spotlight and we are applauded for our actions, we think this is what we were designed to be and need to be. Acting like a fool can get attention; so can presenting a good paper in class. The question is not "Which action defines me?" but "Who am I?" And the answer to that question might be quite unrelated to our actions or our achievements.

For the teen to take center stage among their friends and to be applauded can be a moment when they feel they have penetrated the mystery of who they are and rocketed to pristine clarity on the issue simply because they are accepted! The teen can easily think, "Surely being accepted is a clear indication that this is me at my best." But acceptance is an unreliable measure of our true identity. Whenever we are accepted, we are tempted to repeat the performance for more of the head spinning feeling, even if it is uncomfortable or unnatural to act out in the way we did. Our behavior and the acceptance of it is deceiving us. Friends can be wrong for many reasons about who is the real me and about what constitutes acceptable behavior. See that your teens do not define themselves by their behavior — good or bad — and certainly not by the sole measure of what gained acceptance.

The measure of who we are is not in what we do or even in what we are approved for. It is in the sense of inner approval, the fulfilling feelings that we have when we are behaving according to who we are designed to be. Understanding our temperament requires a self-verification of what really beats to the drum of our true selves — hence, the subjective nature of the questions in the Adult Temperament Key. Help your teen get to this self-validation and feel the comfort it gives to live and act according to their temperament and its preferences.

A trial and error method in search for identity can cause a teen their most embarrassing moments. Wounded pride, damaged relationships, and plunging into unhelpful relationships can all be a bi-product of false self-identification. In trial and error, the errors can hurt and lower the self-image.

Parents who have taken note of their teen's recurring preferences may be better judges than the teenager himself as to who he really is. Although the teen may not agree, listening to parental advice can help, as long as the parent is not trying to make the teen into a clone of himself. The maturity the teen is moving toward involves the willingness and the understood wisdom of listening.

For both parent and teen, there is a better way of discovering our self-identities. Yes, and the parents, too, should complete the temperament key so they see how their teen sees them and how two very different identities can clash unknowingly. Even though the teen has had only a few meaningful years to begin understanding his or her own inner preferences, completing the Adult Temperament Key is the best way to know themselves and to begin the journey of a conscious self-understanding.

A teen should be encouraged to try to answer the questions of the Adult Temperament Key by how he or she truly feels on the inside. Follow the instructions for the key carefully and redo the temperament key annually throughout the teenage years to help them sharpen this inner self-awareness. It is one of the greatest gifts that parents can give their teen.

The Effect on Behavior

When we don't feel good about ourselves, changing the way we act can become the only guiding experiment in finding ourselves, but it can lead to good or bad results. Behavior that follows the way we are designed is self-approving and fulfilling. Also, behavior that is devoid of guilt or embarrassment allows all the good emotions of personal worth to surface. Therefore, knowing themselves will, for the teen, boil down to feeling the fulfillment and satisfaction that living according to their inner blueprint will bring. Good behavior follows.

Self-image can also be helped greatly by a true understanding of ourselves. Teens (and adults, also) who are comfortable with themselves and with their choice of actions will be calmer and appear more in control of themselves. Therefore, they will feel a greater sense of self-worth. Want good behavior? Then help your teen to find the drives that bring satisfaction to them, not just the behavior that generates peer or even parental approval. Once those drives or core strengths have been found, using them and not misusing them is the path to being our best.

Personal Identity Challenges Us All

No struggle for the teen is a greater challenge than the search for who they really are. Nothing will be more helpful than the temperament key and the reading and discovery of their temperament's strengths. The reason is that we must have a measure against which we can evaluate ourselves. Temperament is a discovery of our core strengths and the characteristics we share with others who are like us in their inner design. In other words, it reveals why we and others who are like us think, feel, and prefer to act the way we do. It solves for the teen many of the mysteries of what, why, and how we are what we are and do what we do.

It is not for the parent to tell the teen which temperament they are but to lead them to their own self-enlightenment and self-approval. Everyone who completes the key, including the teen, must self-verify: "This is me."

The benefits of knowing ourselves accurately will be, among other things, a sense of our purpose and direction in life. Also, it gives us a platform for sound decision-making, a foundation for building our values, and a feeling of personal worth. It instills a growing clarity for a satisfying future and a hope that we can be successful creatures. All this the teen needs on the journey to maturity and the parent can help them with the knowledge of temperament.

When We Don't Understand Ourselves

How can we operate our complex human systems well if we don't understand them? If we are wrong in whom we feel we are, we operate outside of our design and that can spell trouble. And as we have emphasized, not all of us are the same design. Using an automobile analogy, do we see ourselves as a Chevy or Maserati? Nearly all teens figure they are Maseratis, but they are not all Maseratis. We set back the attainment of maturity when we misunderstand who we are. We can also have a bad accident if we operate our Chevy as if it were a Maserati.

All the big questions of life are not necessarily answered in the teens, but the need to have a clear idea of who we are can save a lot of unneeded side trips, wasted time, and "bent fenders." Help your teens with self-identification of their true selves and you will have saved them many false starts and damaging side trips. A true platform for good decision-making always starts with this awareness and confidence.

2: Get Understanding or Go It Alone — Your First Step

If your child is a teenager, are you still saying, "I don't understand my child?" Are you puzzled at why your child feels, thinks, and acts the way he does because it's unlike you? Then you have not understood how your child is made on the inside and, therefore, understanding your child's temperament will be the most important source for your information and understanding.

We should never start a building by constructing the roof first or trying to apply the paint and trim to unconstructed walls. Foundations are essential to a successful project. Temperament is your foundation in understanding your child or teenager. Hence, this most important chapter.

Parents should know they need to forge good relationships with their children as early as possible. It will pay off big time in the teenage years for both the parent and the teen if the temperament of the child is known before they enter teenage and both the parent and child sense that they know each other. It creates comfort in the relationship, without which the child will not bond with the parent. Knowing their temperament or why they think, feel and act the way they do is the foundational knowledge for creating a comfortable and desired relationship. How can you relate well to someone you don't know? And from the child's or teen's point of view, why take advice and guidance from someone you feel uncomfortable with?

So, if you are reading this book to prepare yourself and your child for the teenage years and to offset the possible damage that teenagers can do to themselves and others, make sure you have completed the Child Temperament Key on your preteen. But if your child is already a teenager, don't despair. You can still bond and gain all the understanding of them you need. However, you will need to sit down with your teen and complete the Adult Temperament Key together, whether you have already done the Child Temperament Key or not on your pre-teen. They are no longer young children; they are self-evolving personages in a way they have not been before. They must enter the process of self-evaluation and discovery.

The Adult Temperament Key is written in language that your young teen may need to have explained, so they may need your help. You are likely to hear, "What does that mean?" Explain the question for them as best you can. It goes without having to be emphasized that to have done the Adult Temperament Key yourself will prepare you for the questions your child is likely to ask.

The temperament key seems to be an especially hard document to understand because it is asking about subjective preferences that even adults often have never considered. A teen doesn't have this subjective understanding of themselves because they have a much shorter history of self-knowledge and they are also short on the experiences that such questions require. Therefore, don't be worried if they cannot answer all the questions with certainty. Completing the temperament key is the first and most important step to self-understanding and identity. You should complete the key with them each year of their teenage so that their self-knowledge increases and their sense of who they are and their self-confidence improves.

As is repeated below, PLEASE FOLLOW THE INSTRUCTIONS CAREFULLY. Yes, even if you think you know them. Some temperaments may find this grating but in this case, accuracy begins with following the instructions. Read the instructions with your teen. They need to know what is required before they start.

When answering the questions, don't tell your teen what you think the answer should be. At this early stage of the teenage years, you can suggest an answer after they have struggled with the question, but don't tell them what it "should" be. Allow them to disagree with you if they feel like it. Really, the whole process is for teens to discover for themselves what is going on inside of them.

They MUST self-affirm the answers and also the selection of their temperament from the descriptions that they will read after they have completed the temperament key.

Keep your mind on alert as you listen to your teen's answers. You will learn a lot or be happily confirmed about your assumptions of who they are. Listen particularly to what in their answers surprises you. Again, don't try to make them understand what you think they are. By questioning, help them find who they are. You are looking for a self-understanding and self-verification of their temperament.

Finally, your teen needs to know of your interest in helping them find how they have been made. Parenting a teen is not just supplying food, shelter, clothing, shuttle service, and acting as the correction officer. So, completing the temperament key together with them is the start of the process of successful teen parenting and bonding.

Complete the Adult Temperament Key Together with your Teen

The Temperament Key for Adults
Instructions

Both the Adult Temperament Key and Child Temperament Key that I use have been developed using the principles of research into temperament that Myers-Briggs, Keirsey and Harkey-Jourgensen have used for the development of their assessments. These principles, when used in assessments, have proved very reliable and can be depended upon. Any of the above named assessments of temperament are excellent guides to the discovery of how you are made on the inside.

As long as you carefully follow the instructions for each of the Temperament Keys presented here, you should get excellent results.

This is a very positive assessment. We are looking for your strengths, not your weaknesses. There are no wrong answers since it is a self-evaluation. However, be as accurate as possible. Read these instructions carefully since a knowledgeable guide is not looking over your shoulder, and you can't ask for help. <u>It is imperative that you answer according to these instructions.</u>

- Answer these questions according to your preferences (what you prefer), not according to what you think others would have you become.
- Answer each question individually. Don't try to be consistent.
- Aim to get through the key in about 15 minutes or less.
- Think carefully about each answer; but avoid over-thinking, which can lead to confusion. If you are over-thinking, ask yourself: "What am I the most?"
- Again, let me put it this way: You will see yourself as both (a) and (b) in some of the questions. Your answer should be what you see yourself to <u>be</u> the <u>most</u>, or what you <u>prefer</u> the <u>most.</u>
- Your preferences are often different at home than at work. This can be due to the fact that at work certain things are required of you, and therefore they have become your work preferences. You prefer to do it that way at work, since that's what is good for you. If your work preferences differ from your home preferences, answer according to your home preferences.
- We want to know what really beats in your breast, what really satisfies, fulfills, or pleases you the most.

The results should be accurate, but if you attend one of my seminars ask to be checked again. It's a service we provide. When you read the descriptions of the temperaments in chapters 8, 10 and 13 of *I'm a Keeper* you will determine whether they match your results in the temperament key. If they do not match the descriptions, then you answered with something else in mind, and you will need to switch to the temperament most like you.

This check on your answers is very helpful. The ones who are most likely to be confused about themselves are the NFs.

They are the complicated temperament and have the greatest difficulties in understanding themselves for that understandable reason. Now, proceed with careful thought.

ADULT TEMPERAMENT KEY

Check (A) or (B) for each question. Please answer ALL questions.

1. At social gatherings do you prefer to
   _____ A. Socialize with everyone
   _____ B. Stick to your friends

2. Are you more in touch with
   _____ A. The real world
   _____ B. The world inside your mind; the world of possibilities

3. Do you rely more on, or take more notice of
   _____ A. Your experiences
   _____ B. Your hunches/ gut feelings

4. Are you (most of the time)
   _____ A. Cool, calm and collected
   _____ B. Friendly and warm

5. When evaluating people do you tend to be
   _____ A. Impersonal and frank
   _____ B. Personal and considerate

6. Do you mostly feel a sense of
   _____ A. Urgency/upset if you are not on time
   _____ B. Relaxed about time.

7. When you see a mess do you
   _____ A. Have an urge to tidy it up
   _____ B. Feel reasonably comfortable living with it

8. Would you describe yourself as
   _____ A. Outgoing/ demonstrative/easy to approach
   _____ B. Somewhat reserved/private

9. Which are you best at
   _____ A. Focusing on details
   _____ B. Catching the big picture, the connections, the patterns

10. Children should be
    _____ A. Made to be more responsible
    _____ B. Encouraged to exercise their imagination and make-believe more

14

11. When making decisions, are you more influenced by
_____ A. The facts/impersonal data
_____ B. Personal feelings

12. Do you feel more yourself when giving
_____ A. Honest criticism
_____ B. Support, approval, and encouragement

13. Do you work best
_____ A. Scheduled; to deadlines
_____ B. Unscheduled; no deadlines

14. For a vacation, do you prefer to
_____ A. Plan ahead of time
_____ B. Choose as you go

15. When you are with others do you usually
_____ A. Initiate the conversation
_____ B. Listen and tend to be slow to speak

16. Most of the time, facts
_____ A. Should be taken at face value.
_____ B. Suggest ideas, possibilities, or principles.

17. Do you mostly feel
_____ A. In touch with the real world
_____ B. Somewhat removed

18. When in an argument/discussion do you care more about
_____ A. Defending your position and being right
_____ B. Finding harmony and agreement

19. With others do you tend to be
_____ A. Firm
_____ B. Gentle

20. Do you see yourself as
_____ A. Predictable
_____ B. Unpredictable

21. Do you mostly prefer to
_____ A. Get things done; come to closure
_____ B. Explore alternatives; keep options open

22. After two hours at a party are you
_____ A. More energized than when you arrived
_____ B. Losing your energy

23. Which best describes you
_____ A. Down to earth, practical
_____ B. Imaginative, an idea person

24. Which do you finally rely on more
_____ A. Common sense
_____ B. Your intuition/insights or your own analysis

25. In other people, which appeals to you most
_____ A. A strong will
_____ B. Warm emotions

26. Are you more controlled by
_____ A. Your head/thought
_____ B. Your heart/emotions

27. Are you typically
_____ A. Eager to get decisions made
_____ B. Not keen on making decisions

28. On the whole do you spend your money
_____ A. Cautiously
_____ B. Impulsively

29. When you have lost energy, do you find yourself mostly
_____ A. Seeking out people
_____ B. Seeking out solitude/a quiet corner

30. Do dreamers
_____ A. Annoy you somewhat
_____ B. Fascinate and interest you

31. Do you rely more
_____ A. On your five senses
_____ B. On your sixth sense/intuition

32. Are you more
_____ A. Tough-minded
_____ B. Tender-hearted

33. Would you more likely choose to be
_____ A. Truthful
_____ B. Tactful

34. Do you see yourself as more
_____ A. Serious and determined
_____ B. Relaxed and easygoing

35. Do you feel more comfortable when
_____ A. Things are decided
_____ B. Your options are still open

36. Would you say you mostly
_____ A. Show your feelings readily
_____ B. Are private about your feelings and keep them inside

37. Would you prefer
_____ A. To be in touch with reality
_____ B. To exercise a creative imagination

16

38. Is your way of thinking more
_____ A. Conventional
_____ B. Original and creative

39. What motivates you more
_____ A. Solid evidence
_____ B. An emotional appeal

40. Would you rather be known for
_____ A. Being a consistent thinker
_____ B. Having harmonious relationships

41. Do you tend to
_____ A. Value routines
_____ B. Dislike routines

42. Do you live more with
_____ A. A little sense of urgency
_____ B. A leisurely pace

43. Do you have
_____ A. Many friends and count them all your close friends
_____ B. Few friends, and only one or two that are deep friends

44. Do you place more emphasis on what you see
_____ A. With your physical eyes
_____ B. With your mind's eye

45. Are you
_____ A. Thick skinned; not hurt easily
_____ B. Thin skinned; hurt easily

46. When you are asked to create a "To Do" list, does it
_____ A. Seem like the right thing to do and do you feel it will be helpful
_____ B. Bug you and seem more like an unnecessary chore

47. Which word attracts you most or describes you best?
_____ A. Talkative
_____ B. Quiet

48. Which words attract you most or describe you best?
_____ A. Present realities
_____ B. Future hopes

49. Which word(s) attracts you most or describe(s) you best?
_____ A. Logic
_____ B. Loving heart

50. Which word attracts you most or describes you best?
_____ A. Plan
_____ B. Impulse

51. Which word attracts you most or describes you best?
_____ A. Party
_____ B. Home

17

52. Which word(s) attracts you most or describe(s) you best?

_____ A. Common sense

_____ B. Vision

53. Which word attracts you most or describes you best?

_____ A. Justice

_____ B. Mercy

54. Which word attracts you most or describes you best?

_____ A. Concerned

_____ B. Carefree

Please continue to the instructions and the score sheet on the following page.

SCORE SHEET INSTRUCTIONS

1. Place a ✔ in the appropriate column (A or B) to indicate the answer you chose for each numbered question. [*Please note that the numbers run from left to right across the chart.*]

2. Count the number of "As" in column #1 and write that number in box "c," above the "E". Count the number of "Bs" in column #1 and write that number above the "I" in box "d".

3. Count the number of "As" in column #2 and write that number in box "e." Count the number of "Bs" in column #2 and write that number in box "f."

4. Count the number of "As" in column #3 and write that number in box "g." Count the number of "Bs" in column #3 and write that number in box "h."

5. Add the number of "As" for columns 2 and 3 together and write the total in box "i." Add the number of "Bs" for columns 2 and 3 and write that number in box "j."

6. Repeat the steps in instructions 3-5 above for columns 4/5 and 6/7.

7. Which did you have more of, "Es" or "Is"? _____
   Which did you have more of, "Ss" or "Ns"? _____
   Which did you have more of, "Ts" or "Fs"? _____
   Which did you have more of, "Js" or "Ps"? _____

8. In the four letters you listed in Instruction #7, which two-letter combination below is present? Circle it!

S and P   S and J   N and T   N and F

	1			2			3			4			5			6			7	
	A	B		A	B		A	B		A	B		A	B		A	B		A	B
1			2			3			4			5			6			7		
8			9			10			11			12			13			14		
15			16			17			18			19			20			21		
22			23			24			25			26			27			28		
29			30			31			32			33			34			35		
36			37			38			39			40			41			42		
43			44						45						46					
47			48						49						50					
51			52						53						54					
							g	h					m	n					s	t
							e	f					k	l					q	r
	c	d					i	j					o	p					u	v
	E	I					S	N					T	F					J	P

Follow These Steps to Finalize Your Temperament Identification:

1. Read the descriptions of the temperaments that follow and select the temperament that is most like you. You may find that not all the aspects of a temperament truly reflect who you are. That is not uncommon. We are individuals and all are a little different, so what you are looking for is which of the four descriptions fits you best. Which is most like you?
2. You may find that you see a little of yourself in several or all of the temperaments. Don't worry. We all imitate others and therefore "borrow" strengths and characteristics from

20

other temperaments for many reasons, not least to meet what others demand of us. What we need to know is which temperament we really are? As the research indicates we are one temperament, not a mixture of temperaments, and those glimpses of ourselves in other temperaments are simply our adopted strengths. Borrowed strengths or characteristics are just that, borrowed. Our own strengths are the ones that satisfy and fulfill us when we use them. We must know them.

3. Does the one that fits you best agree with your temperament key results? The two letters of the temperament you have chosen must occur in the four letters that your temperament key gave you. If they do, no further decision is needed.

4. If they don't, then you can go back and check your answers to the temperament key. Are they really what your preferences are and not what others have led you to believe you are or what you would like to be based on expectations others have given you? Make sure you answered the questions as instructed. A small number of people who take the temperament key may find it doesn't seem to ring true with who they perceive they are from reading the descriptions. If so, go with what you perceive is the temperament that fits you best.

The Four Temperaments

SP

They crave action, excitement, and stimulation, be it in sport, physical skills with the use of tools of all kinds, the performing arts, or even fine art. They are after a "good time" and only the introverted ones can happily sit still. SPs love freedom and act spontaneously; therefore, they do not take to authority with relish. Possessing a natural talent for all things physical, they can be the world's playmates. They are lovable, exciting, adventuresome, and brave risk-takers.

SPs are pleasant, tactical, and squeeze the last drop of excitement out of each moment. Adaptable, carefree, optimistic, individualistic, they crave self-expression. Tolerance accompanies competitiveness and a generous spirit is usually seen in them.

Does this describe you best?

✦✦✦✦✦

SJ

They are hard-working (many are workaholics) with a responsible work ethic, and they crave a feeling of security, which makes them somewhat cautious in their adventures. They coined the motto "Be prepared," and they like everything in order. Home, family, and responsibilities, all cast around rules and regulations. This makes them feel comfortable. They are the solid citizens and the backbone of society. They feel a sense of duty and feel drawn to be useful (helpmates). If someone does not do their duty, it irks them.

Change can be unnerving and security is paramount if they are to be happy. They are more conservative than the SP and they like to feel in control of their world. They tend more to worry and pessimism rather than an optimistic attitude that all will be well. They must struggle to ensure all is well. Their nature is more serious and they are the guardians of society.

Does this describe you best?

◆◆◆◆◆

NT

We could call this one the ingenious/technology temperament, although everyone craves the benefits of technology these days. They are curious and inventive, often finding their way into science and engineering occupations. NTs want to understand everything and build things. Often they are driven and compulsive, but display few people skills naturally. They are hard-working if what they are doing interests them. Feelings are not worn on the surface. NTs want to find new ways of doing things.

Facts, theories, and strategies fill their minds and fuel their determination and focus. All things logical and only what makes sense guides them. They must feel independent, calm, cool, and intelligent. Scientific inquiry, mathematical, precision, and logical consistency in a skeptical mind describes them well. NTs are *mind-mates*.

Does this describe you best?

◆◆◆◆◆

NF

They care very deeply about people and their world and want to lead people to their potential and to feelings of wholeness. NFs are very passionate, tender, loving, soulmates who want to please. Their inner world is frustrated with struggles, and they are the influencers of society, often finding their way into higher education (as do the NTs) and into teaching, counseling, and personal growth. They champion causes that benefit society and provide for the betterment of humankind. They long to better themselves together with the aforementioned urge to help others be all that they can be. They are emotionally rich and complicated and are easily hurt with their emotions very near the surface.

NFs are influencers, empathetic, passionate, emotional, sensitive, introspective, and lovers of harmony among people. Mostly they are perfectionists, self-demanding, idealists, imaginative, and visionaries living in the world of dreams both practical and fanciful. To these self-actualizers, life must have meaning and significance.

Does this describe you best?

If you are still puzzled or unsure of which temperament you are and which describes you best, then go to my book, *INNERKINETICS®*, and all should soon become clear.

3: The Teen Stands Up!

Temperament Really Matters in the Teens

Temperament is no mystery. Nor is it just another example of psycho-babble. Temperament is a psychological term used to describe the observable differences in people — infants to adults — that form the basic structure of our makeup. It is what I like to call our *innerkinetics* (inner powers), our core drives and urges that shape our lives. Simply put: it is how we are designed.

There is a blueprint inside each of us that makes us want to act, think, and feel in certain ways. It causes us to create our preferences. We know that we don't all have the same basic preferences. Preferences are very important to know and understand. For the teen, this knowledge is the beginning of self-understanding and wisdom — most of the time, the difference between making a good or bad decision.

Many adults do not have a workable self-understanding because they were never helped to understand why they act and feel the way they do. Helping your teens understand themselves is a gift a parent can give that saves the teen years of heartache. Unless we know our preferences (*default leanings,* you could call them) and follow the way they want us to live, we will never find the happiest life we were designed to live.

Children are not blank slates on which we can write a personality or temperament. Think of them as special designs, waiting to be understood and developed. Let's understand that by the teenage years, many of these drives have been well developed, but the teen often does not consciously know them or understand them — nor do most parents. How can we effectively use what we don't know or understand? How can we parent effectively without an understanding of both ourselves and our teenager? Thankfully, if you have read *I'm a Keeper*, you should have completed the temperament key for your child and may have completed the Adult Temperament Key when they were in their early teens. Now you will be able to plunge into **the enlightening world of the descriptions of the temperaments.** A few more thoughts will help you on your way to helping your teen.

Teens are in transition. Certain features of this stage of life need special understanding and intentional development. These stages do not develop independently of a person's core temperament. Temperament permeates all we do, feel, think, and experience on the journey through all of life's stages. That is why it's foundational to all we do as parents.

Think of the teens as a parent's last opportunity to influence the coming adulthood of the teenager and the teen's beginning of the final shaping of his or her life. To do this effectively, ingrain in your mind the concept of parenting, not as shaping the teen you *want* but as helping the teen to be the person they are *designed to be* — shaping themselves with your help. Develop their strengths and inculcate the values and beliefs that will best prepare them for adulthood.

The Importance of Understanding

Let's Summarize:

For the parent

- Understanding becomes the prime source for bonding. The lack of it precipitates a parting of the ways between parent and teen. No teen wants the help of a parent with whom they feel uncomfortable. Parents will be heard and respected or regarded as irrelevant, depending on the strength of this bond.

- Understanding how the teenager sees you as a parent will also be a major help in conducting meaningful communications with your teenager.
- Teens want help but will only accept it from the people who make sense to them. That means speaking to the teens in the way they have been wired (according to their temperament's needs) — not from how the parent is wired — will mean the difference between success and failure. The parent who does not make sense to their teen is not going to be very effective.
- If the parent's help does not ring true to the teen's inner urges, they will reject it as "age irrelevant" or put it down to someone who has never understood them — someone who is becoming more irrelevant each day.
- Teens are focusing more on what exists beyond the home, peers, influential people of all ages, and all those they have to struggle with as they expand and engage with people in their world. Parents are not their only/main focus any longer. The world out there, not the home, is challenging them in this phase of growth. The parent must become more and more relevant. How? By letting the teens know they understand the them. The reading of the following descriptions will soon make this need clear.
- Parents don't shape temperament, nor do they have much influence over personality. Optimize the child you are given!

For the Teen

- A developing brain and the growth toward maturity cry out for help. The teen often asks himself, "Why do I feel, act, and think this way?" It's not just hormones that are puzzling. It's discovering a whole human system — his own.
- Temperament and the influences of environment can be confusing when they oppose each other. Why do they feel their peer group's expectations do or don't match their own

27

urges? Which should they follow? Is fitting in more important than being who you are and following your design? Many teens go astray over this very struggle.

- Learning the importance of their inner drives helps them find their identity and save wasted years. Developing their strengths is something that now needs to fill their lives. "Be all that you can be" is now becoming urgent.
- The teenage years are the start of consciously knowing themselves as adults are expected to know themselves, and the sooner they understand their innerkinetics, the faster they will mature.
- Friends, partners, heroes, and heroines, as well as people they hang out with, are suddenly becoming a significant part of who they are and who they are going to grow up to be. Teens need to know that they must shape their lives on who *they* are, not on what other people may influence them to be.
- The teenage years are when teens must get a grip on their emotions and begin the journey with all seriousness to intelligent emotions. Understanding their innerkinetics plays a large part in controlling their emotions.

Important Things to Know About Teen Temperaments

- All temperaments are wonderful!
- Don't let your teen be afraid to be categorized. Besides, have you noticed that babies categorize everything: all hurts are hurts; funny faces are funny faces. No one teaches them to associate like with like; they just know they must do it. It comes naturally to all intelligent creatures born into such a complex world and who need to connect one idea with another, building the knowledge they need block-by-block.

- When those babies grow up to be adults, they still categorize: all dogs are dogs; all poodles are poodles. How do dogs feel about that? Dogs don't worry about it. They just live above it. And when it is all said and done, their brains have to categorize, too. That's why, at times, a dog will mistake one toy for another and they shamelessly don't try to hide the fact.
- We all enter life with a set of biases (our temperament's strengths). If our temperament limited our accomplishments it would be a curse, but it focuses us and sets our lives surging in the direction where the fullness of life *for us* is to be found.
  - Computer scientists, who try to create models of human brain function, confess they have to build in a bias into their models for them to be able to replicate human experiences. Human systems, by nature, are biased.
  - This human system just does not develop from an organism that has no distinct leanings. Leanings give direction to development and motivation to be who we are from the very beginning. Our leanings are our temperament's strengths.
- Having a powerful direction in life will, in some respects, limit us. A direction or purpose is meant to become all-consuming and it does so by excluding other directions.
- We can excel in any direction we choose to go in life, but to super-excel, we must choose the direction for which we have been designed.
- Life is lived best when we apply most of, or 100% of, our effort in the direction of our design.
- We soak up information from our world all day long and it is all read through the perspective of our temperament. We then apply it to our lives according to the perspective our temperaments give us. (A car is a toy or a sensation, an instrument of transportation, a thing to be understood and tinkered with, or an emotional experience — SP, SJ, NT, NF respectively).

- Precise targets, goals, and aims make sense if we are to optimize and develop as fast as possible. Therefore, teens need to keep refining their goals and narrowing their targets with the knowledge of who they are designed to be.

SP Teen Temperament

The teen SP temperament runs true to the adult SP temperament, except that some features are still in their final stage of development in the teenage years and this alerts us where to focus. SP teens are also being challenged by issues that are peculiarly impactful in the teens. Emotional and social development is in full swing and the teen is looking outside the home at the larger world with renewed interest.

In this temperament, confidence and risk can be easily overused. This teen seeks freedom more than other temperaments and may already have tested boundaries imposed on them by home and society in general.

On First Meeting

Like the adult, they appear pleasant and — in fact, charming — which adds to their attractiveness to other teens. Their optimism, which is also attractive, shows in their being brave, bold, daring, and impulsive risk takers. Some are bolder than others. Their daredevil attitude can be alarming at times. If the confident attitude alone makes an impact on other teens, then you may notice they don't feel the need to carry it through to action. They may find it hard to impress an NT or the overly cautious SJ, however.

Optimism is a characteristic that should be easily seen as they waltz into our lives like a breath of fresh air. In the home, that freshness may be less noticeable, depending on their mood. This positive spirit encourages a love of action, adventure, and excitement — again, very appealing to other teens. Socially, the teens can be the SP's world.

They are all about self-expression in the moment. If the moment passes, it is an opportunity lost. The SP desperately wants to make an impact on those around them, so when that opportunity is not apparent, they either fade into the background, awaiting the next opportunity, or they attempt to create an impactful moment that draws attention by whatever means.

31

The only real world is the world that is happening around them and time to meditate or calm down for mental reflection is rare — usually missing altogether. It's hard to make an impact in your virtual world since no one can see it. Hence, the need to be fully present in the real world of people and things. The present is always their focus.

Seriousness is usually not a characteristic that is readily observed in the SP, except for a serious attempt at anything fun and pleasurable. This lighthearted spirit and their focus on excitement make them the true exponents of happiness and a carefree attitude. Art, sport, and anything that offers speed or physical skill attracts them and holds their interest.

Life is lived at full throttle and they drain every last drop of joy from each moment or feel they are less than what they are made to be. Inhibitions, rules, and boundaries seem to them exist with the purpose of enticing the SP to break them. Being muzzled or hindered in their actions only makes them bolder.

Portrait

Life is, by the SP's definition, an adventure and they have a point. What is not adventurous about it? But life is about how to travel the adventurous road to make the best of it. The SP's adventure is mainly focused on the physical world and aimed at the high end of the excitement spectrum. Adventure is stimulating, usually action-packed, and arouses pleasant emotions. Life is acting as the star in a movie. Grasping each opportunity that passes to explore the unusual seems to make concrete sense to them.

However, the executive functions of the brain are still developing and risk can be under-evaluated more easily by the teen. Many a slip that has affected future lives dramatically when, as a teenager, an SP did not receive appropriate guidance or acted impulsively.

Freedom, for which they would give almost anything, is usually misunderstood. While there is another person on the face of this planet, total freedom is limited. We are also limited beings in every way. We cannot do without sleep or food, for

32

example. We collide with our limitations every day, all day. So, we cannot do whatever we want. We court trouble if we try. Try doing whatever you want when you drive down the freeway. You will soon discover the idea of total freedom is a pipe dream. Freedom does not carry a license that permits us to avoid consequences, either. Consequences come any way. So, the SP teen can best travel life's journey with at least a small degree of caution that will, in the long run, elevate their pleasure and excitement and let them live to enjoy another day.

The desire for freedom develops in the SP a carefree attitude. Life is lived at high speed and every last drop of pleasure and joy must be squeezed out of the present moment.

All physical and emotional senses with their insatiable appetites surge within them and the control of those sensory emotional drives is the task any teen (and especially the SP teen) must learn. The SP teen rises in the morning intent on escaping boredom. Non-stimulating repetition is wearisome. The skill of living well is measured by the fun they have. Variety scores high marks and change is not feared, rather it is welcomed, provided it doesn't take the edge off the zing of emotional arousal they presently have.

For the teen, bravery is more often the challenge they welcome to provide them the opportunity to make a positive impact on others. But it would be wrong to think they are not brave at times for laudable reasons. Noble brave actions furnish the same thrill and even a greater feeling of pride and accomplishment. However, for the teen, bravery is often taking the dare. How can one be known for being brave when they chicken out of a dare? A song I was taught as a child has stuck in my mind...

> Dare to be a Daniel
> Dare to stand alone,
> Dare to have a purpose true
> And dare to make it known.

This **daring spirit,** when life is a risk, can be a very positive characteristic, depending of course on what the dare is all about. All teens, as they face the exploration of their world, will show degrees of daring, but the SP is the one who displays a dominantly daring spirit. The SP teen is born to "dare to do what is right, helpful to others, what challenges the wrong, and what makes this world a better world." To do what is wrong and to go with the crowd is the epitome of cowardice! It is the easy way and is usually smeared with irrational impulsivity, staining the glory of the SP's brave and daring spirit. Therefore, a daring spirit cannot lose touch with thoughtfulness to keep it truly bold, brave, and moving in a positive direction.

SPs hate themselves when they are cowardly, but feel the highest self-esteem when valiant and **lionhearted**. Thinking highly of themselves is not necessarily pride. It is the condition of the human mind that either limits us or lifts the ceiling and provides room for growth. **A healthy self-esteem** is normal for the SP teen. When they think poorly of themselves, something is wrong and thought patterns that are unhealthy for an SP teen have taken over. Confidence is essential to bravery, excitement, and an adventuresome spirit.

We need to understand the nature of risk to an SP. It is raw opportunity. How can one show their bravery without a chance to display what they are made of? Provide opportunities for your teen to risk and do what is right in the face of their friends' scorn and this will challenge them. When surrounded with a crowd that feeds off the strength that comes from numbers, the lone SP who makes a contrary stand feels a surge of adrenalin otherwise unknown. They gain a respect that elevates them in the eyes of their enemies. They are leaders who coax the more timid souls through the fire. Risks are custom-made for the brave. Our world needs the truly brave SP leadership that is guided by a concrete realism and not lone wolf insanity.

From adventure, risk, freedom, and bravery we will move on to inspect the SP's intelligence. **Tactical** is the word Keirsey uses and I cannot think of a better one. **"Fast, in-the-moment decisions"** that have observed the situation with clarity and prepped the mind for instant action is the intelligence of the SP. The teen SP is developing to be superior at this type of thinking. On average, not until their mid-twenties will they have gained the full cooperation of their executive thinking functions and their emotional speed to be their best at tactical intelligence. But they will surprise you long before that time arrives.

Tactical moves are for **manipulating our environment** to produce desired consequences. Most often, those moves must be executed immediately and followed with more tactical adjustments if needed. Often, a tactical move is made to uncover the opponents' next move and ultimately to outwit them. Parents of tactically smart SP teens can, if not aware, be out maneuvered. Like any ability, it can be used for good or bad purposes — for selfless or selfish gains. Because the external sensing abilities of the SP can be very well-developed, they lead in this type of intelligence.

What might fool you about an SP is that they are, when not called to action, **laid back** and pleasantly engaging their world. But present them suddenly with action in the form of excitement and they come alive to everyone's pleasure — or displeasure, as the case may be.

Because of this apparent suddenness to act at some times and display a laid back persona at other times, it can be puzzling to others and to them. The laid back attitude is their preferred lifestyle, but excitement and challenge trump the lifestyle whenever it appears. The laid back aspect of their nature needs to be understood. It means they have no real concept of time as do all the "Js." Therefore, they are often behind in getting ready to leave or don't notice that it is past their curfew time. This lifestyle does not want to run by the clock. It destroys the excitement of the moment if you have to be aware of the time when enjoying yourself. That inner urge for fun feels restricted and derailed. Can they live without a consciousness of time and be successful in life? No. Can they oppose an urge (fun) that shapes who they are? It's difficult. So, what is the answer?

First, they must not try to become regulated, orderly SJs. They must learn when it is that the world demands a timeliness and when it doesn't, and then live accordingly. Living with an eye on the time is needed if they are going to catch the train, but not needed when relaxing for the evening or off work and at play. Becoming aware of what is appropriate and what is not is the learning curve all creatures of time need to traverse. Your teen should be helped to recognize what are appropriate demands of time. Decisions are what life is about.

This lifestyle, which does not want to come to closure, remains open to all its influences. Hence, they can become great **artisans**. **Tools of all kinds** fit comfortably in their hands and they can display noticeable talent with paint brushes, scalpels, the physical manipulation of technology, the instruments of a jet fighter or mechanical tools, plus a weapon of choice. SPs are sensual and respond well to the demands of physical skills. An SP's future may well revolve around some physical skill.

The SP teen will typically display a **tolerance** of others and their values. It can take on a dismissal of values just in order to accommodate all opinions. The SP teen wants to be accepted in order to maintain a high self-image. However, oppose an SP's freedom and all tolerance goes out the window.

Tolerance is never given to others without some reserve, usually an insistence on being tolerant of their own choice of tolerances. Whenever disagreement makes its presence felt, a run to tolerance or, on the other hand, criticism can be nothing but a cowardly escape from the more difficult exercise of finding agreement or loving each other anyhow. Always challenge your SP teen to be courageous and be unafraid of the difficult way. An acceptance of the person (love) and a rejection of their ideas can live together. The SP teen, because they are focused on the world around them, will face having to define when tolerance is helpful and when it is simply a desire to be accepted. Peacemaking without truth and the recognition of all mutual responsibilities cannot find peace. It just delays it.

Driving all these strengths is the emotion of **optimism** (we will discuss this more later) and the SP is indisputably optimistic. Life is to be lived with the belief that we live in a world where good fortune befalls everyone. That we should believe in optimism is the SP's point of view. If something goes wrong, something will go right. It is the opposite of Murphy's Law: "If anything can go wrong, it will." To live under that belief is to drain all joy from the moment. For the SP, there is always tomorrow and tomorrow is not hope; it is a renewal of their optimistic outlook — a new chance.

Put another way, **this world is a generous world** and it will look after us. Don't worry! Worries are not respected by the SP teen. But what about looking ahead and acting today so as to make tomorrow safe and better? That's an SP problem, too. If we are constantly living to take care of tomorrow, we have to gloss over the excitement of today. Catch the moment and live for nothing but now. This sounds so good and makes such good sense of the moment, but it does not make sense of preparing for tomorrow. Consequences can't be just wished away. They are coming as sure as the sun is rising tomorrow. Tomorrow brings new possibilities, but also payback for today and its own missteps. SPs must learn to traverse the learning curve: namely, live wisely for today and tomorrow.

The teaching that "if God takes care of the sparrow and the lily, who don't toil or spin, therefore don't worry about tomorrow because he will take care of you more than he takes care of the sparrow" is a teaching directed at the worrying SJ, not the free-wheeling, optimistic SP. The SP's area of concern is not the use of these wonderful optimistic strengths but the overuse of them.

The SP teen lives to **make an impact**. It's the widening of their social horizons and the developing of their social skills that encourages the taking of all opportunities to make an impression on others or gain their attention. They lighten life for all of us and that is perhaps why they often end up in some form of entertainment or activity where they can make a name for themselves and also entertain us.

Because of this urge to make an impact, they often find themselves in competition with others. Therefore, barely hiding a forceful desire to win in any competitive situation (even the simple competition for another's attention), they forge confidently ahead. They can be generous to a fault. It is hard for them to not follow their own feelings of pleasure when they sense the rise of their self-image. Generosity can be very self-serving but for the SP teen, it is more a means to the end of feeling the rush of adrenalin over yet another success.

If the teen finds himself without the means to be generous, he will often promise what he doesn't have and then set about obtaining it. Imagine where that might lead! All these thoughts make an SJ cringe. The SJ's urge to save for a rainy day is seen as tight-fisted to the SP, who would rather spend and enjoy. Both can be extremes that need to be modified.

All of life is a stage for the SP and it is critical they don't miss a curtain call. A strong urge lies behind this drive in the performing SP: the desire for **self-expression.** It's a form of their preference for freedom. **Individualistic** to the core, they want to carve their own path in life and have great skills to do so. They often learn by failing, which to them is not failure but an indication that something was simply misevaluated. Their optimism says they can always try again and they do so without the loss of self-esteem.

They do not want to be told they are just like someone else. The SP snowflake insists on being seen as unique. The teen will often dress or groom to stand out and be noticed — an urge in all teens, but with greater insistence and purpose in the SP. Therefore, conservatism is not their game because it gets lost in the crowd of sameness. This all feeds back to the need for getting attention.

An **easy-going work ethic** results from the urge to be free and unaccountable. Perhaps this is best illustrated in this slightly altered story of the Ant and the Grasshopper.

> *Ant is busy building his home and laying up stores for the coming winter. Grasshopper is sunbathing on a blade of grass, scoffing at the ant's busyness and trying to coax him to come join in the warmth of the sun and rest awhile. Ant keeps toiling while warning the grasshopper of his folly. Winter comes and the grasshopper is cold and hungry, knocking on the ant's door asking to come in and share the ant's hard-earned bounty.*

"Play first; work when play is done" is the SP (grasshopper's) mantra. The SJ parent wonders if the work will ever get done or becomes obsessed with demanding it be done!

Again, this is an overuse of a strength that, when not over-used, insists that work must not exclude the enjoyment of life while both should be accomplished. Get the SP to strike the balance that achieves both goals.

The introverted SPs are all of the above, but with less public display or insistence on their inbuilt urges.

SJ Teen Temperament

The SJ teen is going through the same physical and emotional changes that the other teens are experiencing, but change is a very real, unnerving feeling for them. It can very easily upset their stability. Insecurity is threatening on every hand when change is faced, and when relationships don't pan out as expected, the emotional and mental earthquake that uncertainty can cause can be staggering for the SJ teen.

SJs who are in a stable home environment will ride the storms of the teenage years much better and those that form solid relationships, better still. However, as the notes that follow will reinforce, feedback cannot be left out of the parenting agenda without suffering the results of aberrant behavior. Feedback is, as they say, "the breakfast of champions" and certainly the breakfast, lunch, and dinner of the SJ teen. This does not mean critical feedback; it means feedback that provides solutions, suggestions, and guidelines for the path through teenage. Criticism negates the positive effect of the feedback. It can always be couched in positive, loving terms.

When appreciated at school and at home, the SJ can be the most stable teen and the leader among other teens. When the atmosphere is too liberal and loose, the SJ will become angry at the way people get away with "murder."

Society needs this "solid as a rock" temperament. It's smart of us to smooth their path through teenage in order to develop those strong stable tendencies.

On First Meeting

As the teen ages, a greater seriousness will probably be observed but earlier, it's the desire to belong that drives the need to be seen as others expect them to be and, therefore, become one of the group. Caution is, however, observable from the early teen days or before, and it is only abandoned when peers pressure the SJ or they force themselves to act in a way they think is going to gain them social acceptance.

Caution can be observed as risk avoidance, taking time to assess the situation and come to a course of action — preparedness, thoughtfulness, playing it safe, and circumspection are the name of the SJ's game. Also, if change is not favored, we can reasonably assume we are looking at an SJ.

SJs, unless worried, are pleasant and socially discreet. Their warmth is cautious warmth as they size you up. Do you belong or do you threaten their territory? Control is also a noticeable trait and one they will display (without consciously intending to) at times.

You will see a practical bent and a strong desire to live a life that is down-to-earth and never lost in the clouds of fantasy or imagination. The real world is their home. To the SJ, it is the only world, which the NF will dispute. As you observe them, rules, regulations, and routines are relied upon to keep their lives from descending into chaos (in many circumstances, another word for "change").

Family and friends are loyally protected as long as they feel a friend is a friend or home is home. And noticeable is their willingness to help. Good Samaritans, they are. In this, they show a high degree of care for others alongside of their urge to **control** everything and everyone about them.

Portrait

If anything, the SJs keep their feet firmly planted in reality. They fly closer to the ground than the SPs — in fact, on the ground and not in the clouds of hope as do the NFs. SJs are **realists** in the fullest sense. Just listen to them talking about people and things in terms of whatever is real, physical, and earthly.

This realism underlies almost all there is to know about them. Realists see what is in front of them and react accordingly. These teens get the jitters when they lose touch with reality. **Security** is what is — not what might be, or could be, or should be.

If you want to keep your feet firmly planted and avoid mistakes and bad decisions, then you must learn **the lessons from the past** and not forget them. Past experiences are their guide and this is where the teen SJ is at a disadvantage. Their repertoire of past experiences is short. Many things have not been experienced yet, especially in the world of social adventures and emotional challenges. Choices are particularly shaky ground. "If it worked in the past, it should work now" is their default guidance.

Because of this need they listen carefully to the **experiences of their peers** and follow them if they have none of their own to fit the occasion. It is **important to them to be right,** so trusting others (which they find harder to do than the NFs) is not solid ground and, in many instances, not even good ground. Parents do well to talk about what the options for action are, which provides what the SJ mind needs. If the parent is trusted, the SJ will open up and receive the guidance of their elders.

The unknown is particularly fearsome for the SJ. If it's a small issue, it matters little; but if the unknown possibly hides big consequences, they begin to be inwardly disturbed. An SJ will proceed when the ground ahead is uncertain, but their behavior begins to be erratic and unpredictable. Solid ground means "I know it is solid ground." The teenage years are constantly breaking new ground and the future is unknown, so just a moment's thought will make you aware of the need for security and solidarity.

The **status quo** becomes attractive and something to rely on. SJs are all about reliability, too. So, this teen should not be pushed ahead when they don't want to venture, at least not yet. They must move through change at their pace. And this brings us to the SJ's driving emotion: caution.

All we have said highlights **caution** as the *modus operandi* of the SJ. When the ground ahead is unknown, treading cautiously makes complete sense. Protecting, providing, inspecting, and supervising are all driven by being cautious and careful. In these words, the SJ temperament begins to take shape. There is a need, in a world that is essentially plunging ahead into the unknown, to protect, provide, inspect and control or supervise.

Caution calls for close attention and scrutiny. Hence the teen SJ is all about the **details**. Progress is to be made step-by-step. These steps must follow in **orderly sequence** and if they do, this realistic teen understands what is going on and feels he is not walking blind. Walking blind means they do not know what is expected. Order and logical sequence provides a way of seeing ahead because it creates reasonable expectations. Caution also provides a measure of control. Leaping into the dark is madness to the SJ and still more frightening for the SJ teen.

"Proceeding cautiously" makes time for preparations. Again, the SJ teens feel more secure when they are **prepared**. Convincing an SJ teen is not easy if what you are talking about gives them no time to prepare. When they try something for the first time, it creates nervousness. Trust does not come easily to them because trust is handing over to someone else and losing precious control.

Control is a natural response to the dangers of insecurity. Control all you can and who you can. But control, when it involves controlling people, can kill the possibility of relationships and being accepted by others. Hence, a tension builds. They want both and can't have both — at least most of the time. The social life of an SJ teen can succeed or fail depending on how they are able to live with less dominance or whether they feel the necessity to insist on control.

If life is an escape from danger, doubt, trouble, and if a struggle to avoid the pitfalls, people have to be rather determined and watchful, and the SJ teen will show this **determined spirit**. They **have to be right**, also, and the two make for someone who digs their toes in and fights for every inch of mastery.

Argue? Yes, they can argue and most of it is in self-defense. Can you imagine how troubling it is to be proved wrong when you hate being wrong and can't believe you are wrong? Being wrong is the SJ teen's version of failure. To have missed some detail in their calculation when they are so good at not missing the details is another blow to the self-image. Therefore, if they are wrong, they must not admit it. At least not admitting it and trying to keep themselves from believing it keeps a modicum of self-esteem in their bucket of personal honor. True, this argumentative spirit does them no lasting favor, but if their peers will support their arguments, then all who disagree must be wrong. Emotions are still trying to dominate a teen's life and reason is fighting from the back seat to exert its influence. Continuing an argument with an SJ teen is entering a marathon in which there is no winner.

It's not always possible to control, so what then? They are forced to trust, and being forced to do anything is hard for an SJ to accept. Moving ahead with trepidation is the only path into the future that is left to them. So they live a life of "faith with caution." Faith with caution is not faith with doubt, and beliefs must be held, even if not held firmly.

The *Serenity Prayer* is a great guide for the SJ teen. It encourages the development of the executive functions of the brain and the emotional element of courage and the joint results of wisdom. Note carefully how it reads…

> *Grant to me the serenity to accept what I cannot change,*
> *The courage to change what I can,*
> *And the wisdom to know the difference.*

What the SJ is longing for is the inner serenity that signals that they have come to peace with the unknown; the ability to accept what is as yet not certain; courage to change what can and should be changed, and the wisdom to figure all this out.

Just as the SP teen is all about self-expression, the SJ version is the opposite. It is not to be different, but to be like the others and **respectable** in dress and demeanor. Don't forget, respectable in dress is not the same as respectable in the parent's mind. The parents and siblings, too, will be expected to be "respectable" according to the teen's ideas of respectability so as not to embarrass the teen. **Belonging** is a big craving and if they don't appear to belong in their peer's estimations, they fear being ostracized. The teen's world, as most SJ teens will confess, can be cruel at times. To be told they can't wear something their peers approve of is like being

44

told to show up in rags. As they age, they will join groups and organizations that they approve of at will and they will be the backbone of such organizations. Recognize the early urge and remember that opposing a core strength, such as having to be respectable, will only result in a miniature Armageddon. Compromise is the parent's best hope and, on occasion, the parent will need to insist on certain attire.

It is not true that the SJ temperament is all about negative concerns. But when the SJ falls into their weaknesses — the negative opposite of their noble strengths — **worry**, **negativity**, and even **pessimism** can emerge with persistence. Remember what worry is: a form of fear. Fear is the emotion that responds to just the thought of chaos or loss. It patrols the perimeter of the unknown. Fear will make any SJ teen or adult look the exact opposite of stable, with feet firmly planted on the soil of reality. Unnecessary fear is not grounded in reality but in what might, could, or may happen. It is a condition in our heads, a mental earthquake. So, worry does for the SJ teen the opposite of what they desperately are seeking.

When deadlines threaten, they turn to greater effort and to what will soon be experienced in their adulthood: **workaholism**, a frantic effort to keep failure at bay. Mostly, such a focused effort to get things done succeeds and then the "fix" is ingrained. When we find something succeeds, we must file it away in our tool box for future use. The determined drive to succeed is not bad, and only when it is overused is it a curse.

SJ teens **think in linear fashion,** so instructions that leave out important steps that are desired, may fail. Tell them the steps that must be achieved, or let them show you they can devise them. They excel in logistical planning and operate with efficiency when they understand what is needed to achieve the goal.

This mental demand for **order** spills over into their lives and takes all manner of forms. For some, it will result in a bedroom with everything in its place and neatly put away. For others, rooms will only become orderly in adulthood, while, perhaps, their hand writing will be near perfect. They will

45

choose and take pride in their neatness and order. It is a reflection that they wish their lives to be orderly — again, the opposite of chaos.

It's no surprise that the temperament that must control becomes, on the flip side, the **helpmates** of those in need. Their fellow teens are in need, and because the teen is now focusing more and more on the world outside of the home, their help is often directed to their peers rather than the home. Encourage their helping spirit. Social connections are important and this community concern and readiness to help others will show more as they run the last lap to maturity. **Good Samaritans,** they are!

Both the SJ and the NT take the prize for persistence. Determination may give up in the face of mounting odds, but **perseverance** will not. *Stubborn* is a word often used of the SJ, but it can be a form of noble perseverance. Examine the roots of this behavior before you condemn it.

Finally, we come to the teen's developing connections to the past. When in the past the methods and practices succeeded, the SJ models their present life accordingly. But this is not all the past holds. Traditions and wealth of history give to us a sense of who we are and where we came from. Identity is strengthened by traditions and the recounting of history.

The early Maoris in New Zealand would sit around the fire and recount the events and family stories of the past (and some still do) to strengthen the children's sense of who they are and who they must be. Family photographs will often adorn the teen's dresser and line the memory banks of their mind. Do all you can to raise their pride in those whose good steps they follow. And if you can find a family hero, the connections and modeling of their past family history will become a strong motivation for all that is noble, brave, and good.

Picture your teenage SJ as the Rock of Gibraltar and do all you can to paint this image on the canvas of their imaginations.

NT Teen Temperament

When parenting either of the two Ns, remember, they live in the virtual world of their minds more than they live in the world outside of themselves. The NT is a mystery to the Ss and, therefore, is not understood as readily by their parents and their peers if they are not also NTs. Just like any teen, they want to be understood. They, too, are going through the changes of the teenage years and both their bodies and their minds are being challenged.

They are different and are usually easy to identify because most of their differences create visible contrasts with the outgoing, social-seeking, fun lovers around them. We'll investigate these under "On First Meeting" and "Profile."

We enter the world of the mind with both the Ns, and what may seem hard to identify in the Ss stands out boldly in the Ns. Two important functions of the mind are the emotional system and the analytical/rational system that sometimes are referred to as the "executive functions" of the brain. The emotional functions surface for all to observe in the NF and the calmer reasoning functions in the NT. This is not to say that the NF is not about their mind or is not reasonable.

We find extroverts and introverts in both NTs and NFs, and also the two different lifestyles: one desirous of coming to closure and the other not. The difference in the lifestyles can usually be seen in the outward behavior: the P lifestyle, more laid back and the J lifestyle, more driven and decisive. In the NT, the difference between the extrovert and the introvert are also easy to spot after a few minutes of conversation or observation.

If you (the parent) are an S, you will find these two (NTs and NFs) bewildering, thinking at one moment you understand them and the next, gazing with no idea of what's going on inside.

On First Meeting

Particularly if the NT is an introvert, you will be struck by their apparent calm. It takes on a coolness that seems to be unsociable and stand-offish. You may stand there introducing yourself and they reply with minimum words and a flat tone that betrays no emotion. Was it a pleasure meeting you? You feel you have intruded or that the teen is in a bad mood and wants nothing to do with anyone. Are they thinking you are some alien from an unknown planet or are you considering that possibility about them? They can make the non-understanding adult nervous and then the adult goes on to the next person, leaving the NT to feel as though they are being avoided, which only adds to their feeling of being different and not somehow acceptable.

Except for the extroverts among them, the NTs may be slow to reply, as though they can't think of what to say, when in fact they are mentally processing as fast as you, but simply finding a need to think about it more and in more depth. You wish they would come out and show some pleasure at the moment, which would at least give you a clue as to whether you were welcome. If the introverts among the NTs are outgoing and warm, it is a very special and unusual day.

Got a math problem? Then standing before you is the best of those who love details and revel in solving the theoretical enigmas of figures and facts. But remember, they long for friendships on their terms, which means with people who value and respect them.

They don't mean to be cold. "Who are you" is the current enigma and while they figure this out, they remain distant and remote. Display a lot of emotion and they may take a step backward, at least mentally. They don't appreciate much emotion, as you will discover as you read.

Under this facade is a pleasant person who wishes to keep his emotions in check. Caring and a true *mind-mate*, these NT teens need the understanding and the companionship of people they can admire and emulate.

Portrait

Montgomery is right in calling them the **technology temperament**. You will find a high percentage of them in Silicon Valley, deep in thought and ingenious in their pursuits. Perhaps your NT is setting her sights on that valley or on an engineering or architectural career. Anything that opens up the day to stimulating, theoretical provocations, the discovery of new things, and new ways of doing things, or even being a science or physics professor will attract most of them. Research is also a field of choice for many.

But make a finer distinction and you will understand better. The SP, or for that matter all temperaments in their teens, will love to play with technology and use it in a fascinating way to their own ends, but these NTs are the ones who show a deep interest in creating the technology and writing the software in the strange language of computers. First, the NT teen will revel in Internet play, especially if the game has a strategic challenge. If hooked, they can be obsessed with this form of mental stimulation to the neglect of all else. It is a side track into the wilderness of underdeveloped strengths — those the games don't exercise. Read about their strengths and find ways to engage them in other pursuits that use their strengths or you may forfeit them to poor grades and ever more distant or combative behavior.

Another challenge accompanies this obsession with video and Internet games. Because they are not the ones to excel in social events, they can readily gather a group of friends on the Internet who they never meet in person but with whom they connect. Their social life is then conducted at a distance and they become less and less socially adept in person. These "friends at a distance" can cause the NT teen to substitute them for the real encounters of life. Face-to-face encounters call for more complex interaction. Appropriate body language and physical responses are not learned when they make their friends via fingers on a key board.

Yes, they live in their heads, but life is more than thinking. **Socially challenged** are words that come to mind, although they would not like to be thought of as socially awkward. A loss of a girlfriend for a male teen, for example, can be a huge setback and a crushing defeat. Try not to negotiate them into another relationship too fast. Encourage and show your faith in their abilities to find their way among people and they will try again. When they do find a mate, it will be a choice that has checked off the items on their list for desirable partners. Once they have determined that they have found the partner of their list (dreams sounds a little too emotional), they will commit and do all they can to make the relationship work, but they will be cautious in their selection.

The importance of intelligence cannot be overestimated for these **mind-mates**. They will **do only what makes sense**, whether it is in choosing a friend or in deciding when or whether to complete a chore. Parentally, all requests must be made to make sense to them. "Sense" means it has to be reasonable by general standards and it has to match *the teen's* interpretation of present facts. For example, if they are focused on a project that they are internally committed to complete, they will view all the other demands of life as time-irrelevant or simply invasive and annoying. "Not now; later," their attitude demands.

They must learn that their interpretation of the facts is not the only reasonable one. When they arrive in Silicon Valley, they will soon discover, if not before, that there are multiple interpretations of the facts. One plus one doesn't always make two. It depends on the characteristics of each "one" and the meaning of plus. Contexts determine meaning.

Usually **quite bright** or even brilliant, NTs can exhibit a pride in their mental achievements and in their mental superiority, whether real or not. This pride is an essential means of maintaining their high self-image. Achieving and receiving recognition for their achievements keeps their self-image healthy and high. A low self-image is the destruction of the NT teen and will set them back a long way in their maturation.

Recognition is not the mushy type of pleasure a parent is inclined to exhibit. Nor is it the equivalent of a gold star. It is the honest praise, full of integrity, from someone they love or admire. Therefore, it is essential to try to be on their list of admired people (which is typically very short). It takes a lot to rise to this level of acclaim. If you are not, *in their opinion,* mentally admirable (never superior), you can climb this ladder with integrity and admirable skills that they don't have, or by simply loving them in a practical way, without too much emotion. This pathway of cool and calm emotions, while being important to them and their needs, elevates you to being admired.

To be **loved by this teen,** you must be admired, respected, and you must match most of the points on the list of their rational requirements for parents. Parents are not admired for just being parents. The NT knows there are many parents out there who demand respect but have and deserve none.

If they do not show the desire to be physically close, don't despair. It may not be you at all that they are **distancing themselves** from. It could be just their lack of desire for closeness. Reason dominates and, therefore, emotion has to be subjugated and, at times, denied.

Here is what you might see in the emotions of your NT teen. They are not usually emotional unless their upbringing has shown them a comfortable experience with emotions. To the contrary, they can be angrily emotional when they have lost control of their emotions. Losing control is disaster brewing for the NT teen. They may also have lost the ability to keep their cool because they have been taunted and irritated beyond their ability to control their emotions when they were younger. They may have developed the unlikely habit of using their emotions to express themselves. An emotional display can be simply where they go for self-defense. If the home is nothing but an emotional volcano that blows often and unexpectedly, they may also not develop the typical NT calm and cool management of their emotions.

NTs don't like emotion. It clouds their thinking, in their estimation. Therefore, they keep their **emotions suppressed,** or better still, locked away in a box, out of sight to others and out of mind to them. In this way they can remain calm and operate with their typical calculating coolness.

Ways to deal with troublesome matters for the NT teen are to avoid them, walk away from them, or suppress any response to them. The NT will do all of these and anything else they think of to avoid being emotionally triggered. Emotional people pose a danger to them and a threat to their calm stance. Therefore, they will not partner with an emotionally volatile person, nor will they respect them. It's like respecting their nemesis. The parent can be emotional with others but appropriately calm and sincere with them. That's all right.

There is a **skepticism** about the NT, which can be destructive if used critically but constructive if used to solve problems and come to the best understanding of things. Squelching their questions will only distance them, but turning their negative approaches into positive language and goals is the way to model how they can best use their skepticism.

With the NT, do all you can to create a positive home atmosphere. When disciplining them, listen carefully to all explanations and act only if you have enough evidence to make a decision. Then calmly and quietly state the discipline. (You might ask for their suggestions as to what discipline makes sense. It is just giving them a "buy in" to the discipline). Do all this with no fuss or bother and with the promise that you are not going to say another word because it is not necessary. You can use the phrase, "I'm making you a promise that I won't say another word." When they complain and argue, remind them of your promise and walk away. Follow through and be absolutely consistent. The more discipline is a matter of reason based on indisputable facts, the better it will teach the NT teen. You will have to persist, at first, to show that your intentions are set in stone.

Create an atmosphere of **discovery** and do all you can to further their "finding, devising, and inventing" as they discover their world. Go with them on discovery trips; sit with them as, together, you search the computer for answers. Do all you can to build knowledge. Take them to the library and indulge their interest in books and science. This is a teen who wants a parent who is willing to be a partner in his or her explorations and who learns with them.

Your NT can lose touch with time. Each temperament is related to time in a different manner. The NT, when absorbed in a project, is unrelated to time — detached, that is, and lost in what they are doing. Their concentration is so intense that they don't want to be disturbed. If you interrupt them, they are likely to snap at you. Focus cannot be broken if their intense pursuit is to proceed without starting all over again. When they finish their project, they "wake up," so to speak, and ask, "What day is it?"

Honor this teen's strengths and help the teen develop them as they will make a great contribution to this world if given a steady and warm (not too warm) upbringing.

NF Teen Temperament

Complicated! Of all the temperaments, this is the intricate, convoluted, and tricky one to parent through the roller coaster of the teenage years. It hasn't gotten any better for the parent as we have traversed the temperaments. The SJ could be the easiest; the SP, the most fun (if you can keep up with them); the NT, a sudden introduction to the virtual world of the mind, and now the NF, the baptism of fire!

I don't want to make it sound bad. It isn't, but be prepared for the heights of parenting pleasure and the lows of depression with nightmares, starring your fears, such as "What did I do wrong?" and the fervent prayer, "God help me!" The morning light will bring the reminder of the best that can be in parenting and the reestablishment of hope. No temperament is bad or less than another in worth; certainly not this one.

What am I talking about? Why is this temperament so complicated? Because emotion is the most complicated function in the human system and the human system is the most intricate, delicate, and most complicated organism in the universe. Let's begin to understand emotion and what it does in us, to us, and for us.

What is it about emotion that is so difficult to understand and control? Just to begin with, it's the speed in which emotions appear and the totally unpredictable nature of how they operate.

First, speed. Reasoning crawls like a snail in comparison to the fast appearance of emotions. Emotions can be in full flight before we can actually know what is going on or what has triggered them. At warp speed, they flash into our consciousness and the first we know is we feel them. Then to our surprise, they are controlling our responses while we are just beginning to evaluate the situation. NFs (and all sensitive Fs) know exactly what I am talking about. The ability to evaluate comes after the appearance of the emotion.

We are going to be meeting emotions again in another chapter, so just a few important details here will help us understand the NF teen (and for that matter the adult, too). Because the emotions in our teen spark before we have time to think, we as parents will have to find better responses than the all too common and useless command, "Stop being so emotional, can't you quit that?" This is a useless command because it won't work, and that is because **it can't be done**.

Are you surprised at this? If you are a cool "T" (look at your four letters, again), you probably will doubt what I have just said. However, we can measure the speed of transmissions in the brain and we have the evidence for emotional responses happening before the analytical brain has even received the message, let alone had time to process it. Simply put, emotions take us by surprise most of the time.

Second, when an emotion is triggered, it doesn't remain the same emotion for long. For example, if an NF is suddenly angry because they have been hurt, the first emotions to appear are a combination of hurt and anger. The two always go together and never conduct their war dance alone. But as soon as the person is angry, whatever the response is from the person who hurt them (or anyone else for that matter), these emotions may have morphed into perhaps another — hate. Microseconds later, the feelings could turn to disrespect, disbelief, and after several other mutations, they may settle as resentment for a while. But by now, the emotions of disharmony have set in and the person who initially hurt the NF is now viewed as an enemy and the emotions turn again to yet another feeling: bitter disbelief. Soon, a loss of all hope for this relationship is felt.

All these emotions that I have described mutate in a matter of a second or two and if not stopped by some means, they may meld together into bitterness. Once bitterness sets in, a long recovery back to emotional calm is the inevitable path.

Can you understand the complexity that emotions create? You see, just one of the problems the NF faces is which emotion to chase and calm. They change so fast that even the fast-thinking NF can't keep up with them. They are at a loss to know which is the emotion of the moment and as soon as they feel one, it becomes another! Emotions in this hyper-sensitive and super-emotional temperament never let go. If they do mellow a little with age, it is not much. Of course, as with all temperaments, a strength such as the strength of emotions in the NF can never be used as an excuse, just an explanation and a challenge to be managed.

Try to understand. Sympathize, at least, with the NF because in order to be the rich, rewarding, emotional temperament that they are, they must live with the perplexity and power of these emotions. They must also discover how to choose intelligent emotions while, at the same time, they try to wrestle and subdue the unwanted unintelligent emotions. When the parent thinks this emotional nightmare must be stopped by force, they are trying to shovel the Rocky Mountains into the sea with a spoon. The NF teen, as they learn how to manage and control their emotionality for good purposes, needs the understanding of the parent, not their condemnation. Parent your teen (for your own good, if for no other reason) by helping, not hindering or beating your NF teen into the ground.

To the teen let me say, people love your emotions when they are positive and fear them when they are negative. Therefore, don't hate your emotionality. Rather, love it, and in a chapter ahead you will learn how to capture your emotion's great powers and be a true blessing to all those around you.

Plato, some 2,300 years ago in his astute understanding of this temperament, also noted that they were all about their mind, not only in the dominance of their limbic system (emotions).   They were agile in their ability to reason, contemplate, and insightfully penetrate the unseen world, in his opinion. They, like the NT, live in the virtual world of their mind and often get lost to the real world by refreshing themselves via retreating into their minds and daydreaming.

Now at the speed of reason, not emotion, we will try to understand the NF teen.

On First Meeting

NFs are pleasant, friendly, engaging, and warm.   You may think immediately that you have met a friend. They make you feel you are the center of their world as they give you their full attention. This openness can create difficulties when not managed.

They are sensitive and will pick up on any disturbance or pleasure within the scope of their radar, but they will be chiefly focused on your needs. They want you to feel their heart, not just their head. If the teen is angered, then the opposite of warmth is instantly felt by others because the NF will either explode in an angry defense or withdraw in noticeable coolness. These are their only weapons against getting hurt more: explode or withdraw.

It should be obvious from their approach that they are looking for harmony and that is indeed a reason for their focused, friendly behavior in the first place. But their antennas are up and if the message they receive is negative, they will prepare themselves for self-defense. They are trusting, at times too trusting, and even by their teenage years they have been burned enough from trusting too quickly to willfully walk into another trap, or so they are convinced. This is the temperament that is ultra-willing to please, in fact feels compelled to.

You may notice they are value-driven more than fact-driven. Most of their decisions are made on the basis of their values. This highlights the importance for them to build sound and healthy values into their reticular activating system (the filter in the brain that sorts all incoming data). It is no bad thing to respond to values rather than facts. In some cases it is the best way to make a decision because the facts don't always reveal the values by which we can best conduct our lives.

Love and hope or the lack of either explains most of their actions that you will observe on first meeting.

Portrait

These teens are all about people. I often call them the **people-to-people temperament**. This characteristic will never leave them. But the parent, upon the discovery of this trait, thinks that the teen will always be kind and loving since that is what *people-to-people* seems to imply. But people are

57

not always kind and loving to the NF teen. They have to deal with all kinds and learn the appropriate responses to those who have doubtful or damaging motives.

Teenage is a time of rude surprises for this **trusting, loving teen** as they turn their focus to the world outside of the home. Many NF teens quickly become more reclusive in avoidance of all the hurtful actions that may assail them. When the parent asks whether they have been hurt, they prefer for their parent not to know, so they respond with, "No, it's all right," meaning, "yes, but I'm trying to handle it and I don't want to be seen as someone who can't handle the hurts of others." They are actually trying to handle their own emotions with this response. Best for the parent to respond with, "That's good, but if you want to talk at any time, I'm ready."

Other NF teens become angry at the hurts that people inadvertently or deliberately hurl at them and they **try to be tough,** acting as though they cannot be hurt and that they, like other people, can let it roll off their backs. They can't, however. The males can become macho in an attempt to match the offensive, insulting behavior of the brusque and ill-purposed teen. If the parent treats them offensively, they become more determined to return evil for evil until they melt enough to offer an apology and seek harmony again. Much of their harsh behavior is an attempt to handle the emotions that are surging inside. It's either a self-defense mechanism or an attempt at controlling their emotions. Being tough and hurtful to others is not "them" and they feel the discontinuity of their actions and a sense of guilt.

People are both their pleasure and their pain. They **want to help people**, anybody that needs help that is, and if a peer is being treated wrongly or is in unfortunate circumstances, they will side with them and seek to help them. Therefore, they can easily take on the role of being the ill-treated or **poor person's friend** and savior. They will also try to befriend and influence the teen who is leading a life frowned on by others. Learning the limits of empathy and influence is a major lesson this temperament needs, not only to protect themselves but to be helpful to the person in need.

This label of being "the people person" is well earned as they will become the **influencers of society**. Language is a skill they are trying to perfect (the introverts may be more reserved) and when it is needed, they can be so convincing with the use of just the right tone for the words. Most of them will develop their oratorical skills and their powers of persuasion. Sharing their genuinely strong convictions becomes an obsession for the ENFJ and INFJ.

The parent should realize that these forceful arguments, of which they become the subject, are in fact an indication of the strengths the teen is developing. All their attempts at influencing others is fueled by strong emotions that will be used increasingly throughout teenage and as they age. They will be quick to defend some cause they cherish and will oppose with equal gusto the ones with which they disagree. Abraham Lincoln is an example of an NF who was very susceptible to depression and its emotional battles, but also powerful and life changing in his words.

A strong **sense of justice and fairness** also beats in the NF's heart, intensified by the powerful rhythm of their disturbed emotions. The cause of freedom for slaves was, for Lincoln, a cause that reflected both his deep values, sense of justice, and his strong emotions that would not let him retreat or fail — and he won. The theme "of the people, by the people, for the people, shall not perish from the earth" would mold this people-to-people man.

Along with the influencer's irresistible mix of emotion, plus the urge to defend a just cause, surges the heat of **passion**. Help your NF teen to choose the highest cause and hone their core strengths in promoting and defending it. They will love you for it and it will tighten the bond as long as you don't try to force your choice of a cause on them. Guide, don't force. The highest causes don't need to be forced on someone. They promote themselves. If you try to make the NF less passionate, you might as well try to remove the leopard's spots.

It may be a relief to note that if they have good values, a **sense of integrity and ethical honesty** beats in their hearts. Again, encourage it. Being a people person is all about seeking to lead others to their potential and to experience the wholeness in which humans who function according to how they are made can bask. The NF is narrowly focused on these things and wants simply to find where they might be able to exercise their influence best in life. There are countless ways this can be done and helping them find their direction is a way to ease the pathos of not knowing and wondering if they will be good at anything.

The NF's **sensitivity** needs to be explained, together with its passage through teenage. Most parents regard their NF teen's sensitivity as something that is damaging and needs to be toughened up or eradicated. That would be a big mistake. They must be who they are, not some other person they find it hard to emulate. Sensitivity is a requirement for giftedness. Destroy sensitivity and life becomes mechanical, losing all its artistry. With such strong emotions, a stayed more mechanical way of living is an impossibility for the NF. Sensitivity has to be managed while being kept intact and healthy. Your NF teen is trying to enjoy his sensitivity and not be overwhelmed by the hurt it can incur. They want it and hate it at the same time. When it hurts them, they suffer and when it fills them with rewarding feelings, they enter for a moment the heaven their temperament provides. Remember to walk the fine line of nurturing sensitivity and not letting it destroy those delicate emotions.

The NF teen is **hurt daily** by what people do and don't do, say and don't say, and what they expect that doesn't happen as well as the obvious attacks that devalue them. All NFs need help with overcoming the hurts others impart. The best help is in rationally evaluating the hurt they have suffered and then helping them change to an appropriate and more intelligent emotional response.

When they are hurt, follow this procedure for a better chance at being an understanding support.
- First, calm them and comfort them. That's what hurt emotions need most.
- Then, think through the hurt with them and sort out what is reasonable for them to accept and what is not.

- Next, talk over the alternative emotions and discuss which ones will hurt and which will heal. Encourage them to adopt the healthy, healing emotions.
- At any point in this discussion, a change of focus such as a place to go, a walk to take, a program to watch, can light up a new energy center in the human spirit and aid its natural healing powers.

Here are two things that will improve a parent's help for their NF teen. First, watch the message that the tone of your voice delivers. How the parent says things, much more so than what they say, is a key to reaching and healing the emotions of the NF. Say it without obvious care and concern in your voice and it means nothing to them. Worse, it carries the message that you don't really care.

The second is to remember that love is an irresistible force. Give an NF teen lots and lots of love and they will be yours because love creates harmony and positively impacts emotions, sensitivity, empathy, passion, kindness, and if it is genuine, integrity. Read through the strengths of the NF and you will soon see that love strikes most of their intense themes creating harmony.

To complicate matters more, the negative emotions of the NF teen can cause a speedy lowering of their self-esteem. The NF is very introspective and is constantly sensing how others think and feel about them. It will lessen with age and experience, but in teenage it can be one of the most important things that affect the atmosphere of the home, for example.

A low self-esteem leads to aberrant behavior and, in the teen, also to depression. These NFs are the ones most likely to get depressed. The parent cannot lift the self-esteem of their teenager. The teen must do this for themselves. Therefore, the parent should not take such a heavy responsibility on themselves. However, the parent can influence the lifting of the teen's self-image. Encouragement and an unconditional acceptance of the teen is essential if they are to feel better about themselves. This unconditional acceptance is not what the parent feels is unconditional but what the teen feels is unconditional.

Intuition, of which the NF teen is well endowed, even if at first they do not realize it, is at times a possible source of both trauma and joy. Premonitions and intuitive dreams are normal to most NFs. They can also readily sense what another person is feeling without any recourse to what the five physical senses are telling them. Some parents think this is strange and that something is wrong with their teen, but this is not so. Intuitive insight is a strength that will serve them well as adults and should not be disdained or stifled, as happens to many an NF because of its mysterious nature.

Imagination and idealism are strengths of this temperament and the NF teen will often let their imagination roam into dreams of their future and even into the world of fantasy. Imaginative dreams are often an element in the teens' search for their own identity and direction in life. They can live a possibility in their virtual world and test its appeal. All people can use their minds in this way, but to the NF, its usage is dominant. "Imagination is more important than reason," so said Einstein, and our teen NF should be encouraged to develop his or her imagination and its powers of discovery.

Another sensitivity plays a major role in their lives. Life must have meaning and if anything does not have meaning, it is soon forsaken by the NF, not by all temperaments. Emotion is what gives meaning to life and once again, we see the core urges of the temperament forming a distinct pattern. Fun for fun's sake is not of great appeal, but meaningful fun is perfect fun.

From meaning comes the need to be significant — significant in the lives of others, that is. This is the feedback that they are effective and successful, and when they are not, they dislike themselves and feel they have failed in life. So, celebrate your teen's feelings of being significant and wanting to be significant. Is your NF teen feeling significant because of your estimation of them? It's not just what you say but what they believe, and the parent can influence what the teen believes about himself by the tone of their voice and the love that transcends the gap between one person and another, arriving in the other person's mind with the intent it was meant to carry.

Welcome to the complicated world of emotion, sensitivity, passion, introspection, and idealism. It's the world of meaning. If you are of a different temperament than that of your NF teen, then walk in step with them when you can and when you can't, love them lots. Positive emotions crave the warmth love offers.

4: Less Is Better! — Mind and Brain

The brain seems to grow at a faster pace than is needed (if by "growth" we mean the number of connections it is making). Just as an oak tree produces more acorns than is needed, the brain produces more connections than it needs in the years before maturity. A simplified explanation goes like this: the brain registers and retains all input from all our senses, external and internal, and then must determine which stay and which must go.

We are told by neuroscientists that somewhere between the ages of 11 and 13 the brain is 95% the size of an adult brain. Growth in all of its compartments is nearly complete. But big changes not reflected in its size are about to take place. Final pruning of unwanted synapses happens in the teenage years and continues until about 25 years of age. Major mental shaping of the adult brain takes place. Less is going to prove to be better and more efficient.

Many of these connections and synapses start falling like raindrops, but not without meaning and planned reorganization. All that planning is determined by our choices. Used connections stay and unused ones are weakened and then disconnected. Ideally, by adulthood, what is to be kept has been kept and the connections that are not helpful have been disconnected, readying the brain for adult responsibilities and challenges.

The maximum number of connections is achieved between 6 and 12 years of age (the precise age will vary with the individual). Growth demands energy, so after this peak, the brain's energy demand is lessening as growth slows and synapses drop. Focus, however, is increasing and direction narrows, causing a more efficient operation of the brain.

The changes in the grey matter of the brain (losses of neurons, dendrites, and synapses) are visible to scientists and during the teenage years, the brain is reshaping itself in a big way. Envision the teen's brain in a vast reshaping mode, which can easily be observed in the differences in behavior and decision-making efficiency between a 13-year-old and a 19-year-old — hopefully! A parent, together with the teen, can be both an intelligent cause and guiding factor in this reshaping. No more a child, the teen needs a reorganized brain that prepares him for adulthood and the responsibilities of freedom.

- This pruning takes place continually, but the major periods seem to be in the second trimester of gestation and in mid to late teenage, as the neuroscientists have informed us.
- In teenage, it seems the focus is on the pruning of unwanted or unneeded synapses (connections), not cells.
- The axons that carry outgoing information and their myelination (think of it as insulation) seems to be one of the last things to fully develop.
- The frontal cortex is also late in developing and this is reflected in the development of self-control, planning, and resisting temptation. It may, in some cases, account for impulsivity in some teens, according to some neuroscientists. "Late" does not mean self-control is not in play earlier or can't be developed earlier, just that it develops more and in a significant way in teenage.
- The frontal cortex also becomes more active with age, while other areas decrease.

Temperament accounts for some of the above, since we see some temperaments pruning some connections more readily or earlier than others. Those inner drives seem to be influencing what is dropped and what is not dropped in each of the temperaments. Also, we may note: adolescent brains are highly dynamic, constantly changing, and energetic. The process slows with age and with the narrowing of life's interests and directions, as we have said.

In this highly active period, independence is sought more and more. And then at 18, when the teen is legally granted adulthood, research shows that the human mind is not yet ready for all the responsibilities and demands of adulthood. The teen may still turn to older people for more understanding and help while not wanting to show a lack of self-reliance.

Also at 18, while still wanting the safety of dependence, the teen may pull away from family and develop closer ties to people outside of the family, searching the experiences that freedom offers and the almost limitless opportunities that their world gives them. This is yet another period of confusion caused by endless options, interests, and not being rescued from undesirable consequences because they are expected to stand on their own feet and bear their own responsibilities.

Remember, what can be known for certain about the brains development in the teens is that we retain what we use and lose what we don't use.

Final Stages in the Synthesis of the Emotional and Rational Departments of the Mind

From two years old, reason and emotion have been trying to work together. The teenage years are the final struggle for a synthesis of reason and emotion before adulthood and if not achieved, at least for the most part, will result in a rocky introduction to adulthood.

Generally, teens decide much more with their amygdala (emotions) and not so much with their frontal cortex (analytical/rational brain). We see an earlier leaning toward the dominance of the analytical/rational brain among most NTs. All teens are learning to make the connection between these two important elements of mental activity more consistently and effectively. All Fs will show a more intense struggle with their emotions and a more sensitive use of them.

Adults use both in a practiced mutual interdependence. Answer for yourself whether that is an over statement or not! To the teen, emotions are not identified as much as they are felt as directional urges. More and more, identification and understanding of these urges are to be expected as they age. The identification of other people's emotions experienced in social situations also develop much more in the teens than was seen in childhood.

Although the analytical/rational operations of the brain seem well-developed by the early teens, the skilled evaluation of the emotions continues well into the twenties and is a leading factor in the maturing process.

When Is My Teen Mature?

It used to be thought maturity was at puberty because of sexual maturation. Some primitive cultures, believing puberty was the signal of maturity, considered marriage appropriate at this early age.

Now it is seen that mid-twenties is more likely an average age for maturity for most people. Here are more relevant observations about teenage and development.

- The "raging hormones" and an unbridled, risk-taking behavior, pointing to an immature decision-making ability are main issues in teenage maturation. Training our teens in good decision-making behavior can be a real gift.
- Teenagers, contrary to their own assessments, need parents — still! Parents should be active in their training all the way through teenage and accept a lessor assisting role more and more as the teen develops.
- Teens need to accept this, of course, since they are still in a developmental stage. It is difficult to acknowledge this since they are feeling more and more mature. It is like climbing a mountain and just when you think it is the last ascent to the summit, you realize there is another, and yet another.
- Part of the indication that things are still developing is the teen's need for extra sleep. My father fought my teenage sleepiness with "Early to bed and early to rise makes a man

healthy, wealthy, and wise," but his admonitions, I'm afraid, were only obeyed when force was imminent. I guess I didn't respond well, if gauged by his persistent threats.

- Suggestions for achieving an earlier pattern of retiring to bed: turn off the cell phone and turn down the lights. Both have an effect on the brain's shutdown mechanism.
- Also, exercise before bed triggers the release of melatonin.
- Inadequate sleep can have detrimental effects on development, health, mood, and performance.

In our society these last four bullet points may not be received with enthusiasm and may have to be flexible as life and our technical world changes.

Risk-Taking

This section directs most of its attention to the SP temperament. They are the ultimate risk takers. A little understanding can help the parent who is faced with a nervous breakdown over their teen's risk-taking behavior.

- SPs will take risks because of their optimistic outlook. Harm seems unlikely to the true optimist. Good things happen as well as bad, they think, and if you want a new experience, you must believe that good things happen to the bold.
- Other temperaments usually take risks to copy or comply with the SP's brave example.
- A risk is an adventure or an interaction with uncertainty, both of which naturally attract the SP.
- All actions are a risk, but teens feel the need to test their limits in order to know where they are in comparison to others and some do it more daringly than others.
- To the teen SP, the unknown must be explored. Excitement has to be found. "Where are the great ecstasies and the natural highs," they ponder? "What do the unnatural highs offer?" they also muse.

Risk, of course, cannot be avoided. Life is a risk. With the quest for more freedom comes choices; choices introduce us to risk. The parent that tries to influence an SP not to take risks is going to meet with failure. Direct. Don't oppose a core urge of a person's temperament.

Anything can happen to the teen who is disconnected and not anchored to some welcome source of information and help. Deepen your connection! The teen must feel you understand. They will pay more attention to direction that does not condemn their feelings but offers exciting alternatives, so show you understand.

The self-control mechanisms are not yet fully mature in a teenager — more mature in some than others. Therefore, the ability to say no or to choose wisely is not yet fully developed.

Saying no is not an easy matter when faced with excitement and adventure and it requires courage, too. Show them the challenge to resist is greater and requires greater courage. Have they got what it takes?

Concerns increase when the teen has risk-taking peers. Involve their friends in the family talks and seek to get them to act for the common good. Challenge all of them to make good choices. Often the way to help your teen is to find how you can help and guide their friends.

Self-Control and Good Decision-Making

Although the brain's analytical ability is near full capacity at the beginning of the teenage years, the emotional component in decision-making is far from complete.

- Excess dopamine and raging hormones send signals too loud for most teens to hear the more refined signals of reason.
- Taking risks, unwise pursuit of excitement, and chasing of fantasies are actions wide open to the impulsive behavior that is typical of many teens. Self-control, when external

controls are absent, is the only option and this is why it is an important goal in parenting teens.

- These facts do not excuse teens for making poor decisions. They simply underscore the importance of taking time out and engaging their reason with their emotions. Even the teen is responsible for choosing the best path of action. It also flags parents of the increased need for their help, not their condemnation.

Therefore, the rational, emotional connection and the practice of mature thinking should be practiced early in the teens, or even before, to mitigate this challenge. For help in developing emotional control, see the next chapter.

Here are more considerations, for both teen and parent, that are applicable to all temperaments:

- A slower thought process and a focus on the question, "What if...," is a helpful training tool for the teen.
- "Do I want this on my résumé?" is also a good stock in trade question for the teen to ask themselves. Another slogan used in the same manner that has helped many was to ask yourself, "WWJD?" ("What would Jesus do?"). Teens might also ask, "What are the consequences of my [skipping class], both short term and long term?"
- Line a wall of the house with posters and quotes that advocate good decision-making.
- Reinforce good decision-making with challenges to show courage. (It always takes greater courage to do what is right than to follow the crowd). Provide opportunities for the teen to earn things they want if good decisions are made. The failed belief that the teen should be good "for nothing" (in other words, be good without having to be rewarded) should die a speedy death. Adults expect a paycheck for work completed! They live for the rewards of responsible behavior.

- Text great self-improvement messages to your teen. Memorizing them can earn the teen something — you decide what. Making the messages temperament-appropriate increases their impact.
- Argue the benefits of boundaries and limits and the wisdom of moderation. Engage reason in teaching and rationalizing good decision-making.
- Let the teen have a "buy-in" to increasingly more decisions and to any discipline that might be applied as they show more wise actions. A buy-in is to encourage their input and for it to be respectfully treated.
- Risky decisions are often taken away from the teen by the parent because of the parent's protective motives, fears, and actions. However, the teen needs experience in making risky decisions and we should give them that chance to develop their judgement and choose between consequences. Consequences have a way of teaching good decision-making. However, don't rely on consequences alone.
- Make most decisions negotiable. Teens don't learn the right thing by being ordered around, but by becoming a part of the process.
- Self-control is essential for teens to lessen aggression and heighten their evaluation of consequences. Self-control is often a matter of emotional control. (See the next chapter.)
- Teens learn best from strong parental modeling. What are they learning?
- Don't enforce a rule that does not have solid reasoning to support it, even if it has been well communicated. Parents who behave exclusively in an authoritarian manner face failure.
- Relax the rules or allow the teen more say in decision-making when maturity of decision-making has been shown.
- Be just, fair, and kind, but keep the boundaries.
- To do all of this, you have to be involved in your child's life as much as possible. Engage!

- Remember, teenage curiosity, independence, and struggle is normal. The challenge is theirs to face and deal with in an ever-increasing display of maturity. Help them!
- Above all, love never fails. Parenting, when love has been abandoned, marginalizes all the parent does and says. But love is not just *anybody's* definition of what is loving. It has to be patient, kind, and not abusive — a love that shows respect and is long-suffering, kind, not rude, (and this is difficult) not easily angered, and keeps no record of wrongs, always protects and trusts, hopes, and perseveres. The author of these excerpts from a two-millennia-old poem is Paul, and no one has written a better list of the essential features of love that causes it to never fail.

DON'T FORGET: Always treat your teen according to their temperament or they will tell you, "You don't get it."

The Role of Memory

- Understand the importance for the teen to build a memory bank of good decisions. Adults depend on their large memory bank of experiences that enable them to make more reliable decisions. The teen is building his.
- Teach the importance of building a solid reference of successes. When facing a temptation, they will then have the experiences of many good decisions to guide them when they feel challenged or weak.
- Most of these memories are filled with emotions and our emotional system is always involved with pulling up past memories from its decision-making library.
- Always be there for the teen when choosing or evaluating the choice of the most appropriate emotion. Their memory bank will increase positively with access to yours.

5: All Aboard the Rollercoaster! Emotions at Full Throttle!

Understanding the Wild Ride of Emotions

During the teenage years, emotions come to the fore for all temperaments and challenge both the teen and their parents. NFs are likely to experience the wildest ride through turbulent emotions. The reasons for an emotional roller coaster don't need much research. For starters, teenagers are looking ahead to life on their own and what it might look like. It can be scary. People are asking them what they are going to be and the question is getting more serious as expectations rise. Times are becoming more serious. With seriousness comes frayed nerves, frustration, frequent lessons learned in the heat of rejections, and the embarrassment of mis-steps. The questions, "Who am I?" and "Who am I going to be?" will finally be answered for good or for ill and the stakes are high.

For preteens, the question was whimsical and playful: "What would you like to be when you grow up?" Any answer was acceptable and sometimes it led to a moment of playful mirth. Now reality is around the corner and the question is, "Have you figured out what you are going to be when you grow up?" The words carry the tone of judgment if not adequately answered.

The teens are a halfway house of sorts. It's the last lap of the developmental journey before the teen is released to freedom, independence, and the responsibility that these realities are going to bring. During the teens, young people are living under the shelter of their parent's home with few obligations and no adult responsibilities, but the future looms larger and nearer every day. Even play and social encounters become more consequential. Things like having a part time job, handling their own money without being bailed out for mistakes, seriously settling down to prepare themselves for a career or choice of college, discovering how to handle their emotions and decisions in their broader social encounters, and finding a mate make this time the biggest challenge of their lives — so far. Fear and confidence fight for dominance in their minds.

Other serious issues face the teen:
- Am I in love?
- Will anyone really want me?
- Why am I not pleasing my parents; I try to make good decisions. They just don't see it my way.
- Should I try drugs like the other teens?

And the list goes on.

Parents do them no favor when they meet their every need and do not let them get their feet wet by experiencing many of these responsibilities ahead of their release date. A few trial runs through the university of hard knocks could help the preparations and speed the maturing process. If for no other reason, the teen needs to meet and become familiar with the emotions that will hit when they do enter the adult world of independence. The over-protective parent is an encouragement for future dependence, not independence.

Independence does not sound so attractive when its full meaning suddenly arrives. Walking a tightrope above a tested and reliable safety net is not the same as walking the same tightrope without a net. Each temperament will approach this with different emotions. Emotions surge around the feeling of wanting the parent to act as their safety net and yet wanting complete freedom. Realistically, they can't have both. A battle that begins inside of them expands to those around them. "I want to keep living at home when I'm 18, but I want my full freedom to do what I want to do in the home, have my friends over, come and go at all hours, do drugs with my friends when my parents are out, or in my room when they are at home, play my music at my volume, be fed, and I don't want to have to do chores or pay rent until I want to move out on my own."

Smart kid, don't you think, but just not living in the real world. The parent is likely to reply, "You are welcome to stay at home, but when you live in this house you live under its rules." This is not usually the end, however. If one parent is firm and the other lenient, the teen will try betting that the tender parent will let them off or negotiate with them over any breach of the rules. Besides, what parent would evict their child? This is the only time the teen will be happy to be viewed as a child.

Much of the emotional roller coaster has to do with the teen going through a period of adjustment to responsible freedom. Until now, freedom has looked rosy.

Of course, there are many other reasons for a teen's emotional ride through the teenage years and here are some more.

Hormones

Hormonal issues begin the last phase of emotional development (teenage), which will last until the mid-twenties. Just because those hormones have started the initial changes on the road to physical maturity does not mean that they ramp up slowly. They can go on an immediate upsurge, their power being felt in scary ways, at times, for the young teen. "What is happening?" they wonder as they seek their peer's advice.

These chemical changes introduce emotions the early teen hasn't experienced before. The word *control* is filled with urgent meaning when faced with these skyrocketing emotions and "in the moment" becomes a critical time period for teenage decision-making. All teens with an F in their profile may experience emotional earthquakes that rattle their confidence and depress their self-image.

In childhood, in-the-moment decisions were commonly made, but now they carry with them greater ramifications. The thought of consequences (hopefully the teenager thinks about consequences) challenges the "in vogue" philosophy. "Just do it, follow your heart!" is the cheap counsel. Now everyone — teen and parents — will learn how strong the teen's self-control is and how influential are the beliefs that the parent has endeavored to instill? Hormones don't back off.

Mind Games

Physical, emotional, and social changes dominate the brain's development in the teenage years. This is why the teen struggles with consistently choosing intelligent emotions to power their decisions or simply with making consistent intelligent decisions. The brain is being organized according to the teen's choices. Consistency should increase throughout the teenage years, so don't expect your young teenager to be as consistent as a nineteen-year-old, but expect constant improvement.

Failure to make good decisions is to be viewed more urgently as a time to teach and methods of discipline must be evaluated in terms of how well they teach. Force diminishes in its effectiveness as a training tool. In deciding on disciplinary measures (the word comes from the word *disciple,* which emphasizes the central theme of all discipline: namely, how well does it teach and train), the following are guidelines:

- If every indiscretion is met with harsh judgment, the teen will feel he is in a correctional facility, not a home. If they feel the parent is beating on them and destroying their feelings of worth, they will withdraw or rebel. Discipline will not have achieved its goal.
- If the parent lectures at each offense, the teen will turn the parent off. No fuss comments work for most minor breaches where guidance is needed and more serious discussions, along with consequences for more serious breaches, are the general way to go with all temperaments.
- Patience is paramount because of the nature of the pruning activity going on in the brain.
- Judgment of the decision is often not as effective as positive, reasoned suggestions. The teen also wants an answer as to why he should do other than what he or she has done. After all, getting the rational activity of the brain to partner and mellow the activity of their emotional brain is what has to happen if maturity is going to advance.
- An effective teacher wants to see the positive results of his teaching and not the progressive alienation of the student.

Teenage signals the change to more of a "stand alongside guidance" than an authoritarian model of discipline. However, for serious breaches, the authority figure (parent) will be required to exercise appropriate authority that achieves their goal as well as the safety and maturity of the teen.

- Remember, angry correction will usually teach anger to the child (there is a place for justified anger as long as it ends in achieving a positive result) and it is not helpful if it ends in the parent's frustrated ability to be effective. To end with "Well, now my teen knows how mad I am," is not successful discipline or guidance. Correction without an effective positive reinforcement or reasonable alternative is only doing half of the task, if that.
- All attempts at discipline can best bear in mind the temperament of the teen and how he or she is best motivated. The strengths of each temperament will take the parent to the core drives that can be challenged and used to motivate a teen. The development of these drives will keep the teen on the track of more consistent and acceptable decision-making. If the parents have not become a good student of the teenager's temperament, they handicap their own effectiveness.

Remember that we are emotional creatures, making most of our decisions based on our emotional responses and in line with our perceived values. Therefore, all guidance is best if it addresses the emotions that led to the unacceptable behavior and argues the benefits of positive, more intelligent emotions. A rational path to choosing emotional motivations is what we really want to develop in the mind of the teen. Patient reasoning, calmly but firmly delivered, best addresses the growing teen's mental needs.

Strangely for the teen (as we have mentioned) emotional development means reducing the number of connections and synapses in the brain, not increasing them. Growth usually means increase, but for the teen, the size of their brain is almost adult size. The process of pruning unwanted and unneeded synapses is still in progress, with much pruning still to go. In this process, the teenager is improving their "free don't" as some scientists call the exercise of self-control. Self-control helps eliminate undesirable connections because it refuses to use a connection that has been used before and, therefore, devalues it.

Too many connections also mean confusion, resulting in emotional inconsistency. Consistency requires emotions that aim at the same goal, such as positive emotions that aim at a positive goal plus beliefs, values, and reasons that don't keep changing and support the goal. When we have two or more established pathways in our brain — one desirable and the other not — consistency of choice is not assured. There needs to be a clear decisiveness and a strong priority. The following story may make the matter clearer.

Evan, an SJ, was brought up in a strict household. He was also taught to dream of achieving and he saw his future as a very successful engineer with all of the benefits such a life could offer. His values and beliefs were built around this dream.

He knew that drug abuse was a path that could derail him. When he was 15, he was cajoled into attending a gathering of his friends with a few others, who cunningly represented the event as simply a "get together." When he arrived, he became suspicious and soon was in the midst of a drug party, the likes of which he had so far avoided attending.

He was pressured by friends who he had felt would not betray him and who he also believed had similar life goals (but were, to his surprise, participating in the drug usage), telling him that one drag would not derail his future. (His values, beliefs, and dreams were being challenged). One friend was a constant user and he could not see that the usage had produced any harmful results in his friend (another challenge to what he had been taught). He had often wondered if his parents were too strict and whether they were right in saying just one slip was all it would take (enter a doubt). Everyone was talking about how it couldn't do any damage to you. Doubts assailed his mind and he refused, but felt himself weakening.

"One experience would not ruin his life," was the thought that kept coming back. It soon became the new belief of the moment and his urge to leave the party left before he did. Now with increasing pressure, a storm of confusion raged in his mind and he was about to succumb when he saw his mother's sad face vividly appear in his mind. The battle was on and the heat of the internal combat was rising. What was he going to do?

His decision, whatever it was, would settle which would become the Alpha connection in his brain, at least for now. Evan's strong beliefs, his dream, his stable self-image and his self-control were about to face the supreme test. In this case, his values won and he slipped out the back door for a lonely walk home, but entering a future now more certain than ever.

From a parent's point of view, can you see how going over scenarios like this with your teen can make the difference in the moment of trial? A teen is benefitted when they know how they function, how they are designed, and what is happening to them mentally when they face the power of changing emotions.

Multiple pathways in the brain give the teen many choices and sometimes they are not evaluated in the moment as thoroughly as they could be, resulting in a bad choice. Pre-thinking likely situations and how they may open up the possibility of taking one of many pathways gives the teen a pre-thought-out pathway to follow and assistance to control their emotions.

When the parent sees teenage parenting as first and foremost a matter of guiding and educating their teen about who they are and how they function, and not as first a matter of using still more force to control their teen, the road is smoother for both.

Establishing Alpha Connections
How do we make a desired connection so strong that it is virtually unchangeable? By repeating it often and by valuing the emotion it gives us.

Sometimes we have many opportunities to repeat a choice and make the connection in our brains a virtual highway for our future decisions to travel.   That helps, but sometimes opportunities don't come along often enough and the connection is not used often, meaning it remains a weak connection. Use is one of the things that strengthen it.

Since these connections are made in our mental world, we can use that mental world to reinforce the connection we want. By repeatedly creating events in our minds where we successfully make the right choice, we strengthen the connection.   The brain does not know the difference between what we do in the real world as opposed to what we do in the virtual world of our imagination. Athletes use this mental practice to improve their performance.   We can all strengthen our connections by mental practice. The parent can help.

> *Samantha had worked toward the goal of being valedictorian and her grades were excellent, but she had sacrificed her social life. She was an ENFP and social events are a big draw for her. She could find time to go to these events, but she was afraid she would become so enthralled with becoming the engaging and vivacious person she is that she would be derailed from her studies and make destructive choices. So far, she had held back from attending them but felt she was missing out. She needed to be the person she was created to be — socially rewarding and rewarded, so how could she solve this dilemma?*
>
> *She must strengthen the highway in her brain that allows her to enjoy some events without fear of being derailed from her studies.   This can be done by*

repeatedly imagining how she will limit but still enjoy the social events she attends. As she vividly lives and relives her ability to limit but still enjoy her events, she becomes the athlete that uses her mental practice to give her confidence that she will make the right choices and keep a helpful balance between her studies and her social events.

Humans are designed to live in their strengths, not their weaknesses, and also to develop strong values and beliefs. We have the mental equipment to achieve and support this tendency toward healthy positive living. Weaknesses only hurt our development and damage our growth. I, for one, believe that we are designed for achievement and healthy living.

Developing Healthy Urges

It's this focus on developing the teen's core strengths that helps the teen with the choice and control of their emotions. If we try to deny our strengths, we become frustrated and weaken our self-control. Parents can help the teenager best by focusing them on the development of their temperament's strengths by giving them opportunities to use their strengths and sharing in their strength's healthy, positive activities. A teenager that is misbehaving can quickly sidetrack a parent to focus on only trying to stop the damaging behavior.

She was failing at school, running with the wrong crowd (being defined as one of the non-achievers and troublemakers). Her attitude was apathetic and she had become angry and confrontational with her parents in practically all matters. Cindy was a beautiful, sweet girl at heart and her parents' minds were filled with one task: namely, reversing everything that was wrong because that was all they seemed to know to do. They corrected her, excessively badgered her about her grades and her homework assignments that were not turned in, lectured her about her waywardness, and thought they were being responsible parents.

Things got worse. She was secretly into drug use and got caught with the wrong crowd, two of whom committed a crime, and all of them were held suspect. Now, without any idea of how to help her, they came for help and a new path began. It was hard, very hard, to convince them at first. To treat her respectfully seemed counterproductive to them and to help her develop her strengths seemed a waste of time when they needed to address her bad behavior. But they did change. What they had been doing wasn't working anyhow.

They loved her, spent lots of time with her doing the things they knew she loved to do, and showed her the life she was designed to live. It took a while, but it worked. She became excited to be who she was. Now they are advocates for developing a teen's strengths as the path to better behavior.

Focusing on their strengths keeps the teen's mind positively oriented and this makes intelligent emotions more likely to be the emotions of choice. Intelligent emotions are positive.

Helping teens identify when they are living in their strengths (positive) and when they are living in their weaknesses (negative) is, therefore, a great help in controlling emotions and also those longer-lasting emotions we call moods.

Bravely Facing Our Emotions

When we are young children, our emotions are simple compared to when we reach the teen years. When very young, we tended to react to the moment and to the surface features of the circumstances that faced us. Seldom did we look behind the actions to see what the intent might have been and how it might figure into an appropriate choice of emotions.

Reason comes more strongly into play as we rationalize our actions, and reason can make our emotional challenges more complex. This means the teen must stand up bravely against the force of emotions as they pause and sort out the increasingly more complex decision-making process. The bravery is the result of a lonely battle inside of themselves. There is no applause or reward, except the feeling of

84

confidence that they are becoming their own person and an effective master of their lives.

Maturity is learning how to stand up with courage to our emotions and sometimes we must resist them, sometimes change them, sometimes redirect them, and sometimes alter their intensity. Whatever the challenge, we must be aware of our emotions first, then examine them, and finally, control them with courage.

Emotions are also more rewarding in the teenage years and, at times, can be more deceptive. Love is experienced in a new and more complex way. Warm emotions are warmer, cool ones are colder, anger is more intentionally directed, and withdrawal is also more purposeful and, at times, more manipulative.

Sam Wang, in *Welcome to Your Child's Brain*, correctly observes that emotions shape and organize our minds. But emotions organize our mind for us without our being aware of what is happening at times. We don't get to choose an initial feeling of fear, for example. We become aware of it after the fact, so to speak, and then must evaluate its appropriateness. The initial organizing is not always what we want to accept. The ability to change the way we think, feel and respond is the path to maturity. The teenage years are the last opportunity before adulthood for learning not to follow these initial judgments without first thinking. "Put your mind in gear before you act" was a wise proverb. Become more aware of what is happening in your mind if you want a chance to control your urges.

Emotions prep our body for action and signal the production of hormones. Sometimes, the teen has to reverse their body's urges or deny them because physical desires and rushing hormones don't think and, at times, have no conscience. It's not just a matter of sexual urges; it's also the challenges of choosing between an emotion that is going to harm us (such as hate) and one that will heal us (such as love). Loving our enemies is not simple, but it can be the only way to heal, regain our self-respect, and ward off the crippling feelings of bitterness and hatred. In that case, it is worth all the effort we must expend to work toward freeing ourselves from the inevitable incarceration that bitterness will force us into.

Emotions Reveal Who We Are
It can help us to bravely face our emotions when we realize they inevitably reveal us to others. Emotions usually don't remain unobserved for long. Result? Either a good presentation of ourselves or one we will regret. One of the best things a teenager can learn is that they can, in most cases, reverse their reaction and start again without total loss of respect.

All teens want to feel they are right the first time, every time! Teens are seeking to feel their freedom and take their place along side of the adults, which they are also about to become. "Surely, I am as smart and as capable as others," their self-image insists. Understanding our limitations and being brave enough to admit them and accept them is a teenage lesson that is hard to learn, but necessary. Most of us don't learn it fully until later in life. So, don't let emotions rule without considering what they will reveal of you.

To face our own emotions and declare we are their boss will require large doses of the following underrated skill: self-control.

Emphasize Self-Control

There is no better gift that parents can give their teen than the ability to control their emotions. It's a repeated theme, one we look at several times in this book from different perspectives, not the least of which is this practical one of how to develop self-control.

Self-Control Requires Effort
Self-control is not an "in-the-moment" strength that we conjure up at the time we need it. In that case, it usually doesn't show up. Most people treat self-control in this way: "I'll call on it when I need it," they declare, and then find it is not up to the

task when called upon, not strong enough. It is a structure built block-on-block, an inner fortress that can protect us against any powerful urge we want to resist. We can't give another person self-control. It is, by nature, only self-generated, but parents can teach it by example and lesson. So, helping a teen build it is a parenting priority.

We can lose the self-control we had yesterday. In fact, yesterday's self-control seldom appears with equal strength the next day. We burn a lot of its energy off with every use. To not use it is to lose it. Self-control is built and rebuilt over a life time. It is the power to say no, and that takes energy. Apathy desires its destruction. Doing nothing takes no energy, of course, and is the road of least resistance. The phrases "just do it" or "just follow your heart" are just such a road. We have to exert an effort to master our lives and whenever we don't, we lose precious self-control. Therefore, it must be intentionally and continually built.

Goals and Self-Control

To control ourselves effectively we need to have a goal and value that goal. Perhaps understanding self-control as making choices that lead toward our goal can make it more palatable. Every New Year we make promises to ourselves and try to keep them only to fail after the first few days or weeks, in most cases. What's wrong? It's no good making promises to ourselves without a goal that we don't value enough. Self-control is lacking when we have not first built a mental and emotional value around our goal.

The problem with most of us is we don't have solid beliefs and values (building blocks for our reticular activating system to identify as important) to insist on when challenged by tiredness, apathy, or other distractions. Remember, no temperament functions well without solid, healthy beliefs and values. These start being instilled in childhood and act as fences for the teen to live within safely.

I was raised on a ranch. Alongside my dad, I built fences and repaired broken ones. I learned the different number of wires required to restrain the different animals. A seven wire fence was best, especially if you had sheep. Anything less and they

87

would wiggle their way through between the wires. Likewise, more than one belief, beliefs that support beliefs, and reasons that support other reasons keep us in bounds and help with self-control. Build strong fences with enough unbending beliefs.

The wires were stretched and only when under tension were they any good. We often went around testing the wires and retightening them. A loose wire was the beginning of breakdown. And so it is with us: a belief that is losing its grip on us and gives under pressure will be the beginning of our self-control's breakdown. Check your beliefs and values often and repair what is weak.

A powerful fence is needed in all our interactions with the world and the teen is finding this out in their social encounters, personal achievements, or lack thereof. In *Welcome to Your Child's Brain*, Ammodt and Wang tell us that a child's ability to resist temptations is a better measure of school success than IQ. If self-control is not well developed in the teenage years, it will negatively impact grades and academic achievement. Self-control will certainly be required for success in advanced education. Help your teen build fences.

Once the emotional development is complete, the matter of emotional control and management that is the catalyst for maturity will still be needed over a lifetime.

The Hot Spot for Emotions
The *amygdala* is the emotional hot spot in our brains that receives messages at all times from all our sense mechanisms and regulates our initial responses to whatever is happening in our world. To do this, it must coordinate and interpret the signals. It coordinates and interprets by assigning a value to all incoming data that comes from our memory, from all our "in-the-moment" perceptions, from all our physical senses, from such diverse sources as our beliefs and our imagination, and eventually, it pays attention to the cognitive interplay of reason and emotion.

The amygdala is not perfect and can make mistakes just like reason makes mistakes at times. Because it must respond with lightning speed to any and all situations, its emotional judgments are often based on first impressions. Many neuroscience writers have pointed out emotion's speed of response and tendency to make fast initial judgments that need to be conditioned by reason and further reflection. Therefore, we will need to remake its decisions at times to meet what we see is a more appropriate response.

Emotion's fingerprints are all over our decision-making. It is helpful to remember that when emotional responses are intense, they can also improve memory, visual perception, and strongly focus our reasoning. Strong emotional responses are not all bad. We all must develop emotional control or be under the mastery of our initial emotional judgments. The NF will have the hardest task achieving this self-management.

The teen needs to feel the forgiveness and the renewed trust of the parent when the teen fails to make the best decision, not hot criticism or icy sarcasm. Such judgmental reactions only set off another emotional reaction from the amygdala and make no sense to the parenting task.

Because of the noisy emotional chatter of a busy amygdala, the teen may not have heard the message as the parent intended to phrase it, even if carefully framed. Expect that you will have to repeat the message and help the teen to hear it correctly at times. We all need that moment of grace. It is well known in human experience that emotional turmoil may interfere with the clarity of our understanding as well as our reason.

When we understand, all this patience seems to be pure wisdom. Greet all immature answers with understanding and a measured patience.

Section Two: What's Happening

6: Fuel in the Tank

The Dominant Emotions of Each Temperament

Temperament Is Fueled by Basic Emotions

It can be very insightful to understand each temperament from the point of view of the dominant emotion that drives them. Emotion is the fuel in the tank and our inner engine won't run without it. Not only must we put the right emotional fuel in the tanks of SPs, SJs, NTs, and NFs, but we should make sure it is good fuel and not contaminated by being overused or misused.

What do we mean by an emotion being overused or misused? Let's take the SP's dominant emotion: optimism. Optimism can be overused. It can blatantly disregard danger signs or the need, at times, to be cautious. Just because we have narrowly missed danger this time does not mean we are going to escape next time. If misused, it can be used to avoid facing the disturbing facts of a series of bad choices — a kind of quick fix to make us feel good. If not used when it should be used, it can cause us to miss opportunities, delay when we shouldn't, or become negative and pessimistic, which for the SP is the pits.

Raw, unbridled emotions, devoid of their positive values and proper use, are arguably the most potent and destructive force that can inflame a human. The teen years are when these power-packed emotions, unless tempered by self-control and the taming experience of having to face undesirable consequences, can run wild and lead to disaster for the teen and others. Temperament and its emotions are then expressed in all their negative weaknesses.

The struggle that the teen has with emotions is first, whether to honor the call of their pure core preferences or to follow some other call — in other words, being who they are designed to be or trying to be someone else. Mimicking others is like wearing a fake mask.

Bright futures can fade into the darkness of night when damaging emotions are allowed to have their own expression regardless of the harm they might do. Free choice (the one thing none of us wants to give up) means we all must face the consequences of our actions and make healthy positive choices or pay the price. All free actions have consequences. Free choice also means no direction that a human can take is denied them — anything that is imaginable can be chosen, even if it spells disaster.

A teenager who is facing a serious temptation for the first time is devoid of the personal knowledge of what happens if a wrong choice is made, unless previously taught. "If in doubt, don't!" is good advice. But remember "Curiosity killed the cat." This is the counter play of our unbridled inquisitiveness. The need for intelligent emotional choices should be clear.

We CAN choose another emotion — one that will help us, not hurt us. Don't let your teen be taught the lie that such a choice is impossible. "We can't help our emotions" is hearing the weak voice in our heads, and we need to resist the temptation to be unduly influenced by the too simplistic advice to "just follow your heart."

Therefore, it makes sense that we become familiar with the basic emotions that drive the temperaments so we can direct our teenager wisely. Each temperament is driven by a dominant emotion and because it is dominant, it will be their number one challenge to control it and express it wisely.

What Are Each Temperament's Emotions?

Note again: the core emotions that drive each temperament can be overused or misused or not used at all, and then they are no longer the beneficial power they are intended to be.

94

Here are the emotions that are dominant within each of the temperaments, along with some ways to help a teen use them wisely and powerfully.

SP — Emotional Fuel Is Optimism

- Optimism is seen in the SP teen's desire to show themselves and others that they can do anything. Invincible is not a dream in the moment of the encounter but a perceived reality to the SP. "I am invincible," they truly think at times. Even death, to the extreme SP, seems like a boundary that can be pushed and played with.
- In the SP teen, a belief is developing that the world is a generous world and there is always tomorrow to recoup whatever they lose today. This is an attractive way to live, since it avoids having to worry too much about consequences. They believe they can always bounce back. Surely the world will forgive the indiscretions of youth and they will be allowed to heal and have another chance.
- Optimism is a tantalizing emotion and other teen temperaments may seek to mimic it, even when it feels uncomfortable for them to be so optimistic. Mimic, yes — on occasions — but optimism is not cautious enough for SJs and is carefully evaluated by the NTs to see if it passes the "rational" test.
- Optimism can forget to look both ways and forges boldly ahead on occasions only to run into trouble. Optimism is an emotion that must interact with reason to maintain its balance.
- In the SP, optimism and self-expression become their default emotions.
- But optimism is a noble emotion and only needs wisdom and analytical evaluation to make it one of the best emotional states. It is to be lauded and wisely applied to all of life.

Therefore, encourage optimism but insist the rational brain be firmly in play so that optimism does not become a foolish action.

SJ — Emotional Fuel Is Caution

- Parents may love this emotion, but the teenage years are not where caution is the most popular or most valued emotion. Those SJs who give this emotion its due respect and value will usually carve a straight path through the teenage years, if a somewhat prosaic one. The thoughtful use of caution connects the analytical/rational brain to the emotional brain, effectively grabbing what I call the window of opportunity to think about the best response.
- Consequences are evaluated by caution. Positive values are respected, but the fear that the SJ teen could be wrong in their choice can become, for the over-cautious SJ, an obsession that avoids anything that smells of risk.
- Caution is a strong drive just like optimism. It can be overdone, or at least misused, especially where risk and faith are called for.
- Caution can lead to fear, where it becomes a crippling emotion. But there are times when in company with caution, fear can save the day and save lives.
- It appears then that moderation for a teen is a safe path, if not the most exciting path.
- In the SJ, caution can turn to pessimism quickly and this is a real danger. It can generate a negative approach to all of life, which will limit the teen's potential and create a mind that wants to settle for less — fearful and nervous. This can also be reflected in an SJ's choice of friends. The positive, optimistic friend is liked but often avoided for fear of the SJ being influenced.
- Caution also helps the SJ teen avoid insecurity, which is their loss of stability that results in unpredictable behavior.

Therefore, encourage caution, but don't let it turn into worry and fear. Imbue it with a tinge of optimism to keep it healthy.

NT — Emotional Fuel Is Calm

- We could, as parents, be excused for thinking this is the most desirable emotion to fuel a teen's temperament, especially because it tempers any display of inappropriate emotion. However, it too, has its limits.
- In the NT, calm is the suppression or limitation of all expressive emotions. We don't want to do that because emotion is essential to the full enjoyment of life and when suppressed, so is the meaning that life can impart.
- For the NT teen, it is learning how to balance the positive effects of calm with the possible loss of meaning in life's experiences, together with the loss of the appreciation of the flights of ecstasy in others.
- Calm results in a steady focus on whatever the NT values. But beware. It can become the parent of non-action and apathy. Watch this, particularly in the INTP.
- Perhaps the NT teen's challenge is to find their path and focus on it while they walk it with enough passion to keep themselves motivated and on task. Where the path is unknown to them, they can become derailed and become stationary wrecks while life passes them by. Calm, in this case, has demotivated them.

Therefore, create opportunities for discovery for the teen NT to stimulate their inquisitiveness and keep them moving with an intense drive. Whatever they do, they will not want to lose their treasured emotional state: calm.

NF — Emotional Fuel Is Passion

- Passion sounds dangerous to parents. It can be! But it provides acceleration for the voice of hope in the NF. All things that the NF is engaged in must be pursued relentlessly and continuously, with and by passion.
- Passion builds up the meaning in every moment of their lives and creates a determination and a direction in the teen. "Which direction?" can be the troubling question. Passions don't pause for too much evaluation. Nor is it finicky about whether it is helpful or hurtful. Therefore, for the NF, passion and analytical/rational evaluation should be constant bed fellows.
- A lack of passion in an NF is certainly a cause for concern. It means their spirit has been deadened by some hurt or the loss of hope. When an NF is bored or apathetic, always think first of the two "H's": the presence of hurt and the loss of hope.
- To create healthy passions, it is imperative to feed healthy beliefs and values. The teens are when the passions of a lifetime are often discovered and, for the studious NF, where they set the compass, learning can become an obsession.
- Healthy companions and constant encouragement to employ logic and reason in their search for their best passions are the general guidelines for the parent to follow.
- For the NF teen, here is a phrase that is a steadying voice in the midst of their passions: "The good is the enemy of the best." Settle for only the best and believe you can achieve it.
- Harmony in the parent's relationships with the teen will keep the door open for the parent to influence and guide the NF through the push and pull of their passions.

Therefore, the evaluative brain and the passionate brain must be lifelong partners, and the NF must learn how to make this marriage in teenage or their passions will lead them in the wrong direction.

All temperaments are moved and motivated by their strengths. Encourage the use of their strengths and don't deny them their emotional fuel. And if they use them, teach them how not to misuse them.

Read all about intelligent emotions, the emotional world of your child, and how to progress toward self-mastery in *Intelligently Emotional* and in *Your Child's Emotional World, Parts 1 and 2.*

7: Fire and Ice: Parent-Teen Relationships

Can you imagine a more basic parenting requirement than to understand your child? By the teenage years, the teen can reasonably expect that the parent understands them. The parent has had 12 years of observation. When parents don't understand their teens, the teens feel they are at war — with the parents and also with themselves — and their main help, the parents, have gone AWOL. Of course, the early teen does not understand this from an analytical viewpoint. They simply feel it.

A strong feeling of rejection in this period of emotional challenges can upset a teen greatly. Since their body has undergone big changes, they will naturally wonder whether there is something lacking in their development.

When criticism hits (and many times, a surge of emotion feels like a punch to the gut), it can morph into anger or any number of other feelings, like resentment, disengagement, rejection, worthlessness, confusion, self-defense, etc. A teen is best served with support and assurance, along with a short explanation to engage the analytical mind during these times.

But the teen is not the only one who is confused. The parent is wondering why their teen has not learned to live like they have been taught. In short, the parent has not remembered that their teen is not made like them and they are most probably a different temperament. This mix of temperaments in a family is what this chapter is all about. You are not required to become a student of temperament psychology, just a parent who understands their teen's temperament. We'll break it down to how each temperament relates to each of the other temperaments — sixteen combinations.

Factor in the different effects parents of different temperaments will have on the teenager, and read both combinations of both parents and teen to have the best guide to good parenting.

SP Parent

SP Parent — SP Teen

The charming, laid back, tolerant, liberal SP parent will find a commonality of expression with an SP teen. Both will feel they know each other and recognize each other. The teen will, however, not feel that all of the decisions the parent makes are fair, since fair is relative to our point of view. However, on the whole, they should get along well. The teen's love of excitement, self-expressiveness, and celebration of freedom will usually find approval from the parent who also wants to join in the fun. Boldness, acting out, and all the shared love of activities, such as adventure, pushing the physical limits of sports a little (or a lot), the love of wheels and balls, tools, and machinery, technology and communication devices, or arts and crafts, dance, music and a host of stimulating experiences that, on a whim, fill their lives will create a perfect parent-teen partnership.

Discipline will be a problem when the teen feels the parent is too heavy handed or is not willing to approve the risks that the teen's peers are urging. A teen wants to believe that approval in general means approval in everything. Anger will flare when the teen feels confined or limited. Impulse, at times, will need to be restrained by the parent, and this will cause some rough weather ahead until the synchrony of temperaments fall into rhythm again.

Being an easygoing and free-handed parent can result in the teen pushing the limits of the parent's liberality. This feels to the parent like an inconsiderate over-reach of their kindness and, to the teen, like an encouragement to test all limits. The two don't jive. Perhaps more concerning is that the teen may feel that all authority figures are or should be like their parent. This will cause some unexpected clashes in society at large. Remember, the parent is responsible for training their teen to enter the experiences of a wider society and to be productive within it. Give an SP teen an inch and they will take a mile, while arguing there is no difference in principle between the two variables.

This reinforcement of their core strengths (by like strengths encouraging like) can quickly lead to overuse by the teen of their inner urges and, as a result, to destructive use, which the parent did not intend. The SP parent must be conscious of this multiplying effect whenever a temperament engages another of the same kind. Enjoy the similarities (temperament is all about the similarities), but show where the line is skillfully drawn.

SP Parent — SJ Teen

Notice that both have an S in their designations. This means a lot is still shared. They are both focused on what is happening in the world outside of themselves. But they have opposite lifestyle designations and that translates into so many differences in core strengths that in many respects, they are opposite temperaments. Parenting seems now to be traversing a turbulent sea that, even with all of the parent's encouragement, seems never to be going to calm down. Of course, there are many calm moments where both parent and teen dance to the same drummer, but when they use certain core urges that are strikingly different from each other in these temperaments, they fall out of rhythm.

Several results of the SP's boldness and adventuresome spirit can occur when matched with an SJ teen. The teen can be stimulated by the SP's fun-loving nature to try more adventures than they normally would feel safe doing. They may then become too bold and overexert themselves to gain favor with their parent. Trouble lies ahead on this path. The cautious SJ can't be made into a freewheeling daredevil and they don't want to feel they are a failure in the eyes of their parent, either.

On the other hand the SJ may fear the risky adventures of the SP parent and become risk averse. If they are then pushed to do what their caution screams is unnerving, they will stubbornly refuse and also disappoint the parent. Bonding, trust, and comfort zones are then all jettisoned. The parent is best to encourage risk-taking little-by-little and be content with small increases in their SJ teen's journey with adventure. Nobody likes to be seen as a coward and your teen is not a coward, even if not a risk-taker, and wants to feel the parent approves of their feelings.

The SP wants to do what works and the SJ, what is right and law respecting. Rules and regulations are there for a purpose and need to be respected. This is the teen's stance on life. The teen can be led to be less concerned about what is right, but is that going to encourage their happiness in the long run? No. We only operate with comfort and fulfillment when we are who we are designed to be. All kinds of aberrant behavior may result from the attempt to change this basic inner drive.

Other differences can surface — an impulsive person with one who does not prefer sudden change, for example. This is a clash between spontaneity and orderliness. Impulsivity in the moment also contrasts with the need for preparedness, optimism with caution, play before work and work before play, a sense of freedom versus a sense of responsibility — all these and more. The SP is characteristically lighthearted, while the SJ is serious and the two will criticize each other. Know your teen and parent them to be who they are so that they may live in comfort with themselves and be all they can be. The key is understanding the differences and similarities. Ask yourself whether you truly understand your teen.

SP Parent — NT Teen

There exists a common desire between these two temperaments, but with a slight twist in its direction. The SP is individualistic and, therefore, does not want to be bound and inhibited — especially when it comes to self-expression. The NT wants to be independent and wants to feel self-sufficient. Self-expression is a little different from self-sufficiency and that, in part, distinguishes these two temperaments. They both want to do what works, though, and that is a place to bond.

The parent may not appreciate the long hours the teen happily spends at work on an ingenious creation or playing with intensity at video games with little outward evidence of excitement. The parent may also fail to appreciate the cool, calm exterior of this teen. It's hard to get a wince out of them. Strategy, with its convoluted path through all the imagined contingencies, may bore the parent, but remember, it is exciting the teen. "How does this temperament live so rewardingly inside their heads?" the parent may be asking. There is a world of excitement out there in the real world and when the NT teen engages in it, they can turn its moments of excitement into a kind of studious evaluation, or so it appears. Long hours at the library will not readily please the SP parent either. Even when the NT plays sports, they gain most of their satisfaction from their cerebral exercises. So, the SP parent is puzzled and finds this is a teen that is hard to divert from their goals. They possess a marked strong will and determination that is stolidly expressed.

In most cases, this teen will probably size up the parent and go their own way, regardless of when or to what degree their inner urges surge. However, skills with tools can bring parent and teen together as they design and build things. Only beware, the NT will want to experiment with doing things differently and disdains doing it the traditional way. Adventures into finding out all they can about their world, mutually engaged in by parent and teen, should have a strong possibility of bringing them together. This parent will also encourage the teen to enjoy more things physical. But don't forget what I have said: the mental evaluation and strategy that belongs to the exercise is of equal, if not more, importance.

Another challenge awaits the parent: the avid interest in math and study. The SP parent is likely to become impatient and call for getting their teen's nose out of the book to have some real fun. Science can entrance both parent and teen, but theoretical interpretations of science will be much more the fascination of the NT teen. So, making the fine distinctions and pre-thinking what the parent can do to engage successfully with the teen is an important parenting technique.

SP Parent — NF Teen

The difficulty for the parent to understand the teen now increases with this combination. Teenage for the NF is all about engaging a wider social world and struggling with powerful emotions while trying to keep everything that is academic and personal in their relative places. Show parental concern for their struggles while remaining optimistic about the teen's daily success. The NF teen is engaged in an intense inner struggle with their emotions, sense of identity, meaning, and personal worth. Therefore, a parent's dismissive approach can seem to invalidate their struggle and create disconnections.

Both the SP and NF find fun rewarding, but for the NF, only if it is meaningful — especially the introverts. The NF teen is now beginning their lifelong search for meaning and personal identity. If the parent does not understand the seriousness of this quest, the teen will find those who do. An earlier bonding will be dissolved if meaning and understanding of the inner struggles of teenage NFs are not understood, appreciated, and empathetically supported. This is a tall order and one the SP may well find is a difficult challenge.

The SP parent is optimistic and typically has a higher self-image. This can be a gift from the heavens for the low self-image of an NF who has a hard time maintaining feelings of self-worth. Just the presence of a lighthearted and fun-loving temperament can lift the NF and change their focus instantly because they are totally engaged with whomever they are with. The parent who lives in the moment can also offer a refreshing focus to the teen that lives in wonder about the future and its unknown possibilities. If the lightheartedness and fun-loving nature of the SP are viewed as too shallow, the introverted NF will become irritated, withdrawn, and impatient.

An SP seems, to the NF, to be comfortable with themselves and that calls for the NF's admiration. Perhaps the parent's greatest confusion and lack of understanding about their teen is, as mentioned, the inability to fathom the NF's constant inner struggles and turmoil. The intensity of self-judgments is not comprehensible to the SP parent and the teen feels judged and alone. Long talks and a patient listening ear is one way the parent can support the inner struggles of this teen as long as there is a constant recognition of the teen's worth. Finding what interests the teen and engaging with them in it is a sure way to open the door that leads to bonding.

This teen is very sensitive to criticism and when the parent does not pick up on the feelings of the NF teen, the teen feels as though each lives on a different planet. It's not going to be possible to pick up on every change to an NF's emotional winds, so talks designed to catch up and understand are attempts that warm the teen and to which they will respond.

An NF teen's imagination and daydreams that are so rewarding to them can be interrupted and demeaned by a non-understanding parent. Watch this certain path that leads to disconnectedness. The SP parent does not readily get drawn into the inner world of the NF and, therefore (although not as critical of it as other temperaments might be), is also likely to be less involved in the virtual world of the NF teen. Those talks and walks and times of closeness with a listening ear are, again, vital to a meaningful relationship. Congratulations if many of these cautions were not needed in your case.

SJ Parent

SJ Parent — SP Teen
Both SJ and SP share the same interest and fascination with the real world, not the virtual mind-world of the Ns. The real world is made for the Ss and by the Ss, so this brings an immediate feeling of comfort with each other. The way SJs and SPs view the real world is not that different and even their language is the same: concrete and focused on the people and happenings of life around them. Even when they talk about abstract concepts, like love, they prefer to talk in concrete terms. That means they translate abstract concepts in real-world terms.

But the emotional approaches of the SJ and SP are very different. The SP teen prefers optimism to rule their lives and the SJ, being a little anxious about optimism, feels it must be tempered with a substantial amount of reality (as they would put it). *Caution* is what they mean by "reality." Being real is having your feet solidly on the ground and walking with practical purpose and a thoughtful goal.

That kind of living will create conflict with the SP teen. They are itching to run with pulsing adrenaline through all the experiences of life, and to do so with little regard to preparedness. "Why prepare?" they ask. We don't know what the future will bring and it might present us with more exciting options. The SJ parent wants a steady and safe footing while the other wants to shake things up and enjoy the movement, salivating at the impulse of the moment. Can you see how the teen might think the SJ parent is old-fashioned and irrelevant?

While the SJ parent can be a perfect fit when the child is very young, when it comes to the teenage years, this parent will be seen as too stiff and restrictive for the adventurous SP teen. The very images of how a teen should behave are poles apart for these two temperaments. Nor can the SP teen see how the SJ can be right — only authoritative and demanding for no good reason.

The SP teen wants to experience all that life and its widening teenage social world can offer, while the SJ parent becomes more and more nervous. The values of the SJ parent — trustworthiness, responsibility, respect for the rules — do not mesh well with freedom, self-expression, tolerance, and do your own thing, which are valued by the SP teen. Not pushing the boundaries for the parent means the curfew was 11:00pm not 11:15pm, which seems ridiculous and more like the demands of a prison officer than a parent to the SP. The SP teen simply can't see the sense of being upset with someone being 15 minutes late. "It was only 15 minutes late; that's not late!" they remonstrate with anger. Perceptions driven by different values spark battles readily for these two. The parent will run into the proverbial buzz saw and then readily turn the buzz saw on the teen.

The secret to these clashes can be negotiations with a teen buy-in as to how much flexibility there is and clearly stated and accepted consequences if they don't comply. Example: The time is discussed, the allowance of extra time agreed upon, and the consequences clearly spelled out and accepted by both.

Caution! This matchup of SJ parent with SP child can result in violent eruptions on the part of both, and the SP teen will then pay the parent back with shocking behavior, drugs, sex, trouble with the authorities — you name it. Parents need to create a clear buy-in to all results and, better still, return to the positive building of strengths that will make sure they engage with their SP teen in their teen's healthy activities, like sports and adventures. Sometimes the reason why the SP teens bury themselves in video games is because the outside activities are not on the menu.

If there is one match (SJ parent with SP teen) that needs a caution sign, it is this one. Parenting must change dramatically in order to achieve success as the child turns the corner into the teenage years. Deep involvement in the teen's interests and openness over all requirements are a must.

SJ Parent — SJ Teen

It would seem that this is the best of all match-ups and it can be, except that there are things that can go wrong and make it one of the worst. Both have the same urges deep within and the same sense of responsibility and trustworthiness. Each reaches for similar goals and approves similar behavior models. They know what pleases each other and what angers each. Understanding should be in place and all it takes is a caring mutual respect.

But respect can be far from reality in this home. Given the relative good behavior of the teen, the parent can become more demanding, looking for an unrealistic superior behavior from this compliant teen. Such over-reach uses authority to control rather than serve. Control is an SJ's way of keeping the boat steady and when used with discretion, it works well on SJ teens. Overdo it and the runaway train is bearing down on you. Authority is respected by an SJ teen if that authority is fair and not overbearing. When overbearing, the teen revolts — not just against the restriction, but against the parent and a relationship of dislike is on the way. Solution? Take the teen into the discussions about the rules and requirements before the event and release some decisions to them to develop their responsibility.

Insecurity is another dreaded SJ state. When SJs become insecure, their lives begin to show signs of disarray and the teen's behavior changes for the worse. An SJ parent may become so upset with the change of behavior that they don't see the forest for the trees and apply more pressure, trying to make the teen step back into line. That approach has little chance of success. Remember, SJs — both parent and teen — have a need to control and over-control is always in the wings, ready to demand center stage. Control means some kind of pressure is needed. Pressure on a teen that is falling apart because of not being in control of their own life will cause them to fight back or disengage, neither of which the parent wants.

In this match of SJ to SJ, care must be used to treat the cause of the problems, not the symptoms; treating the cause of the insecurity, not the behavior it produces, and reshaping an overzealous parent's oppressive authority. Do this and relations have a good chance of returning to normal and the parent can once again return to a place of respect. The teen, also, will feel they have been respected. If the relationship has deteriorated so far that no respect is left, then help is needed and a complete overhaul of the relationship is called for. Get things resolved before this perilous place is reached.

What seemed ideal can fall apart.

SJ Parent — NT Teen
The connections between parent and teen are not so obvious with this combination of temperaments. SJs are serious about life and so are NTs. This does not mean there is no humor in the home, just that life is visited every day with a commitment to do their duty or to work their strategies. Even though the NT teen will be pushing for their full independence and the SJ parent will be cooperative to a point, it will not become an issue of serious contention as long as the teen is granted a respectable amount of independence. That can mean their logical contributions to the decisions that affect them are respectfully accepted if at all possible. NTs have the ability to live life, meeting their own goals and letting others do as they please. Of course, they expect the same treatment in return.

110

But the parent has to insist on the rules being kept. It is then the manner in which this is done that makes all the difference. "You'll do such and such because we are your parents!" Result? The NT teen will refuse to do it. The authority is over-reaching and besides, NTs don't do things because they are commanded to do things. If they do, it is with deep dislike of the parent. NTs are rational beings to the core. They will insist on a good reason that makes sense to them in the given context. The parent's task is to make it make sense to them. Present the case so it does make sense. Forcing an NT into obedience is a road that will lead to stubborn refusal, then disrespect, disconnection, and (at least mentally) the repudiation of the parent as a guide or a desired companion.

SJ parents have a positive effect on the NT. They keep this pragmatic temperament solidly grounded, insisting on realistic goals, championing achievement, and loving the fierce focus of the NT that speaks to them of a teen that will be industrious and go places in life. There is much to please and make the SJ parent proud. With their mutually strong drives and the emphasis on persistence, the SJ can lessen control and watch the teen develop, especially intellectually, without the scary emotions that are found in the NF.

Caution is the emotion that drives the SJ and calm the emotion that moves the NT to their comfort zone. The parent will soon realize calm in teenage is a great advantage. They have already been pleased with this in the teen's passage through childhood. As long as the SJ parent can keep the urge to control an NT down to a crawl, their calm will continue to please.

The NT teen is confident in most things and may or may not love sports and physical activity as much as the SJ parent desires. The NT can be lost in books and in their heads, and some SJs wrongly think this is not healthy. Therefore, the parent needs to develop the teen for which they are (an NT) and not force them into things that lie outside their strong focus.

However, argument is where the symbiotic match ends. Both argue to win — the SJ, because they sincerely believe that they are right and nothing but the right must prevail; the NT

111

argues simply to win, even if they do not believe what they are arguing about. Debate is a field they own and, therefore, they will argue until the cows come home. It is an exercise of at least two of their core strengths: the successful use of logic and success of strategy, both of which are used in finding their way to the goal of winning.

SJ Parent — NF Teen
This is a mix of both good moments and absolute frustration. There are many things the NF teen will do that can make the parenting task pleasant. For example, they like to please, so if the home ship is sailing on calm seas, this core drive of the NF makes parenting a pleasure. The teen wants harmony and, therefore, it behooves the parent to keep their own emotional sea as calm as possible.

An NF is all about relationships, so if the circumstances are rough for the family but the relationships are harmonious, the teen will see it as a golden opportunity to encourage and bolster hope and faith so the family can see its way safely through the storm. Yet, another help for the parent is to understand that the teen wants harmony to keep the threat of conflict away and will, therefore, resort to the exercise of love and loving expressions, if they are accepted, to keep the harmony. But harmony is more than calm, since calm can be nothing more than a false peace in the center of the storm. Because of this knowledge, the NF will constantly want to know if all is right and everyone is truly feeling happy.

Most of the conservative values of the SJ seem to be honored by the NF, like doing your duty, showing respect, using respectful manners, doing well at school (which the NF desires to do), being respectful to parents, showing an interest in spiritual matters, and showering those that are hurt with heartfelt empathy.

Looks like a great parenting match doesn't it? Well, wait. Two major things can turn all this upside-down: emotion and sensitivity. Remember, the teen years are the time for the final development of emotional wisdom and the management of sensitivity, which if not managed well, triggers the emotions.

The emotional intensity of the NF can throw an SJ parent into a panic and drive them to their default means of gaining control: namely, force and unbending harsh commands. These measures will only make matters worse. The last thing an emotional NF teen wants is anger and force causing more conflict. They want understanding and comfort, and when they are calm, the soothing effect of reason. Some SJ parents think that forcing them into subjection is the only way to teach them, but that is so very, very wrong. You want to lose the connection with your teen or lower their self-worth till they feel they are worth nothing? Either will result in really bad and "worthless" behavior. Worthless means the teen thinks they are worthless and then nothing really matters in their perception.

This teen will fight for harmony and the parent often misunderstands what is going on because fighting does not seem like reaching for harmony. Tread on an NF's escalated emotions (fear or anger, in particular) and you will find it bites like a venomous snake, leaving hours of painful emotional agony to be endured, sometimes by both. Meet the emotions with loving care and an obvious attempt to seek harmony and most of the time you will succeed in reaching the NF teen's heart. Once this is accomplished their head is easy to capture. They will also apologize and most of the time, quickly.

Another issue that will often surface is the NF's imagination and the strong influence of their virtual world where they live and play out their responses to the turbulence of their teen relationships. As children, some of them had imaginary friends who were the ideal companions to play with and to help them develop ideal relationships. Now in their teens, the real world of imperfect friends must be encountered, related to, and nurtured. The relationship road in the NF teen's world is never smooth. It does not follow the idyllic paths of imagination, rather the trails of hurt and challenge at every turn. If not helped through this idealistic pursuit, they will either withdraw into themselves, turning their failures into negative self-judgments, or try to change and be like all the others, hardening their hearts, which they find no comfort in doing. Your NF teen will often daydream, either to return to the world of their imaginations that they can control or to refresh a loss of inner energy to keep going.

When emotions are high and the hurt is a deep wound, the NF teen will be most difficult to help. Parents will not know what to do and the worst is to apply force at that time. Boundaries must be kept for the normally compliant NF, but how you do it is the secret to the parent's success. Try lovingly and calmly, because the NF believes at heart that "love never fails."

NT Parent

NT Parent — SP Teen
The SP teen can be quick to anger and constantly searching for fun and pleasure without much cause or concern for getting on with life. They live in the moment and are content with what the moment offers as long as it is not boredom and drudgery.

The teenage years are a real adventure for the SP teen. If not pure excitement, the chance to use their cunning tactical skills presents opportunity at every hand. Guidance seems unnecessary to them because they feel they can make all the smart moves that life calls for and if their moves fail, they simply try again without remorse for the wrong move. The teenage years are a super adrenaline-packed adventure.

Now, give them an NT parent and what happens? The wise NT, with their calm approach and belief that the teen needs to learn by making their own choices and facing the hard knocks, does not trigger the anger of the teen like the more concerned, emotionally driven NF or the authority motivated SJ. Unacceptable behavior is met with a calm insistence on the loss of the privilege that has been misused. The NT parent also believes that people are to "let the teen be" and become who they are. The fun-loving SP teen is to be the pleasure seeker and pursuer of happiness and they will find it, says the NT parent, as long as they don't abuse their privileges. This teen gives the NT parent a reminder of the sparkle of happiness and joy which is medicine the intense NT needs to relieve their single-minded focus.

What pleases the NT parent is the SP's adept use of tools in creating and building things from Lego creations to useful woodworking or impressive art. The achievement of the NT works well with the creativeness of the SP.

The NT parent will, in turn, help focus the scattered teen and keep them on the path of development. When the SP teen is off in one of their rebellious moments, the NT will calmly and firmly redirect them with a no-fuss discipline that is beneficial to both parent and teen. Why get upset when all you have to do is remove the privilege? The best application of this "losing what they abuse" method is to inform the teen beforehand about the boundaries and the consequences so there is no surprise, and the discipline is enacted with the reliability of a mathematical equation and with about the same emotion.

What holds this relationship together is the NT's lack of speedy judgment of the SP's expressionism and the feeling that the teen's individualism is a companion to the independence that the NT parent honors.

Two worlds have met — the world of the physical and the world of the mind — and they have found a bridge that the NT can travel to appreciate the SP, even though a sense of distance is also felt because of the SP's lack of interest in theory and the conceptual universe of ideas. If we could look for a bonding over interests, we might highlight the interest of the NT in the ingenious world of technology and the SP's delight in the use of technology and all things mechanical.

NT Parent — SJ Teen
Another interesting match is the earnestness and calm of the NT parent and the seriousness of the SJ teen. SJs are bent on being successful and the NT, on achieving a goal. The difference is insignificant when it comes to a parenting relationship working. Often in the world of business and research, the two work together and enjoy each other's focus on the details. The NT parent will see greater purpose in leading the teen to think ahead and plan for the "what ifs," which the teen will not reject. Strategy and logistics are partners in devising and making things work, and so it is with the NT and the SJ.

The NT will not have a tendency to control the SJ, which will leave the SJ teen open to attempting to control the parent, but this won't work with the quiet, determined, strong-willed NT parent. The battle will be short and intense, with the SJ teen failing to be able to manipulate or control the NT. Because the NT will grant considerable freedom to the teen to develop their own independence, it will not be a volatile relationship. In most cases, it will be a respectful engagement.

Also, the teen will be pleased at the NT parent's obvious pride in good grades, a serious approach to learning, and a diligence in study. Because the SJ is more logistical (a skill the NT needs to be able to turn their theories and inventions into reality in the commercial world), the NT must not represent their theoretical approach as superior to the SJ's honoring of systems and their step-by-step breakdown of theory into reality. If the teen feels the parent represents themselves as superior intellectually, battle lines will be drawn — even if not made known — and the self-image of the teen will suffer. Trouble lies ahead.

The SJ teen comes in two styles:
1. If they have a T in their profile, they will be more demanding of principles and rules and less responsive to feelings. However, the STJ teen sees life in black and white. The rule is the rule and feelings seldom matter unless they are successfully pointed out to the parent as important facts. This "harder" version of the SJ blends more comfortably with the NT parent. Only the parent's mental world, as opposed to the teen's real world, will highlight the temperament's differences.

   The teen's desire to help can be less appreciated by the NT parent and if not noticed, will make the SJ teen feel less than approved. A lack of approval is a lack of feedback and this can be a source of bad behavior that amounts to payback for an unappreciative parent.

2. If the teen has an F in place of the T in their profile, another element will enter the parenting mix. "F" stands for feelings. Feelings are a people phenomenon and rules are kept or broken by people largely over their emotional reactions to them. This cry for emotions to be understood

116

is what the NT parent must factor into their actions and judgments. Although the SFJ is as rule-oriented as the STJ, they obey the rule with an eye on emotions. "Do the feelings demand the rule be bent?" becomes an issue. With the NT parent, emotions are not front and center in their world and with the ESFJ in particular, emotions can be quite intense and demonstrative, causing discomfort and trouble for the parent-teen relationship.

All SJs will show some emotion in wanting to like other teens and be liked by others because they are social. This can cause an NT parent to look on this desire as a weakness because they see independence as the desired strength. Boundaries must be kept, but honoring the emotions without rejecting or demeaning the teen is the key to less trauma for the parent.

NT Parent — NT Teen

NTs display a common life, pursue like desires, respect each other's mental focus, and feel proud of each other. Reasoning is the "go to" in all matters of training and both feel comfortable with its authority.

What a happy match this can be, but only if the impact of the first and last letter in the profile match is understood. There are two extroverts and two introverts among the NTs, and that can be the source of unexpected clashes. When drained, they can irritate each other and can cause a display of temper that is not typical to the NT. To recharge their spent inner energies, they need opposite conditions that are not disturbed. The introvert needs solitude and if another person disturbs them while recharging, they will snap back or sometimes erupt in anger. When drained, the introvert must be allowed their solitude to recharge and the extrovert, who needs people, must be allowed to connect with people and exciting things to replenish their lost energy. When we are tired we become irritable for the same reason: we are spent and need to replenish our lost energy. Parents should be ever conscious of when a teen is drained and help the teen become aware of it themselves, teaching them what to do to remedy the temporary need: introverts need space and solitude and extroverts need connections with people and/or excitement.

The last two letters, J or P, represent a lifestyle difference. The driven lifestyle of the J can become very impatient with the laid back attitude of the P who seems to not be achieving or, in the case of the INTP, not able to translate their ideas into reality and usefulness. Parenting is often a matter of asking, "Which type is my teen and who am I?" For the theoretical NT parent, such differences can become a matter of study. We have to understand the differences before we can find ways to mitigate the struggles each has with the other.

A dislike of another lifestyle or manner of recharging may arise that can destroy respect and eat away at the success of this excellent match of temperaments. Competition is built into the NT temperament. Both parent and teen will need to win and if maturity has not yet tempered the parent's behavior, competition to win will end up in a fight. Also, what is normally a happy blend of minds will become a struggle for mental dominance. There is a point where the parent must recognize that the competition must end. If not, the game is no longer a game; it is a serious struggle for supremacy.

Last, but not least, is the fact that similarities of temperament may blur what is lacking in the NT teen's development. For NTs, the parent should pay attention to the social development of the teen. This is the time when it becomes a major growth issue and preparing the teen with social manners and social know-how can save the teen some very awkward and embarrassing moments. Life can also become too inward for these thinkers. The teen needs the urge and opportunity to have a little fun and not miss the refreshment that the nutrient of joy can and must bring into their lives.

NT Parent — NF Teen
Contrasting behavior is obvious in this combination. There are many reactions and responses that the injection of emotion into the relationship will cause. But even though there are contrasts, there are also many similarities that point the way for the two temperaments to travel together successfully.

Let's start with the difference in the way their intellects operate. The NT parent is strategic in his thinking, seeking to map a way through the contingencies of life, and the NF teen is diplomatic, seeking to bring people together and find personal solutions to almost everything. The source for this difference is in the way the mind of the NF is emotionally driven and that of the NT is logically directed. The NT will find it hard to constantly take the emotions of the NF into account and value them. It will require an understanding on the part of the NT parent that emotion is the only thing that gives meaning to life and that not to honor its supreme place in the success of relationships will destroy on a daily basis what could be a growing bond.

The NF teen needs the rational and calm approach of the NT, but if the NT does not respect and value the emotions that the NF values, the personal connections will never deepen. It helps for the NT to recognize that they can benefit from a deeper appreciation of emotion, too. The volatile emotions of the NF can unnerve both the NT and the NF, but for totally different reasons. Because the NT parent is not as aware of their emotions, they can be lost as to how to help the teen manage them and they typically withdraw and leave the teen to work it out for themselves.

This feels like abandonment to the NF. The NF is uncomfortable with their own emotions most of the time because they can end relationships in a flash and they can hurt so cruelly. Yet they also reward abundantly. Emotions are both the NF's blessing and challenge.

The passion of the NF is loaded with emotion and sensitivity, which can quickly be too much for the calmer, cooler NT temperament. The parent must not show dislike or disapproval of the NF's passions unless harmful, because they are a central strength without which the NF feels blah. Passion comes in a package of urges that, together, shape the temperament and should not be the focus of the NT displeasure. Again, the NT parent must relearn the value of passion and emotion, which was, if they think about it, the only form of communication with which they, too, began life.

Imagination is another cause of friction between the NT and the NF. It has free rein in the NF and although it is important in the NT as well, it is not confined to reason as the NT may want it to be. In the NF, it can be a wild adventure, uninhibited by rationality. In fact, imagination is often the NF's great adventure land and fantasy land. The NT parent can only wonder if this is unhealthy! In itself, it is not.

Although the NF teen is logical and will listen to reason (provided the emotions are calm), feelings make all things personal for them. "Why do you make everything so personal?" cries the NT parent. Answer: "It only has meaning if it is personal." The trouble is that relationships are personal, feelings about oneself are personal, all learning for the NF is personal to the extent that it helps them live more meaningfully. Realizing that they are coming over to the NF as so impersonal is the NT parent's clue that they need to make their parenting a warmer experience for their NF. NT parents will benefit greatly by warming up the relationship.

The interpretation of what is moral and what is a matter of integrity also plagues this parent-teen relationship. The NF teen makes decisions based on his or her powerful values and convictions, which are being built daily and which can never be separated from the meaning of their lives. In reality for the NF, values interpret the facts. For the NT, the perspective is different: the facts must speak alone, stripped of all personal conviction or treasured values and without any subjective influence. An attack on the NF's values declares war. First, honor the feelings and strong values of the NF and then a calm discussion can help direct their values, if needed. Again, no help will be given if the values are first attacked! The NT has a habit of doing this.

Since both temperaments live in the same virtual world, much discussion and understanding that comes from living in an intuitive mind can take place and knit a rewarding relationship. Emphasize what is shared and develop the teen's strengths, even if to the NT they feel like opposites. We all complement each other.

NF Parent

NF Parent — SP Teen

NFs love anything about the functioning of the human system. Action is a function and the SP teen's interest in being physically active attracts the NF. The SP's actions are even artistic at times, graceful, and beautiful. That, too, stirs deep feelings inside the NF. SPs are *artisans*, as Keirsey calls them. He got this notion from Plato, who called them *iconic*, makers of icons (symbols, works of art). SPs are also optimistic and for the hopeful, future-oriented NF, again, there is a kinship and an appreciation.

But SPs live in the moment and NFs, while having to exist and find pleasure in the moment, live with the meaning of the future bearing down on them constantly. Happiness is *in the moment* for this teen, but happiness *with a meaning that may extend beyond the moment* fulfills the parent. The difference can make them feel poles apart. Creativity, as seen in the SP artisans, is expressed in all the traditional arts from stage performances to music and painting. Because of the dominance of emotion in the NF, a bridge of interest becomes an easy appreciation of the contribution of the SP to society. In fact all things beautiful are valued by both temperaments and both find art a way to express themselves. These connections, among others, bring much pleasure to the NF parent. There is an excitement for the NF parent in being blessed with an SP, typically an exciting, charming teen.

NFs find challenge and pleasure in all temperaments. They will want to develop their SP to the best they can be and this lifts the spirit of the NF to say the least. SPs will welcome all this support and play to the audience.

Now for the challenges: SPs are not inward and introspective, not even in a positive healthy way. They move on quickly with no time for introspection and crave the next of life's experiences. "Pause and smell the roses; search for the meaning behind the facts and happenings of life," is the NF parent's cry. They do not see this same spirit in the SP teen and if it is there (as in the ISFP), it is less inward and more of an insightful interpretation of the outer world of things and people, not the inner world of the mystical spirit. The NF parent must be careful not to convey this feeling because it can be misinterpreted. Intuition will often guide the NF to say and do the right thing.

All those inner strengths of the NF are also missing or less dominant: imagination and the world of fantasy, intuition, the deep search for harmony with others, and more. Their SP teen seems bound for a shallow experience and the NF parent finds it hard to imagine that it will be satisfying for long, but it is. Again, this feeling of the SP being short-changed on the count of the lack of contemplation of life's meaning must not be expressed or leaked to the fully satisfied life of the SP teen.

Celebrate with them. Have fun with them. Explore with them. For the SP teen, even relationships are easily dispensed with as another fills the horizon. In fact, SPs in their relationships are the heartbreakers, while the NF parent is the heart healer. A lack of understanding fills the SP teen when the parent tries to mend all their relationships that have fallen by the wayside and litter the SP's path.

A major problem lurks. When the fiery SP explodes in anger, so does the NF, but the NF hangs onto the event far longer, creating yet more explosions or hurtful comments from their teen. It is a good thing that the SP teen can move on from hurt and anger so quickly. Emotion must be managed and in this case, it is the parent who must master their emotions. The earlier they can do so in their relationship with their SP child, the better. If they wait until teenage to manage their emotional responses and get over them, they may suffer some disconnections with their teenager and the loss of treasured bonds.

The soulful relationship that the NF parent desires needs to undergo a change. Relationships can best become more playful engagements with their teen. However, the SP teen will find their parent's understanding of relationships and all things personal a great benefit when they fall into the rare moment of contemplation.

NF Parent — SJ Teen

Here we see values coming together. The SJ teen is largely conservative, trustworthy, responsible, reliable, honest, a doer of what they see is right, and a Good Samaritan, all of which the NF approves and also exhibits to some degree. The NF parent finds satisfaction in such conservative ethics unless they have made a shift to an ideology that disdains these standards.

What is acceptable in our society is constantly changing and the parent will need to become familiar with where the teen's values have gone in order to provide help. The parent makes decisions largely based on instilled values while the SJ teen may not. Traditions may form their value or they may move toward the values of their peers in order to gain acceptance.

If the NF parent understands how to handle the SJ teen, this is going to be a happy nurturing for both. The SJ is sympathetic, the NF, empathetic, and a mutual caring is the goal that will bring most of the desired harmony. As a social creature, the SJ is seeking a sense of belonging, which contrasts with the NF who is all about building happiness among people. Understanding the teen's need to protect status and to belong will avert some unneeded criticism.

With emotions to the fore, the NF will have a bumpy ride with the SFJs (emotion sparks emotion) and a more distant relationship with the STJs, who care little about emotional meanings. The NF parent can get hurt easily and withdraw or explode at the very moment when they need to increase their loving contact. It will be a hard lesson to learn not to show hurt to the "harder" SJ. SJ teens can see the NF parent as weak when hurt or reactive to what the teen feels is a matter of no significance.

NF parents can also be overbearing with their romantic connections, frequent touches, tender words, and desire for more physical closeness. To feel smothered by a parent in the teenage years is going to cause the teen to distance themselves. Independence is not gained when the bond is overbearing. And let's not forget that the teen years are the beginning of severance from the home.

Painful as it is for the parent, this is the direction in which things are moving. Care should be taken not to distance themselves because of a disappointment over the SJ teen's lack of imagination, idealism, and sensitivity. Focusing the attention on the development of the teen's strengths and helping them mature in their own design is the best path for the NF parent to pursue.

Seldom does the SJ teenager look beyond what is in their immediate real world. Possibilities are not cherished since all is more earthbound and practical. NF parents must get used to this. The SJ teen will crave the material things when the parent wants them to focus on the more lasting, meaningful values of the spirit. A lack of intuitive insights by the teen can make the parent wonder about the teen's understanding of their world. Many of the adjustments will be the parent's responsibility in guiding an SJ teen.

NF parents must learn to be more thoughtful about their expectations of this well-meaning and earthly focused teen. These are the ones born to make the world go around. They are the doers who express their love in a practical way. With so much to be thankful for and with hurdles not too frightening to leap, the NF parent should count their blessings and enjoy this true helpmate and partner in life, guiding them to a smooth passage through teenage.

NF Parent — NT Teen

This is a very good match for the NF parent. They see everything the NT brings to the relationship as positive, except for the lack of emotion. In the teenage years, the NT increasingly parts company as independence calls all the louder. Dropping the emotional ties of childhood, but still wanting the support and pride of a parent who understands them, they look for release from the apron strings.

Their lessening need for emotion, closeness, and their rejection of nurturing is the passage to maturity for the NT teen. In fact, nurturing now feels like an insult, a pathetic misunderstanding of their needs. They want the parent's trust, not their concern. Independence means release to a life on their own unless they have financial needs, of course, in which case they will come calling.   Is that not true of all temperaments! So release them faster than you would an NF, for example.   Speak with favor of their good decisions and their developing self-reliance.

The NT teen will welcome the guidance of an experienced "people person" because when entering a serious relationship, they feel their lack of personal skills. A few think they are as skilled relationally as any other person, but they will soon discover reality. In all matters social and personal, the NF will typically guide and help with encouragement and many words as they take an intense interest in the choices of their teen. Most often, the NF parent will settle for their teen's choices and warmly welcome them. Sometimes the NF parent will be too trusting of their teen's choice of a friend and the relationship will unravel before their eyes or, worse still, be a cause for the teen's demise. Perhaps the best social trainer for the socially awkward NT child is the NF parent who is not over-trusting.

All achievements — both mental and logical — of their teen will be the pride of the NF parent. Study, books, and the world of discovery can be entered into with pleasure by the parent and in this they will be the equal of the NT parent. If true bonding has already taken place — namely, a mutual understanding of each other — bonding over interests will spread the icing on the cake.

Remember, that the optimistic connections between the SP and NF temperaments will mean they will both bring to the NT teen what the SP parent would bring, only in the case of the NF parent, it will be brought with a dose more of meaning and intuition than the NT teen will find magnetic.   The NT teen needs the lighter touch of optimism and hope as they look into the future.   NFs can't help but do this with their generous encouragement. It will help keep the NT on track with a long-term vision. Intuition is shared and the NF parent will be wise to encourage its development in the form of rational insights. Rational intuition makes sense to the NT teen.

Becoming at home with the NT teen's cool and calm approach, their seeming lack of a need for romantic moments, and their emotional distance will take some doing for the NF parent.

The reward will be a relationship that will build with the years and make for a steady, well-grounded and developed NT adult.

NF Parent — NF Teen

Fire and ice, love and hurt are the expectations of this relationship. It can be a remarkable display of emotion and sensitivity. Wouldn't you think that all would be well in this relationship? Each should sense each other's similarities and needs and get along so happily. But, not so. Like sparks like, and emotions being worn on the sleeve of both makes for a turbulent relationship at times and a deeply loving, empathetic one at other times. Love is never forgotten and flashbacks to childhood closeness, tender moments, and the warmth of mental and emotional embrace can bring a foretaste of still more rewarding future experiences.

In so many ways, these parallel each other and encourage closeness and a soul bond. If the major problem of emotionally sparking each other and hurting each other with statements made in the moment of hurt can be modeled positively by the parent for the teen, this can be a match made in heaven. However, perfect relationships don't exist, only fantastically rewarding ones. Please note, even in this potentially wonderful partnership, hell can often intrude, so watch the back door!

The joys for both in sharing moments of imagination, dreams, intuitions, and fantasies can tighten the bond of an already tender and close relationship. The love of beauty and the sharing of their special places, moments, enjoyments, and hopes bring to the fore sympatric emotions. This, potentially, is the true soulful connection. Therefore, as a parent, bend all your efforts to enjoy someone who can on a deep level enjoy you.

In emphasizing the positives and in living as though the future is already here, this can become the greatest opportunity for the parent to develop the teen's strengths. Influence, don't take over their lives and their decisions; they are individuals who are valuing more each day the feelings of becoming an adult. The parent and teen are both influencers. Keep it positive.

126

Influencers have to be sensitive, so please watch that sensitivity does not turn the slightest suggestion of disharmony into hurt. It's a tall order for the hyper-sensitive NF, but a necessary goal and a great model of self-control for the parent to give to the teen.

Don't overemphasize the negatives between each other. Place the focus on personal growth and meaningful significance in each other's lives. Teenage is the time for NFs, both parent and teen, to become mutual pilgrims through these stormy formative teenage years.

8: Out and About — Social Wisdom

Choosing friends with serious social connections is an education the teen is plunged into without any real prior training. The teenage years are the main period where we are to gain in social intelligence.

Social development is different for each temperament. The parent's expectations should be different, too. The issues around which most of their social challenges revolve are, by temperament, the following:

SPs — The social adventurers

- Impulsivity
- Optimism and a lack of fear
- Everything is a challenge and, therefore, calls for a daring action
- Opportunities to make an impact
- Self-expression

SJs — The more cautious socialites

- Am I missing out? When is "being responsible" too cautious?
- How do I control this experience?
- How do I control myself and others?
- Insecurity keeps assaulting me.

NTs — The distant social want-to-be's

- It has to make sense — yes, even all social encounters
- Over evaluation — difficult to strategize relationships
- Where is my list of requirements for my choice of friends?
- I clearly am not attracted to many.   Is there something wrong with me?

NFs — The social emotionalists

- Passion in social encounters
- Introverts can be drowned in the emotion of fear
- Driven by the need for harmonious connections
- Doing anything to please
- Is passion the same as love?

Section Three: Into the Future

9: Maximize Your Teen!

Serious Development for Life

Let's call the strengths of a temperament *core strengths* — our basic design. The word *core* is used with nuclear energy, the center of great power, and in this sense, it is an appropriate designation of the center of human design and functioning. These core strengths are the factors that need to be developed and valued so the teen can progress toward their maximum, their fullest potential.

A Journey

How can we help our teen become all they can be? Notice, I did not say all they <u>want</u> to be, because their wants may not be what will lead them to their best. I remember, as a teen, gazing at a beautiful red piano accordion, prominently displayed in a Whakatane shop window and rationalizing my desire to be a musician. Others that I knew had learned to play them and I could do anything — so I was told. So, I dropped my hard earned money on my heart's desire. Musician? I had no training and soon found I had little skill— rather a fast-mounting heap of frustration. I kept it, kept trying, and finally, after several other instruments, admitted I would love to be the next maestro but didn't seem to have the "gift." What was more obvious to me was that I didn't find the satisfaction I thought I would find. I was made for something else. Could something else work better?

Physical development? We know how to be all that we can be at this: pump, run, sweat, repeat! That worked. Yes, and there was some satisfaction in physical development. But was this my lifelong goal and occupation? I concluded, no!

The teaching of my parents and youth leaders said I was unique; everyone was. So, if we are all unique, we must somehow be designed or create ourselves. I knew I was not creating myself. I had no idea what I wanted to create or how to create it. If I were creating myself, this was a non-planned journey. Was my environment molding me? Only by convincing me I didn't want to be what my environment offered. Nor did I desire to be like the people around me. Don't get me wrong — they were great people, but I knew they were not me.

I slumped into the one thing I seemed to be left with, and that was reading, study, books, the bedroom I built under the house that contained my 30- by 20-inch self-made desk and an old chair — and, oh yes, solitude. But what for? I didn't know with any precision. It just felt right. I gave up asking others what they thought I should be because it only made me despair that this was an unanswerable question. Unwittingly, although I didn't realize it, I had found one thing that fulfilled me: learning, study, that accumulation of knowledge and insight. Now, that's a great future, isn't it — a professional learner?

Someone told me I didn't know who I was, and that rang bells. Years went by and at 21, I had my first glimpse when my college president taught a course on temperament. Temperament at last seemed to offer some help. I saw how I was made on the inside for the first time. I was excited, relieved, mystified, and scared, all in one complex emotion. I was also in a state of both acceptance and denial. What should I do? Study this strange revelation of inside urges. And I did, with no goal in mind except self-discovery. But I knew at this point, that in some way I wanted to be a help to others.

Self-Discovery

How can we maximize what we don't understand? Does the phrase, "anyone can be anything," help us to maximize our teen or help the teens maximize themselves? Hardly, because although that is almost an absolute statement, it lacks several extremely important points. I can do almost anything, but not necessarily well or equally well as others might be able to do them. I know I can do some things better than others. And there is the bigger issue: I don't want to do "anything." I want to do and be what makes me feel chock-full of satisfaction, pleased with life, satiated with that sense of being what I was designed to be, functioning smoothly with a happy feeling. "Anything" is not necessarily what is best for a unique individual.

Recently, I read an article on the attempts to write computer software that would cause a computer to make decisions like humans do. It reported failure. It also concluded that it cannot be done without first building into the software a bias. Humans make decisions with the bias of their values and passions. A computer can never be a human and vice-versa. I am unique and one element of that uniqueness is my biases.

I can see my uniqueness on the outside. All I need is a mirror. *Unique* makes me think more of what's on the inside, my inner design.   That's the knowledge we need to help our teens develop.   The temperament key is where we begin.   From there, it's this personal verification of the life forces within us that will shape us and give us that reward of being filled to the brim with contentment when we use and develop them.

We are talking about an inner core, where the non-physical DNA is to be found: the real me, the way I think, feel and act. My preferences, if you like, that my basic design (my temperament or innerkinetics) has given me.

Nothing trumps this in importance.   Supporting, aiding, and developing a teen's core strengths (the strengths of their temperament) will smooth the path through the teenage years and give them direction in and for life. Here is where to start...

Help your teen develop the strengths of their temperament, the temperament they have verified is truly them.   I would argue developing a strength is:

- The best way to develop purpose in a teen.
- The way to avoid boredom. A teen who is not developing their core strengths is bored, directionless, and has not "found themselves."

- Focusing on who we are and where our design is leading us.

Much of the attraction to drugs and other damaging behavior is offset when a teen finds themselves. Behavior needs direction from our values, beliefs, and core strengths.

Therefore, the next chapters on developing the strengths of the temperaments may be the most used part of this book.

10: The Core Strengths that Shape and Fulfill the SP Temperament

My name is Joel. I like the name; it has a punch to it. Say it with a little force in one short syllable, cryptic like, and emphasize the J — Joel! I want you to remember it.

If you don't know me, you will. Now that I'm a teen, I have learned things about myself. My excitement is not all about toys and games any longer; it's about me. Wow! Those hormones are up there! You know what I mean? You'll soon find out I'm a real risk taker, too. Tell me "no" and you challenge me at the core. "No" means there's a lot of excitement to be had on the forbidden side of life. Did you realize that's how it hits me?

It's true. Only the present moment is my playing field. That's all any of us have, isn't it? I feel my senses on red alert most of the time. You can only feel all there is to feel if you use your radar and read the morning news in every face. And I like to react. You know, be quick to the draw and ready for whatever life brings me. I'm spontaneous and I love it. You won't miss me because I make an impact on everyone, unless they're half dead.

People don't think I take things seriously enough. I do. I'm optimistic and I walk through most of the swamps of life fixated on the mountain peaks. That's where I live, and I'll climb any peak that faces me. Is there any action around here?

The path for teenage development is written in the SP teen's core strengths. A parent may also choose to develop some gifts, talents, and skills that the teen displays or shows an interest in to become a part of their lives. However, if preparation for adulthood is the focus of parenting a teen, the core strengths must be developed so as to not damage the teen or damage others and in order to give the teen an understanding of where their fulfillment in life will be. This will aid greatly in their making good choices.

Try this exercise: Ask the teen to list each of the core strengths of the SP in order of importance *to them*. As they go through their teens, get them to re-list these core strengths in order of importance to them. Do it every year or two and let them see how they are developing and appreciating their core strengths and what changes in their preferences are taking place. Further self-understanding can be achieved by asking them the reasons for any changes in their rating of their strengths. We want to achieve both awareness of their core strengths and a growing appreciation and understanding of them for both the parent and the teen. The parent is not the judge of which core strength is more important than the other. The teen must verify for themselves.

If this is done, the parent can watch the growth of their teen and the teen's self-understanding will be a tremendous help in this final rush to adulthood.

Learn your teen…

A Convenient List of the SP Temperament's Core Strengths

Lives happily in the present moment

Brave, bold, daring

Spontaneous, impulsive

Effective, tactical, aggressive

Easily excited

Wants to make an impact

Lighthearted, playful, tolerant

Ultimate optimist

Action

A focus on the physical senses, graceful

Generous nature

Dramatic concrete language

Lives Happily in the Present Moment (Orientation to Time)

Living in the present moment can cause a constant flow of distractions. Time is passing by like a river and every moment is revealing some other attraction or distraction. If the teen wants to keep focusing on something, they have to grab it mentally and hold onto it or it will disappear down the stream of time. If the SP sees something more interesting to them, they will let the current attraction go and grab the more interesting one. Nothing must slide past that is pregnant with more excitement or possibilities for the moment.

What an exciting, impulsive way to live! But problems, like being easily distracted or being told they can't concentrate, are common judgments hurled at SPs — they don't see the point of concentrating on one thing and letting all others go by without taking a look at them. Is an SP easily distracted? Yes! Can they concentrate when they want to? Yes! This is a natural phenomenon in this temperament and one we all do, to some degree, at times. We have to train ourselves to focus and the SP has to do the same.

Will the SP teen train themselves naturally and instinctively? Not in all circumstances. If an attractive male or female goes by, they will focus on the attraction as well as, if not better than, any other temperament. If it's time to stop shooting hoops in the yard with their friends and do their homework, the chances are remote that the homework will attract them. Impulse means a motivation to do something has arrived, and there is not much impulse in doing homework unless the teen views getting it done will present the chance for a more wanted activity, one they absolutely do not want to miss. In other words, the SP focuses on whatever motivates them. Expectations motivate them as well as the present opportunities.

Just like the NF must learn to manage their emotions, the SP must learn to control or manage their urges for excitement and pleasure. It's not just a matter of what the moment presents but teaching them to make the most of what the rest of the day presents. It's always "how can I take advantage of the most excitement and action?"

Happiness (joy) is a nutrient and we need it. The SP teaches us its importance for all of our lives. However, like some vitamins, it can be taken to excess and poison the system. All nutrients for the health of the human spirit require some degree of self-control. Getting the teen to plan their time, not on paper but in their mind, and learn to make the most of each hour is a needed training. They will do it if the motivation is there. Ever noticed how they can be ready on time if it is something they desperately don't want to miss?

The present has to be lived with gusto, which means excitement is not experienced to the fullest if you hold back. But if you abandon yourself totally to one thrilling activity, you may lose an even greater one. The SP has to learn to look ahead a little and not be consumed in the moment to the point where they miss more important things. Their tactical mind needs to pause to think more about what the alternatives are and what will serve them best. Pausing to think a little more about what they should do does not mean they are being less tactical, either. Speed is only one aspect of the tactician's skills.

140

The constantly refreshed energy of the SP is in part due to the constant changing of their focus. Switching from one thing to another holds boredom at bay and boredom can drain us of energy as fast as activity can, if not faster. The parent must note that the SP teen can teach us how to get the most out of the moment. They have no problem concentrating. It's a matter of asking, "On what are they focused?"

This energy, enthusiasm, and focus is a perfect example of how to maximize the power of our core strengths. When the SP teen adds determination and perseverance to their efforts, it puts the icing on the cake of success. Have you noticed how the SP athlete is determined and perseveres in practice? They can devote themselves to practice as well as anyone else. As long as they practice as though it is a performance, the adrenaline flows and the thrill they feel motivates them.

If asked to sit still and do nothing, the SP fidgets, squirms, looks for distractions, and gets into trouble because they will create a distraction if there isn't one to ward off the boredom. Living in a moment that presents nothing stimulating is painful for them. To ask them to sit and meditate without movement can be torture.

The teenage years have plenty of distractions and heaps of fascination available. Moments can easily be filled with pleasure. If nothing else is available, there is the cell phone, their tablet, or the computer. The world works against the parent who is trying to help their SP focus and persevere because it advocates immediate gratification and constant distractions. However, sports are still ideal for the all around development of an SP. Remember: make it a game or a competition if you want to grab their interest.

Facing a long lecture or (perish the thought) banished to a room with little or nothing to do is when the SP will show the greatest distress. A moment with nothing exciting is torture indeed. Trouble will usually result.

Living in the present is what we all have to do because we have no other moment. But all of us who are not SPs, either live in the moment while focused on the past or we are planning the future, or we are busy with the task we are

141

engaged in. The SP lives in the moment while focused on the moment. Training this "in-the-moment mind" to find the best way to live can be done. What you will need to do is help the SP pause and use their tactical mind more effectively to focus on what is needed most.

Developing this Strength — Things to Share with Your Teen

- Become more aware of what the moment is offering you.
- Learn to choose the best out of the moment. Remember, the good is the enemy of the best.
- Ask: "Is this the best way to spend this moment in the light of the fact that you may miss….?"
- Be who you are — live in the present and learn to hold onto what is best.
- Ask: "Which is the best: doing what you are doing or getting your homework done and then being able to do…?"
- Compete with yourself or others over the tasks you are currently doing.
- Make a competition out of homework each day. You can compete against others or against your own ability to keep focused.
- Learn to live happily in the moment.
- Remember, whatever you focus on becomes more energized, so use this knowledge wisely and make good choices for where you focus.
- Be creative. There are almost endless ways to help a tactical mind pause and think of the best rather than just fall prey to the moment. A happy SP is pleasant, motivated, and their behavior improves.
- But you will probably be asking, "What about values and making good decisions?" Glad you asked, because teaching good decisions and beneficial values is a matter of modeling these things first and then helping the teen to act in such a way as to not damage themselves or others.

Brave — Bold — Daring

Risk is adventurous! It is often accompanied by optimism, action, and wanting to make an impact on others. Most SP teens will display their daring nature when they have an audience. A risk, just for the sake of the risk, is not as rewarding as a risk with others watching or knowing of the exploit. Risks are not limited to the outdoors. Classrooms, homes, public places, adventure parks, anywhere is a stage for risk-taking.

Each of the four SP variations (ESTP, ESFP, ISTP, ISFP) will show different degrees of boldness, but all will feel the call to be daring in some form or another. The ESTP and the ISTP will excel in this department, while the ESFP will risk when it serves their purpose and the ISFP will usually be much more subdued in their bold exploits.

Flouting the law or doing drugs can be simple experimentation for the other temperaments but for the SP, it is taking a risk and experimenting with the added thrill of a precarious activity. Both the NT and the SP are adventurers, but the NT is searching more for a new way to do things and the creation of a new invention or for increased knowledge. The SP is on a quest for the surge of adrenaline and the rush of dopamine that will bring moments of excitement to remember.

It may seem strange to some that the thrill does not have to last. Why risk just for one fleeting high when there are many adventures that carry a long-lasting but less thrilling recognition and delight? A suggested answer is that the SP is measuring excitement by the intensity it offers them. It is as though excitement and pleasure rises with the sun every day and sets long after the sun has descended, so take what it so generously offers and do not focus on the long term.

This theme of a belief in each moment containing more possibilities for the SP to enjoy is deeply rooted in nearly all of their thinking. Beliefs drive the human system and all pleasure starts in the mind. Just as stress is in our response to whatever is happening to us, so pleasure is in our mental grasping of the silver lining that exists in every moment.

Bravery can be defined, for the SP, as more than just risking life and limb in the rescue of someone in danger. It is in doing what others hesitate to do. The SP teen will be seen to be a fast reactor to any situation that presents opportunity for sensual stimulation or the stimulation of others as well.

For the parent who sees their task as preparing the teen for adulthood, their speed of reaction is concerning. What if an unwise decision is made due to the speed at which the teen made the decision? The parent wants to slow the teen down. And there is wisdom in this approach because what the SP needs is more time to think, but that time frame is still small in comparison to others. A brave act that is unwise loses some of its payback to the SP. It is this training that will impact them most, so the parent is trying to show them a better way to make an impact or show their daring nature with a greater payback. If in our training we show the teen a better way to achieve what thrills them, we have a greater chance to affect change.

"Slow down" means to pause for a moment and think. It's just a temporary stop before an action to achieve greater effectiveness. It's a moment to figure out more than just the next move. Skilled basketball players can be seen doing just this: dribbling for a moment gives them a greater chance to see how the play is developing and what might be the next best move. True strategy is thinking far enough ahead to foresee several possible actions. This is the skill the NT exhibits best since it takes time. Think of a chess player and the pregnant pauses that last for minutes before a move is made. This strategizing is not the SP world — too much waiting. They are the action temperament and fast thinking in momentary pauses is the SP at their best. Train them to see the value of a momentary pause. They should quickly catch on. If you (the parent) are an SP, make sure you model the "in the moment" pause and not a thoughtless action with unwise speed.

But what risks should a teen be taking? A teen who has no vision of what they want to be in their future has no guidelines for what risks they should or should not take. "Would I like to have this on my résumé?" — that's an important guideline. "Do I really want to live with the consequences if this risk goes bad?" is another steadying thought.   For the SP teen, it's a matter of their mindset.   One mindset sees only the moment. The other sees the moment in the backdrop of the future.   The moment is in the foreground, but the future is not out of sight. Teach an SP teen the art of thinking in the context of their future.

The teen will need to create this backdrop by thinking a little of their future.   Parents can feed in lots of ideas, but a parent is never wise to formulate an SP teen's future for them unless it is the one they do not want their teen to pursue!   All temperaments imagine their future, and the more the SP sees their future, the stronger the influence it will have on them.

Remember, if you want your SP teen to <u>not</u> do something, rather than telling them not to do it, dare them to do what you want them to do.   Dare them to do what is right, always with the reminder that doing what is right is always harder than doing what is wrong or what the crowd is doing.   Great courage is in going against the flow of opinion and doing what no one else is willing to do.   Gandhi, in his quiet way and although not an SP, showed remarkable courage in choosing to do what all others were not willing to do or felt was foolish. An SP teen with their penchant for bold, courageous acts should be helped to see where the real courage lives.

Developing this Strength — Things to Share with Your Teen

- Understand this brave, bold image of courage. Use it and don't misuse it.
- Courage is a way to control fear and drive its negatives out of your life.
- If ever you feel uninspired, do something courageous and wise.
- Direct the daring risk-taking nature of this SP to positive pursuits where it will have its greatest impact.
- Channel the SP into productive areas, such as sports or actions that benefit others, and teach them not to overuse or misuse this strength.

- Help them develop a vision of what they will become and what they long to be.
- In all tactical decisions, help them develop a pause that will give more wisdom to their tactics. Speed is not everything.
- Remember, risk too much of life and limb and you will risk no more — you'll be dead!

Spontaneous — Impulsive

Think of all the good things an impulse can initiate: works of art, a productive meeting, a life-changing experience, a kind word, an inspiration, a moment of joy, and on and on. Life is not planned and structured, nor are all the good things in life carefully orchestrated. Welcome the moments of unplanned happenings and let your SP know you don't despise this thrilling gift that lies in seizing the moment.

All these strengths of the SP are interrelated. Impulse is an unpremeditated risk. It can turn out good or otherwise. Some premeditation is wise, of course. The SP is not likely to pause unless trained to pause. To be spontaneous and impulsive is to live in the moment, which SPs do. The teen will follow this urge without hesitation at times. A mental image of pausing to choose the best move and evaluate the other options that any moment will offer is something the parent can help build into the teen's mental processing.

Before a likely choice has to be made, a simple reminder that does not put the teen down or treat the teen as though they have to be parented can help activate a "think before you leap mentality." A reminder is a prompt, not an instruction. This soft communication in the spirit of "just flagging" can be used early in the teenage years most effectively, informing of the parent's intent to signal that they will be guiding.

Modeling how the parent thinks before they leap is very helpful if the parent is an SP, not as helpful if the parent is another temperament. Therefore, if the parent is not an SP, learning how an SP will make speedy but still thoughtful decisions will guide them in teaching the young teen.

146

Teaching the teen can be a simple no-fuss condition for being allowed more independence. "We think it's time to release some more independence to you, so let me outline what we mean and please ask if anything is not clear." A teen wants to be spoken to as an adult, even though they may not be an adult yet. We all want to be treated respectfully before we actually have the rights of complete independence. "Give respect to earn respect" is a good mantra for the parent. Dad and teen or mother and teen outings can be woven into all the demands of a family's life and become special times of companionship and offhand training. Where possible, share and compete in their skills and make these times talk times, not just competitions.

After-the-fact reporting can be a fun experience. An SP, when asked to share their exciting adventures of the day, finds an opportunity for self-expression and gives the parent the chance to know what is going on in their teen's life. Where possible, share the teen's excitement. If you want this time to become productive, don't make it a time for correction or the teen will not share without fear of reprisal. Talk later about any issue that needs your input and your help.

Spontaneity, for the SP, is release and adventure, room to move, and a chance to impress, to feel the rush of freedom under their wings and the adventure of change. The SP values this strength because they must feel free to move when the urge calls. The teenage years are when they follow these urges with increasing responsibility to own the consequences of their choices. Consequences don't scare the SP like they do an SJ, for example. They don't lose any joy over a bad decision because they know they will have the opportunity of another decision and get it right the next time.

Spontaneity is the condition that presents them with the chance to use and develop their tactical skills. SPs want to be the first to act, and the speed in which they act is their advantage.

Looking at this strength from another point of view, it is an act of faith — a belief not so much in the rightness of the action but in the ability of a skilled tactician. SP teens are developing this belief in their own ability constantly and feel bad about themselves if they don't believe in themselves. Ridicule their impulsiveness and they feel you are ridiculing them. The best training for the SP teen is how to be spontaneous and yet thoughtful. Fast but accurate thinking is what they like to be known for.

Fear is the enemy of impulse. When we are controlled by fear we lose the desire to act impulsively. Your SP teen must give fear no quarter or they will hate the person they have become. To be spontaneous is to be creative in the moment. Welcome this strength that comes and goes like the wind and, at times, blows with force over our dull spirits to enliven them.

Developing this Strength — Things to Share with Your Teen

- Help your teen become increasingly aware of their use of spontaneity.
- Point out the mental and emotional lift spontaneity produces.
- This strength requires confidence in yourself and, therefore, is a self-image builder when resorted to in times of depression.
- Feel the surge a sudden impulse can bring and pay attention to its inspiration when there is one.
- Don't forget to carry a little thoughtfulness into your spontaneous moments and let spontaneity and thoughtfulness enrich each other.
- Keep fear out of your life and your impulses will reward you more frequently and more fully.

Effective — Tactical — Aggressive

Effective
The SP is all about producing a desirable result and will stop at nothing to achieve that result. This single-minded perseverance is one of the reasons for their success. If you

fail, try, try, try again. Do so in different ways and leave no stone unturned. Once, as teens, they have gained independence from the home, this determination is the line between living well and losing. As a teen who is still within the security of the home, this determination is more about finding which stones are the ones to turn in order to get them what they want. Experimentation ranks higher than single-minded determination for the SP teen.

To be effective is to impress. More than one SP drive is involved in being successful when an SP achieves. They use tactics, aggressiveness, making an impact, boldness, excitement, optimism, and have also engaged action in the cause. Whereas the NT is more about being efficient, the SP struggles for effectiveness.

Powers of persuasion, execution, influence, and competitiveness, are all in play. The ancient proverb, "easier said than done," does not distract the SP when a goal is firmly chosen. When the SP has run out of ways to make something happen, they do something — anything that has a chance. If left with nothing else to do, they will spin their efforts to you as success. They are impressively optimistic in all things. Slumping into the pit of surrender and giving up is unthinkable.

What an impressive image of the powers of the effective SP! This winning, never-die attitude is the SP's path to greatness. The SJ will plan and act, taking one step after another and then, if all fails, resign themselves to defeat but rise to fight again. The NT will strategize and theorize and when their theory fails, invent another and yet another. The NF will delve into the nuclear energy of emotion and with undying passion, give all and die in their cause. Each has a way to ultimately look like they are made in the image of indestructible power, vanquishing all odds. SPs only fail when they give up. We want our SP teens to learn how to be all that they can be.

Therefore, as parents, we don't want our SP to give up, but we want them to also treasure the power of wisdom and know when to bow out and fight another day.

Aggressive

The determination that leads the SP to effectiveness is also the force that makes them, at times, aggressive. Aggression, for the SP, is a readiness or willingness to apply force and attack. It can lead quickly to physical violence, which the parent should set their sights on discouraging, of course. Once it enters the stage of being physically destructive, it has often crossed the line of no return. Wherever moral standards of right and wrong are not taught, the SP can become the villain of the neighborhood. In most cases it is first observed as an aggressive or "won't die" attitude. This is the stage of all-hands-on-deck to influence the teen in a positive direction.

Aggression in the teen and the adult is causal. A human cause begins in the mind and flowers in the actions. Lying between the thought and the action is the belief. A belief is a conviction of the right or wrong of something and we will always act according to our beliefs. Therefore, great importance should be placed on the formation of good and productive beliefs. The parent can model these and teach them in the spirit of a guidance officer. They can warn of the damage done to the aggressive person and to others. But above and beyond this, they will need to keep all the positive forces of example and guidance in play to offset and avoid their teen becoming consumed by the destructive forces of aggression. Discipline may be necessary.

Keep this in mind: a belief that has become an extreme conviction can result in what we see daily in our world — people who have become fanatics and who will do anything to destroy and kill in the name of their depraved beliefs.

Tactical

Tactics are the means used to achieve effectiveness or aggression.

There's little time to waste. We must do something now! That's the spirit of tactics. Tactics is the art of maneuvering in order to win or come out ahead. Armies, ships, and aircraft employ tactics to order or arrange their forces for effective attacks and defenses. The SP teen is a winner and tactical movements are the weapon of choice to defeat the slower thinking opponent. In social situations the SP employs tactics often, much to the despair of others. To keep the moment moving and exciting, tactics are also used to produce desired effects.

The mind of the SP is ever-searching for the tactics that will give them the advantage. It is a tool that enables effective action and can result in aggressiveness. This strength is not to be discouraged because it will be one of the most important reasons for the SP's success. But it can also be a cause of their downfall.

Being the means to an end, tactics can be evaluated for both their successfulness and their ethical rightness. Our tendency is to judge them for their successfulness alone. This is the spirit of our age and even political behavior can be seen as doing just that.

Ethics is a word that has been devalued in our society and culture. Effectiveness, aggression, and success have been elevated to a more important status. The ethical rightness of an action has become one of the last things to be considered. The end truly justifies the means these days. But this is the path to destruction that all nations and empires have trod. Humans must limit their actions to those that do good to themselves and others. Therefore, tactics are to be judged as advantageous or otherwise according to the ethical effect that they have. The teen can be helped by a study of ethics and an understanding of how their actions can be judged as constructive or destructive.

How are you going to influence your teen over the matter of right and wrong? Nothing more powerful in ethical training is the instillation of the golden rule as a firm belief. "Do to others as you would have them do to you."

The heart of the SP temperament is really not action or excitement but effectiveness and an unsurpassed determination to bring that about.

Developing this Strength — Things to Share with Your Teen

- Being effective has to do with timing, arrangement, and methods. Help the teen be aware of the timing of their actions and the way they go about achieving a goal.
- The tactics for being effective will determine the degree of effectiveness. Tactics are not just the first solution that comes to mind. Good tactics are chosen to best achieve the desired result. The fast-acting SP teen can be helped to consider alternatives, even if they consider them only briefly. It is the pathway to selecting the best tactics in adulthood and succeeding greatly.
- Aggressiveness should be taught as a tool to be used appropriately. Help the teen develop firm boundaries for the use of aggressiveness. If our aggressiveness does damage to ourselves and others, it is questionable.
- Tactics or aggressiveness can eat away at our personal integrity if carelessly used. Being a person of trust and honor is a value to carry into adulthood.
- Remember, the wrong use of these drives can destroy your life.
- When losing, help the teen to fully appreciate that losing is the signal for us to rise to the next level of effectiveness. Failure is often the only teacher that elevates our success.

Easily Excited

Is this a strength in teenage? SJ parents might view it as potential trouble, and it can be. It can also be a strength and a wonderful positive nutrition for the human spirit. The teen that falls into depressive gloom is in just as much danger as the teen who is overusing this strength. Overuse is being too responsive to indications of pleasure and, therefore, looking for them to the exclusion of exercising responsibility.

By definition, being excited is being at a level of stimulation higher than normal. We are talking about "above normal" most of the time for the pleasure-seeking SP teen. Excitement is enjoyed in the moment for them. It is the quest of the SP and brings with it health and happiness of spirit. One thing we do not want is an SP who has lost their optimistic, excitable spirit and has sunk into a depression.

Excitement for the SP teen is mainly a stimulation of the physical senses. Adventure, trips to exciting places, and physical thrills of all sorts will stimulate an SP teen and give them the feeling of a natural high and can offset the tug to experience the unnatural highs of drugs. With that in mind, the parent can appreciate the value of physical challenges and experiences for the easily excited SP.

The parent is looking for the exhilaration and adrenalized effects of action. Sports are, therefore, a natural for the SP teen because they not only provide action and adrenaline but approval, applause, and the development of discipline. Just one glance down the list of core strengths in the SP temperament will reveal how physical achievements in the company of a crowd of people can elevate sport to the perfect avenue for the development of the SP teen.

Can a teen be over stimulated? Yes, but it is less of a concern than under stimulation. The SP maintains a high self-esteem because happiness is not found in a low self-esteem. Bouncing off the walls with excitement will usually be calmed with the burning up of energy, whereas the lifting of a low self-image is a much more demanding and difficult task.

Joy and happiness don't last. They have to be renewed daily. Yesterday's joy doesn't make the same impression on an SP as the joy of the present moment. In fact, it can be easily forgotten with the arrival of new pleasures. Excitement is motivation. Absolutely essential for the developing teen is excitement that leads to motivation. For the SP, the loss of motivation is a loss of excitement. To keep our actions balanced, let's remember, excitement is not an end in life; it is a means to an end.

Developing this Strength — Things to Share with Your Teen

- Catch the moments of excitement with your SP teen. Let them feel the impact they are making on you as well as feel the impact they are feeling themselves.
- Celebrations of their achievements are not to be missed.
- Excitement feeds optimism and optimism is their dominant driving emotion, so we want to encourage both excitement and an optimistic spirit.
- When your SP teen is feeling down, criticism will not serve either their purpose or yours. Lift the sunken spirit of an SP and they will return more quickly to their normal optimistic spirit.

Wants to Make an Impact

SPs seek to be noticed. Making an impact on another person means they are being effective by some measure. Beating another person in a race is making an impact, so is stealing the affection of a lover away from another (a misuse of a strength).

Making an impact has a positive effect on the self-image. The adrenaline rush of applause or the reception ceremony in the winner's circle does the same. Most of us do not realize the need for keeping our self-esteems high. I have mentioned several times how a low self-image results in poor behavior. How can someone who thinks they are not worth anything act with the same motivation as someone who has a high self-esteem?

Some authorities feel that helping teens to a positive self-esteem is the parent's greatest task. I don't know if I would say the greatest, but it is of notable importance. Parent's suffer, too, when a teen does not love herself. Self-esteem is a protection against delinquency, drugs, and the eager quest for relationships at all costs. Of course, it can be misused, but the healthy use is of value.

For the SP teen, making an impact is a way of proving to themselves that they are worthy of their positive feelings. Parents have the greatest impact in the formative years of life in molding and shaping their children and how they think of themselves. By far, their influence on how a child thinks about himself has the greatest impact. The same is true of the teenage years when the emotional and social intelligence is being formed. Teens are learning to make the best decisions and that is not the easiest of accomplishments. Only if we feel good about ourselves can we expect to learn to make good decisions.

The SP can make an impact on others in either a positive or negative way, and persuading an SP to accept the challenge of making a positive impact is to call on their courage to be outstanding as a leader for what benefits others most.

Developing this Strength — Things to Share with Your Teen

- Make a positive impact! Keep looking to make positive impacts.
- If performing or any acceptable skill is their way of making a positive impact on others, then help them train and practice their skills.
- Life itself is making an impact on things and on people. Opportunities are endless. See your life as a parent in terms of your making an impression that will change the lives of others.

Lighthearted, Playful, Tolerant

Lighten up to light up. Happy people lighten their hearts with optimism, trust, and faith. The flame of our positive beliefs ignites the fire of happiness in others. This is one reason why the SP is so attractive to all and to SJs, they appear as being able to handle life with ease — at times, a near impossible task for the SJs.

Lighthearted

Lighthearted is a contagious concept and one the optimistic SP lives by. The opposite, heavyhearted, plunges us into the gloom of sadness and the pit of dejectedness. An SP shudders at that thought. When that happens, life has lost all its pleasure.

The SP teen attracts attention, also, because of their pleasant approach to life, which draws others out of gloom and into moments of happy abandonment. As far back as literature goes, people have felt the need to escape the seriousness of life, so they have danced, sung, and expressed their happiness with abandon.

If the SP teen has an SJ parent who is too serious, the parent will stand in stark contrast to the SP's sense of lightheartedness. A disconnection occurs. There is a time and place for both lightheartedness and seriousness, and the parent is wise to make sure they do not present themselves to their SP teen as the killer of their joys. It may not be too far-fetched to say, but the SP is made to lift the sullen heart and spread joy and brightness wherever they go. The human race needs both the lightheartedness of the SP and the seriousness of the SJ.

It's in the widening circles of teenage social life that the SP finds the chance to spread their lightheartedness to others and feels the lift it gives them when they impact those around them.

Playful

Playful is a lighthearted concept and is the common SP expression of lightheartedness. Play is a tool that the SP teen finds hard to discard or tone down when they are faced with a widening circle of friends. As kids, they played with gusto and happy purpose. Now as teens, the urge has not diminished. It is only the search for relationships and for status that has now increased and play is an important part of how they sort out their mates and sense their importance, which often revolves around their skills at play. Often the skills and the lightheartedness are combined, as in a recital, a show, a musical production, or drama.

Sport activities are a chance to play and, although an SP may take the competition and practice seriously, they do not equate the effort with the drudgery of work. Play is for a purpose and work also, but the acceptability lies in the purpose for which either is performed. Therefore, for an SP, work can be made more attractive if it gives pleasure, is competitive, and contains an element of fun. A close feeling to playfulness is when the SP teen is acting, as in a play. Also, action can be a substitute in the workplace for playfulness

Tolerant

Tolerance is a form of lightheartedness. It means we are giving another person the right and the freedom to think and act as they will. Judgment becomes the enemy of tolerance; rules and regulations must, therefore, bend. The word means to permit to indulge (if not to endorse), to turn a blind eye. The SP's style is a permissive approach to life.

Tolerance has limits, unless we want to remove all laws and condone all actions. What usually happens is that the one who wants tolerance for all is intolerant of those who disagree with them. So, the SP either must change what society will accept or accept what society will not change, and that means a limit to absolute tolerance.

Help your teen to assimilate into society without damaging themselves or others with their demands for tolerance. Most people put tolerance in a sensible place and recognize that we can't be tolerant of all things (an obvious example is willful murder) and being intolerant can, at times, breed hatred and resentment, which we don't want in a healthy society, either. A guided decision is what a parent can hope for. Creating a belief system that serves us well has been the struggle of people in all ages and the breeding ground for great good. When the belief is destructive, the breeding ground for great hurt.

157

Developing this Strength — Things to Share with Your Teen

- Remember, optimism is the emotion that will make this strength possible.
- As soon as worry and pessimism raise their heads, help your teen refocus on something good and enjoyable.
- Positive beliefs create light hearts.
- Refashion your belief so you see play as a positive use of your time.
- Create a balance between refreshing activities and work.
- Be tolerant of others, but don't destroy the backbone in your own beliefs.
- Encourage others to lighten up and then show them how.
- Don't forget that true happiness is born in our beliefs.
- Always hope. Then doubt and despair will find it hard to find a resting place.

Ultimate Optimist

The SJ parent will immediately think of risk-taking and an irresponsible attitude because they are the watchdogs of danger and breakdown in society. The balance is a place all families and cultures must seek to find.

Optimism is a healthy mental and emotional state. It is also the SP's dominant emotion that fuels the strengths of their temperament. It is their way of seeing the world. Take it away from the SP teen and they feel the drumbeat of pessimism. To your teen, anything less than optimism is pessimism. A parenting model that meets optimism head on will incur a rough ride.

The benefits of optimism are the ease in which the teen will move from worrisome concerns to lightheartedness and fun. If the parent is a worrier, the parent is the one that will be taught the lighter side of life. In fact, parents of SPs usually find themselves having to meet their teen halfway. A conversation about how risky some activity is will likely make the SP teen feel controlled and they can choose to tactfully take the risk on the sly to prove to themselves that they are the spirit of freedom. Parent with calm guidance and not with anger or heated debate because that only increases the chance that your teen will take matters into their own hands. Share life with them as much as possible.

Depression is not a common occurrence in the life of an SP teen and when sadness assails, they will usually pull out of it quickly, desiring to feel the fresh air of optimism again. Optimism is a healthy spirit most desired in a troubled world. Wisdom is what optimism needs.

The pitfalls, hardships, and disappointments of life are experienced with a detachment that circumnavigates worry and pessimism. The SP teen finds it easy to believe something if there is a driving sense of optimism about it. Keep this in mind as you parent with guidance and appropriate discipline. Show the upside of a behavior. Those who immediately expose the downside of whatever is being discussed will find the SP teen feeling the necessity to oppose all that is being said. The SP teen wants to know what can be done, not what can't be done.

The optimist also feels that the company of pessimists or worriers is depressing, an air too heavy to breathe. Therefore, they detach from not only the discussion, but the person. Does your teen feel you are a depressing influence? If so, it is probably because you started by telling them what they can't do and by delineating all the dangers and troubles that lay ahead. With this teen you must start discussing any issue with its benefits and possibilities, not its downside. Flagging the downside after relating the upside is much more acceptable to an optimist. Optimists live on dopamine and pessimists starve themselves of it.

Optimism demands a faith and trust in ourselves. The self-image is usually high and healthy. Confidence is the air the optimist breathes, whereas it chokes the pessimist. When the parent gives the impression that they feel optimism is foolish, they have lost their SP teen. As a result of optimism, the SP can be a great encourager of those who are timid. Where bold attitudes are needed, SPs become intrepid leaders.

The parent who has most to be concerned about with the SP teen is the SJ, since they are "bearish" and their SP teen is "bullish," to use the language of Wall Street. The parents should be watchful of their attitudes and their language that gives the feeling that confidence is over-confidence, optimism is a rash judgment, and positivism is a foolish and unintelligent way of life.

Developing this Strength — Things to Share with Your Teen

- Create a positive and optimistic atmosphere in the home.
- Encourage optimistic beliefs.
- Encourage a positive self-worth. Being down on ourselves and our world leads to worry and depressive beliefs that the SP finds hard to understand.
- Encourage the wise use of freedom.
- Indulge in positive self-talk.
- Detach from negative people and negative influences as much as possible.
- Celebrate your successes and all the good that you hold dear.
- Belief in the Divine has been found to be healthy and uplifting by researchers and billions of people.
- Check each other's confidence daily.
- Look everyone in the eye and say to yourself, "I am at least as good as they are."
- Be thankful in all things.
- Be a family that finds the silver lining in every dark cloud. Learn to search for and focus on the good, the wonderful, and beautiful.
- Become an encourager of others. Encourage each other.

Action and the Physical Senses

When action is a dominant theme in our lives, boredom and the downside of life find less opportunity to uncover a resting place in our hearts and minds. An active teen is less likely to find trouble or get into trouble — more likely to find pleasure.

Action for an SP is anything that stimulates. Sports of all kinds — art and artisan interests, creative writing, games, competitions, all these create excitement and offer creative possibilities. Depending on which you, the parent, see as appropriate, some are more beneficial than others.

How valuable is this SP teen? If an ounce of action is worth a ton of theory, they are very valuable to society. But the teen is not always active. Action should be encouraged and be a large part of the family's agenda. Movement is essential to life and movement shapes this teen. SPs live in the world outside of themselves, searching its offerings and experiencing its exciting actions. Keep them active and you will mitigate many troubles. Activity also lifts their self-image and their confidence in their abilities.

An SP teen should be encouraged to excel in some physical way, be it team sports or skilled use of a paint brush or a pen. Physical success builds self-confidence in the SP.

Because they live in the moment, they need to fashion some dream for their future. The attraction of future possibilities can keep their active lives on track. Don't demand it; just encourage it.

Developing this Strength — Things to Share with Your Teen

- Know your teen's active interests and plan your encouragement of them and your parent involvement where possible.
- Explore new activities.

- If an SP teen is depressed, increase the activities and explore new ones. With an SP you have the easiest task to get them out of depression. If it persists, get help.
- Model your own interest in activities.
- Employ the help of a coach or an InnerKinetics® specialist to maximize the teen's capabilities.
- Make their performances a family time.

Generous Nature

This strength is not just generosity. It's an attitude to life and a driving force of much that the SP feels and does. Perhaps it's best expressed by the phrase, "Easy come, easy go." We have already referred to the SP's belief in a generous world and if you really believe that, then generosity is not so much a sacrifice as it is a sharing. There is even a lightheartedness, a happiness in sharing. The pain of loss seems alien to the person who believes in easy come, easy go.

The SP teen doesn't usually save for a rainy day, either. Why? More will come their way and living in the moment is spending the resources they have been so freely given. The SP sees life as much from the receiver's point of view (good will come) as from the giver's (I'm simply sharing of the abundance that I have).

Pleasure is not to be possessed. It belongs to us all, and sharing the joy of the moment is an act of love and kindness at its best for the SP. There is another positive aspect to generosity for the SP: sharing what they have with others makes a great impression and they are all about making an impact on the people in their lives. From a parent's point of view, understanding where all this generosity is coming from is a most important step to understanding your teen.

However, hidden in this kindness is a warning: motives must be kept pure or the act of generosity sours. If the teen is seen as after some selfish gain, they will not be seen as generous. Unselfish motives make this teen very attractive to all those who think of others and value a basic ethical stance in life: "Do to others as you would have them do to you."

Magnanimous, not mean, is the meaning in the Latin root of the word generous and it was carried over into French and English. The French word, *genereux,* also means fruitful or bountiful, containing the thought of a generous world, just like the SP would tell you. So, it is clear that this strength is to be observed in the world around us and we cannot forget that we are a part of that world, too.

Therefore, it may not be surprising to find your teen giving away your time and possessions, too!

Developing this Strength — Things to Share with Your Teen

- The more the teen sees the use of this strength as an act of love, the deeper its meaning.
- Kindness is love in action and kindness encourages generosity.
- Be an example of love in action and your SP will "get you."
- Focusing on others and what we can do for them makes this strength stronger.
- Keep the motivations pure and your SP will shine with unconditional love.
- This strength is not for making an impact; it makes its own impact in the process of loving.

11: The Core Strengths that Shape and Fulfill the SJ Temperament

Richard: *"Richard here! You want to know about me? There's not much to tell. I plug away at my classes and I don't know if I will do well because I don't know if I should believe them when they tell me I have done well. I guess it's true that I take life seriously, but most of the other students don't seem to me to be responsible."*

Interviewer: *"By the way, Richard, tell me of your recent excitements."*

Richard: *"Well, I did well in my math class and I got onto the football team. I like to keep an even keel. I get nervous when I don't know what is going to happen next. Ever since I became a teenager, I've been anxious about all the changes that are going on in me and around me. I try to do my work, but I'm worried that I won't get a high enough grade average to get a scholarship and if I don't, I'll not be able to get an education."*

Richard, after a pause: *"All this change is upsetting. Now that I'm in high school, I want to be valedictorian, but there are too many things to do that I don't have any control over. Whoops, I got to go or I'll be late for class!"*

The path for teenage development is written in the SJ teen's core strengths. A parent may also choose to develop some gifts, talents, or skills that the teen displays or shows an interest in other than their teen's core strengths, and that is good, too. However, if preparation for adulthood is the focus, the core strengths must be developed so as to not damage the teen or damage others and to give the teen an understanding of where their fulfillment in life will be. This will aid greatly in their making good choices.

Try this exercise: Ask the teen to list each of the core strengths of the SJ in order of importance to *them*. As they go through their teenage years, get them to re-list these core strengths in order of importance to them. Do it every year and let them see how they are developing and appreciating their core strengths and what changes in preferences are taking place. Further self-understanding can be achieved by asking them the reasons for any changes in their rating of their strengths. We want to achieve both awareness of their core strengths and a growing appreciation and understanding of them. The parent is not the judge of which core strength is more important than the other. The teen must verify for herself.

If this is done, the parent can watch the growth of their teen and the teen's self-understanding will be an awesome help in this final rush to adulthood.

Learn your teen...

A Convenient List of the SJ Temperament's Core Strengths

Lives tied to the past

Careful, cautious, concerned

Thoughtful and prepared

Responsible, dependable, solid work ethic

Do what is right, law abiding

Strong need to belong, social, respectable

Steady, not easily shaken

166

Trusts authority

Supervisors, managers, systems, routines

Stoical

Logistical in work and play

Communicates with the details

Good Samaritans, helpmates

Non-dramatic in speech

Lives Tied to the Past

The first Greek philosopher is often said to be Thales (c.620 — c.555 BC), and to him is attributed the statement, "The past is certain, the future obscure." We have no way of knowing what temperament he was, but that statement is certainly the viewpoint of the SJ parent or teen.

This mental approach to life affects the SJ teen more than they usually appreciate. What *is* eclipses what *might be*. The cautious, thoughtful approach to life, the strong need to belong, the desire to be steady and secure are some of the characteristics that shape and set this teen on a solid path, if they so choose.

But the teen does not have a lot of personal history to draw from. Without this "reference book of past lessons," they move into their teenage years experiencing anxiety more than most adult SJs. The extroverts are more confident and the Ts determined not to show their nervousness. With less of a past to depend upon, the SJ teen places more emphasis on what they have just learned. The authority of teachers becomes a needed source for their growing knowledge.

The past and its recently acquired knowledge are relied upon, and to challenge what they have learned, for example in school, will likely call forth a rebuke. Because of this dependence on their past, the SJ teen treads into an unknown future cautiously. If a relationship ends, they can become over-cautious about another one. It is not just the loss of the relationship but the challenge to their trust in people and to their ability at being right and making right judgments that concern them, and they see that as what led to the split up. An SJ teen appreciates a careful step-by-step approach to helping them adjust to big disturbances in their lives.

Parents should also encourage their SJ teen to learn from the past, to value the past, but not to drag its pains into the present. There is nothing wrong with the SJ's reliance on the past to guide their future, only in an over-reliance.

Don't try and make your teen forget the past or live with a "don't care" attitude in the present. You will be mistaking them for an SP. They will plan for the future, but they don't want to emotionally live in it; it's too uncertain.

Living with the guidance of the past is also to live nervous about change. They do not want to change because it challenges the tried and true past experiences and rocks their boat. Change, however, is necessary because the past lessons they have put their trust in may not apply any longer and it is a matter of searching for security somewhere else. But where do you find the feeling that everything will go as planned if not in the past. To change is to venture forward without guidance, having to gather trust as you go. Always give them a sense of security because their happiness depends on it.

Developing this Strength — Things to Share with Your Teen

- In our fast-changing technological age, change is forced on the SJ teen constantly. But change in operating a device that works according to certain principles and that can be verified as safe and secure by a few strokes on the keyboard is not a real test of change. This kind of change is far removed from changes in relationships and the unforeseeable behavior of people. Help your SJ teen to accept change in small steps when it comes to the unpredictable world of emotions and people.

- Change is inevitable. To walk through it cautiously is the key.
- Honor the SJ's desire to be cooperative. It helps them with feeling secure and links with what others have done or are doing.
- Make sure the teen builds structure and routine into their own life.
- Help them choose wisely who it is in their experiences they can trust.
- The successful SJ is the one who interprets the past correctly. Help them interpret the lessons of the past with greater accuracy. It is a valuable skill.
- Refer to the past yourself and show how it is of value to you.
- Teach how to question change without rejecting what it offers.
- Routines that work do not need to be disturbed. Remember, the cry is, "Don't fix what isn't broken."
- In accepting change, help the SJ teen to check the results. This way they will feel more secure.
- Discourage a slavish trust in the past.
- The problems with accepting change are largely emotional. Address the emotions of anxiety, not just the rational explanations for change.
- The future will always be scary, so always face it with courage.
- Control is not the best response to change since we can't control everything or everyone. To be over-controlling is to face defeat or rejection.
- Help the SJ teen to factor into their thinking that all of life is a risk and they had best examine things in terms of calculated risks.
- The past way of doing things will eventually become irrelevant. The issue for the SJ is not shall we change, but

when shall we change. Timing is a learned art, so model the appropriate time to make changes.

Careful — Cautious — Concerned

The teenage years are fast-paced and in the face of this, the SJ teen struggles with the slow movement of a cautious attitude. Confucius said, "The cautious seldom err." It's not absolutely true, but the SJ would lay great stock in it. The SJ teen does not want to be wrong or err or, especially, have to admit that they were wrong. Self-defense comes out immediately. Care and cautiousness is used in order not to err.

For most SJ teens, teenage is not the time of life when they can develop firm routines for their behavior to make sure they do not err. The teen will often pull away from the crowd if they feel too pressured. Caution is not refusing to move forward. It is yet another way of making sure the move will not create insecurity. This caution focuses them on the details. They will often get stuck on some detail they don't understand. Once the details are related understandably with the other facts, the SJ moves ahead without concern.

Because they are focused on the world outside of themselves, they are also focused on reality rather than imagination. They call their world "the real world" and have less patience with the world of ideas and a "reality" that is unproven or yet to be. They have found the "devil to be in the details." Caution can breed this suspicious approach to everything, including looking for the devil in everything. In this, the teen needs guidance. Too much concentration on looking for what might go wrong makes for a very negative view of life and saps it of its joy. Make this clear to your SJ. There is nothing wrong with looking carefully at the details of life. The answer for a happy life is what we do with a negative attitude and how quickly we adopt a positive attitude.

Concern is also a wonderful attitude, but when it is negatively energized and seldom seeks a positive outcome, it is a certain spoiler of pleasure. The positives in life, like trust, faith, and hope, depend on the absence of concern or on the presence of positive concerns.

There is a lot of mental training to be given to an SJ who has become negative and pessimistic. In order to help your teen, don't try to eliminate their negative attitudes. Rather, try to instill positive ones. Trying to root out the negatives only focuses the life on them and creates more negative energy. We then fail in creating a positive atmosphere.

"Careful" requires being meticulous — paying attention to the details. In doing so, the emotions of anxiety and fear can become the emotions of the moment. This is a prime example where overuse of a strength can create emotions that will make it a weakness instead of a strength. Parenting an SJ teen is about keeping the positive side of life to the fore.

Carefulness can easily create anxiety before the event, such as when we sit in the dentist's waiting room. Anxiety can also be crossing our bridge before we get there. You may notice that these fears may cripple your otherwise confident SJ. The period before an exam is a case in point. It is best to keep busy so as not to make room for a crippling fear. A crippling fear can become an obsession or a full blown panic. Teach your teen to face events with care, but also with a positive attitude of confidence and hope.

Concern is often of a higher value than fun for an SJ. Fun for fun's sake is not their way of living. There has to be a purpose in the fun and keeping your eye on the purpose for the fun is where the attitude of concern comes in. This strength has to be watched or it will become the killer of all joy.

Concern will also bring about the need for rules to protect the downside of everything. Rules are then put in place by an SJ teen to protect what they feel might go wrong. This attitude is a return to placing more emphasis on the negative, somber side of life. Teaching a balance between a healthy, positive outlook and a concerned one is a crucial task for the teen's parents who are acting as guides.

Developing this Strength — Things to Share with Your Teen

- Keep drawing attention to the positive side of things without condemning the proper use of care, caution, and concern. Point out the silver lining in the clouds of doubt and the good in all things.
- Pausing to be cautious is all right, but pausing too long can quickly turn to an overuse of this strength. The teen should understand the damage of continually focusing on the negative.
- It's not a balance between being cautious and confident that we are looking for. It is the appropriate use of both. Some things call for caution and some for a bold confidence.
- When depressive attitudes appear in your teen, it's time to take steps and find help for them to be able to discover how to do what is needed to keep them from falling into depression or apathy.

Thoughtful and Prepared

You will find this feature of the SJ teen coming to the fore in the teenage years. More preparation for classes and for all the extracurricular activities are going to exercise this strength. Being prepared gives a sense of comfort to the SJ. It makes them feel as though they have some sort of control over the future. A lack of control is frightening.

Preparations involve thoughtfulness. Thoughtfulness sharpens an SJ teen's planning skills and this makes for a teen who is building the skills of a solid mental foundation on which to live their lives. Everything the parent can do to encourage this thoughtfulness will help the teen stand strong in the widening world of the teenager.

Henri (Louis) Bergson, a French philosopher, wrote, "Think like a man of action; act like a man of thought." His words capture the spirit of the SJ temperament. You want your SJ to do just this. Thinking through the steps that need to be taken is acting it out in the mind. Then acting according to their thoughts is showing their mental preparedness. All this is the concrete thinking of an SJ mind. Homework, papers, schedules, practice, and the demands of social acceptability are all creating the opportunities to shape the mind of the SJ. Don't forget to approve all their industriousness and encourage it, if it is lacking.

Is your SJ making lists on paper or in their mind? Lists help the SJ remember details that are not in the path of their focused mind. They clear the mind of disturbances and the SJ teen is not happy with disturbances that surprise them and mess up their orderliness.

It's difficult to prepare for something you don't know. A goal is the concern of all SJs who are taking their lives seriously. Early in the teenage years, they may worry about what they will do when they grow up. Few go to college without knowing what they want to be when they enter the work world. Many worry because they have not decided who they will marry. Relationships for the SJ are planned, not just happenings, as they are for the SP.

Belonging to clubs, gangs, and organized groups of all sorts gives the SJ teen a chance to feel respected and discover the solidarity that is in a group. There is more than strength in numbers; there is comfort and the all-important sense of being accepted. Therefore, show your pleasure in their belonging and guide them in their choices, always pointing out the best choices in terms of their goals. Being their guide is, for the parent, engaging in an advisory partnership in their late teen decisions.

If changes are taking place in the family life, let them know in ample time for them to mentally prepare and become involved in the preparations for change. But in all of the seriousness of the SJ teen's life, guide them to include some more lighthearted activities to keep them from becoming dull and planning the joy right out of their lives.

Developing this Strength — Things to Share with Your Teen

- Give attention to how your teen is being thoughtful. Notice what needs help and direction.
- Approve this strength whenever you observe it because it is the basis for their productive life.
- Lighten and spice up their seriousness with occasional light-spirited outings.
- Always help the teen to be aware of their goals. Losing sight of their goals results in nonproductive preparations.
- SJ teens can benefit from a simple form of time management. Help them design their own self-management tool.
- For the SJs who have a T in their profile, keep encouraging their concern for the feelings of others.
- Every now and then, do something on the spur of the moment to inject the experience of spontaneity into their lives.
- Be watchful for an overloaded life that has been poorly planned and has become overbearing.
- Redirect any planning sessions that become worry sessions. An SJ teen must learn early to keep worry out of their creative planning.
- Beliefs play a large part in what kind of planning we do and for what purpose. Help them build constructive beliefs that support good planning.

Responsible — Dependable — Solid Work Ethic

It seems impossible to talk much about an SJ without using the word responsible. A teenager may not seem responsible because consistency of behavior has not yet matured, but the longing to be seen as responsible is there in force.

It is difficult to be responsible and reliable if a solid work ethic is not also in place. If the teen has an SJ parent, this trait can be taken for granted and not focused on because it should be second nature in the home.

The teen, if not receiving approving feedback, can resort to irresponsible behavior. Feedback is not only needed, it is an important indicator of what you can expect from the SJ teen. Give them good feedback and they will normally live up to it. How does the teen know what is responsible behavior if there is no feedback to teach them?

Complaints may abound about homework and chores, but if an underlining streak of dependability is not observable, it can be assumed the teen has not received sufficient positive feedback to make them into the teen they need to be. Feedback is the breakfast of SJs.

Discipline will be responsible for a consistent responsible attitude. Remember, the word *discipline* comes from the word *disciple*, one who learns. It is training people to do what is required of them. Without this parental training, self-discipline is hard to teach oneself. The discipline does not need to be punishment; it can be reward or positive feedback. It can also be training, teaching, and encouragement, which can be in the form of feedback. Use all forms of discipline and don't rush to punishment because it seldom motivates, unless it is strong enough, and then the question remains, "What has it taught the teen?"

Some sort of control is needed to teach discipline, and control is what an SJ is all about. The application of acceptable, not unbearable, control should be obvious. Some parents are afraid to discipline their children in case it harms their development. A lack of it will harm the child.

In a developing period of the English language, called Middle English, the word *discipline* meant mortification by scourging oneself, and in early French and Latin, it meant instruction or knowledge. The different cultures resulted in either a negative or positive viewpoint of discipline. Instruction and teaching is, in many cases, all that is needed and by the teenage years, it is the main means of guidance if self-discipline has already been taught. An SJ teen should display a developing degree of self-discipline. All that we have noted about the strengths of the SJ — careful, cautious, concerned, thoughtful, and prepared — are elements that, if taught well, will result in responsible attitudes.

Responsible attitudes result from self-imposed rules and regulations and these things create a structure for society. So as a parent, all of these characteristics form a list of things the parent needs to teach their SJ, in particular. If the teenage years are reached and these strengths accompanied by self-imposed rules are not present, the task to teach them becomes very difficult. Our society is built on laws and when personal responsibility is not expected, the society begins to breakdown. All the great empires were constructed around personal responsibility to obey certain rules and expectations, and the same is true of the great worldwide religions.

A balance between the freedom to self-express and obedience to laws should also be kept in mind because a human has a craving to be an individual and also a respectable member of a society. The SJ teen wants to be accepted in society and, therefore, has a drive to belong and be accepted. To do so, they must conform to the organization's rules.

The personal reward for the use of these strengths is great. When teaching discipline and responsibility, the reward should always be kept in focus. Attraction is better than force. But since self-discipline involves forcing oneself, we may need the help of external pressure at times. The SJ's reliance on routines is all part of these basic urges surfacing and aiding the process of self-discipline.

Developing this Strength — Things to Share with Your Teen

- Teach the benefits of responsible attitudes and behavior in society. Do so by modeling it for your teen. Whatever temperament the parent is, the SJ teen needs to see responsible attitudes and behavior modeled or they will not respect the parent.

176

- Belief results in behavior, so do all you can to instill solid, responsible beliefs about the need for rules, regulations, trustworthiness, and a solid work ethic.
- Teach that being responsible is a way of honoring others and ourselves.
- The SJ builds societies and they should be made to see their part in a smoothly functioning world.
- Without pleasure and the lighthearted moments in life, being responsible can become a bore.
- Responsibility can be taught, but no one likes to be controlled, so a happy medium — particularly in the teens — between control and guidance will get the results required.
- Model self-discipline and personal responsibility.
- Since being personally responsible and reliable is a trait all temperaments need, all parents can display it. However, the SJ will demonstrate its dominance in their temperament.

Do What is Right — Law-Abiding

All of the core strengths of a temperament appear as a macrocosm, a unified pattern of urges that support and elevate each other. This one overlaps what we have seen so far of the core strengths of the SJ and, therefore, repeats them, but from the stance of providing an underlying belief that gives structure to being responsible and dependable, etc.

"Right is its own defense," said Bertolt Brecht, who fled Germany during Hitler's regime and exiled in the USA. He demonstrated his own belief in doing what he knew was right. He did not believe that right had to be defended. But since that day, right has been demoted in our society from being a law or an axiomatic belief to being a mere opinion. If right is an opinion and opinion is right, then who and what among the millions of opinions is right?

All ethical beliefs are now seen as nothing more than opinions. Rules are simply opinions, too, for most folks in our society. Opinions shake and flap with the winds of personal desire and have no more substantiality than the wind.   But still in our society, murder is regarded by most people as wrong and defined so by law, not just an opinion.   Sense still holds on amid the fading moral standards of our day.

When right and wrong are only an opinion, it is going to be hard to raise a temperament that honors doing what is right and is, by definition, declaring that there is a right and a wrong. The SJ's urges are being watered down when society believes that obeying the rules are for our convenience and not to be regarded as a duty.

SJs are often accused of thinking in black and white, with no room for gray. Gray is perceived as a fuzzy middle ground for folks to hide from the necessity of making a clear cut decision. You will notice it is the J in their profile that calls for a lifestyle of decisiveness and closure that makes this black and white mentality a necessity. There is nothing wrong with this stance either, as long as it doesn't result in judging.

The SJ teenager is going to be torn between what to believe and how to act if this preference for black and white is being seen as wrong. To the person with this preferred J lifestyle, right and wrong makes absolute sense; keeping your options open does not. If you have exceeded the speed limit by seven miles-per-hour and not twenty miles-per-hour, an officer will be hard to convince that the seven mile-per-hour offense is not an offense. Gray does not exist in the law's mind. There is a lot to be said for this decisiveness.

At the moment of this writing, it is raining outside. That's a black and white decision that is correct even though it is not raining hard.   The SJ teen needs a legitimization of their decisiveness and, in order to live harmoniously with others, an understanding of the hypocrisy of being critically judgmental.

The SJ teen is faced with another confusion: If they insist on doing what is right in the face of criticism, they may well find that they are ostracized and are not accepted by others. There can be a conflict between the urge to be right and stand for the right and the need to belong and be accepted. Humans have faced this as long as they have existed.   Standing for your principles and what is right is still seen by most of the world as the noble and right thing to do for the betterment of society. If tolerance is the spirit of the age, should the SJs not be tolerated for their opinion?

This is the place to remember the definition of the correct use and development of our core strengths: namely, not to damage ourselves or others and, preferably, to benefit ourselves and others. So, the SJ teen will correct the parent when the parent has strayed from the rules and they will even feel the necessity to correct the teacher. To accept their correction as at least understandable would seem to be a good use of tolerance.

Developing this Strength — Things to Share with Your Teen

- Every human builds their beliefs and values. Help your teen to build them in keeping with their core strengths.
- Help your teen to understand what is a right and wrong use of their strengths.
- Help your teen build a consistent set of values and beliefs.
- Courage, for the SJ, is seen often in the way they stand for what they see as right, no matter the consequences. Encourage this and support their introspection of all they are believing.
- Call for a consistency between what they believe and what they do. We live happily with ourselves when we live with personal integrity.

Strong Need to Belong — Social — Respectable

The SJ teen is a social animal. The introverts among them seem more reserved at times, but still have a longing for acceptance among their friends. They build friendships and feel secure when accepted by those they have chosen. It is this social side to their strengths that creates a need to belong and to be respectable.

A sense of belonging in a community must begin by knowing how to belong to oneself. If we do not accept ourselves, we will find it hard to accept others. An acceptance of ourselves means facing our imperfection and our mistakes and loving ourselves nonetheless. It is only our love of ourselves as imperfect beings that makes us able to love others unconditionally. To teach this to an SJ teen is life changing and stabilizing. Most introverts and NFs are also in need, but for different reasons.

If your teen hates themselves, they develop a fear of not making it in society or becoming a loser, which leads to thinking about checking out and becoming mediocre. An SJ teen is not as likely to hate themselves as an NF, but the lesson is needed: love yourself and as long as that love is not an obnoxious pride. To do so will display an attractive confidence to which others will be drawn. We feel we can rely on the person who has confidence. So, if your teen is not being accepted by others, it may not be what they are doing as much as the image they project. Work on the issues that are creating this low self-image.

The opposite of a sense of belonging is to feel like a stranger. The whole issue of loneliness and isolation can be a force that shapes the life of a teenager. Belonging is the glue that holds the strands of society together. Remember, they are focused on the world outside of the home now and what they are learning about their acceptance will make a lasting mark on them at this stage in their lives. Introduce them to others, boost their confidence, have friends over, and help them see how they can change people's opinions by being the helpmate they are and the astute planner and loyal partner.

If they are not accepted with one group, introduce them to another. The thermometer that will tell you of the need to step up and help with introductions to new groups will be their confidence and comfort level with the friends they have at the moment. If they show confidence in social settings, then all is well for the time being. Social connections is a drive the SJ must fulfill. One major reason for this drive is the need to feel secure and the SJ who builds societies needs societies.

180

SJ teens will also want to find a place in the group they belong to. Status within the group is the next need after belonging. Typically they will offer their services to the group, become a member of a committee or rise to leadership. A great deal of their self-image is dependent on being of rewarding service in a group, whether large or small. To rise to importance in a group escalates their feelings of self-worth perhaps faster than succeeding at exams or being approved by a teacher.

As the parent, elevate their importance in the family and give them more responsible involvement in the affairs of the home. Be careful not to give them too much authority to change the rules or the home may undergo a complete renovation. When they say they don't feel at home in their own home, it is most often a cry that they have not been given a place of respectability in the affairs of the home.

Developing this Strength — Things to Share with Your Teen

- Join a club, church, organization of any sort, and guide your teen to a place of importance within it. This will cement their feelings of importance both in the group and in the home.
- Find a need they can fulfill in the larger community, like helping organize a clean-up of the community or anything that fulfills a practical need.
- Protection of a society's goods and its life is a service that gives a sense of belonging and authority, achieving two major needs of the SJ.
- Steer them to finding solutions for problems and not sinking into concern and worry over things that are failing in the society.
- Help them know the difference between concern over things they can change and worry over things they cannot change. (The serenity prayer is a great model).
- Watch their emotions when they return from a group meeting and be a non-pressure guide to help them find solutions to problems they might have encountered. You might suggest,

"Why don't you think about it and tell me tomorrow what you consider would be a solution." This way you encourage their powers of resolution and are able to check into the emotions they are experiencing the next day to know whether more help is needed.

Steady — Not Easily Shaken

Feeling safe and secure is a big issue for all SJs and a vital indication of their mental and emotional health in their teenage years. "Steady does it," is the cry of all SJs, as well as statements like "Don't rock the boat." The ground under the feet of an SJ teen needs to be kept steady and earthquakes caused by social or personal disturbances, the subject of rescue efforts.

More than any other single condition, watch to see that your teen is feeling secure. One gauge is their happiness. A happy SJ teen is one that is feeling secure. Increased anger and aberrant behavior that is unlike them is a strong indication of presence of insecurity.

Sometimes the cause of the insecurity is known to them, such as when they have been rejected by their group or they have failed one time too many at their studies. Other times, the SJ teen will not know why they are feeling down and angry or simply emotionally off kilter.

Why is a feeling of insecurity their Achilles heel? Because the SJ is all about keeping the ship steady and feeling more like a rock than a blade of grass tossed at will by the wind. This need to be stable causes their dislike of change. They like things to be the same tomorrow as they are today. Lessons are learned from the past and, therefore, consistency with the way things are done pleases them. If all things are predictable, then trouble is unlikely to strike.

You see, the SJ is all about avoiding trouble. Therefore, they look for breakdowns of the norm and for aberrations and mistakes. It is one reason why they make so many rules and policies to offset the failures that are so concerning to them.

182

When the negative side of life is being carefully watched, any change or departure from what is normal must be immediately addressed. They often live by the rule that if anything can go wrong, it will. Therefore, build protective walls, lay up supplies against the bad day that might come, make sure everything that can be controlled by any and all means is controlled.

We have to admit the wisdom of these preparations against possible failure, but also the lack of wisdom if the possibilities and the upside of life are not at least given equal attention. To parent the SJ teen through a period of life that is full of change, rejections, and failures on the way to success we need to help them keep a balance between their focus on the problems and on the possible solutions. Solutions cannot be just measures that stall or offset problems. They must be real solutions.

Creating a positive outlook is healthy. Insecurity and nervousness can create an emotional sickness. The SJ enters the storm with grave concern, while the SP enters the storm with a sense of excitement over the challenge ahead. A positive approach to a potentially negative situation keeps the vessel of our emotions steady. How the teen SJ will face problems in the future will be largely shaped by the way they learn to handle them in teenage. SJs play defense more than offense and must shift the focus to a point of balance.

The goal is to teach the SJ to move with measured step and a hopeful optimism through the ups and downs of each day. As they do so, they must learn to absorb the blows of trouble and find solutions to all the issues while at the same time keeping their lives hopeful and happy. We are responsible for our own happiness.

The issue of control should be raised again in connection with insecurity. The teen who is trying desperately to control everything around them in the home and outside of it is feeling insecure and will resort to a negative solution and outlook. Control is not the answer to feelings of insecurity unless we can control what is making our world shake.

If it is a person that is causing the quaking, we should understand we can't always control people unless we use enough force to make them comply. Methods other than forced control must be resorted to. The SJ will naturally go to control unless taught more appropriate and successful measures. There are positive control measures, such as appealing to a person's good side, rewarding good behavior, teaching, training, and warning of danger ahead, to name some obvious methods. Society needs stability and an SJ teen needs to learn where and how to make it happen.

Developing this Strength — Things to Share with Your Teen

- Model and teach a calm approach to solving the day-to-day problems. To do this, create a mindset of calm and unshakable resolve. See yourself as in control, not needing to control.
- Model and teach a determination to find a solution other than force or inappropriate control measures.
- In your calm and struggle for peace, don't lose the backbone of a principled life.
- A person who is not easily shaken is a person of convictions. Help your teen develop beliefs that will see them through the rough patches of life: confidence, belief in themselves, willingness to seek help and advice, choosing what does not damage themselves and others, choosing to benefit others.
- For the SJ teen, make sure they keep their feet firmly planted in reality as they will reject any flight into fantasy.
- Teach how to take insults and rejection with dignity and poise. If all someone has to throw at you are insults, they have a weak case. Teach them to show others that insults are harmless ammunition against a person with confidence.
- When others have shaken your confidence, retreat inside and positively evaluate your position.
- Know what really matters and what doesn't.
- Don't become stubborn when you think you might be wrong. Examine your position for its possible weaknesses.

Trusts Authority

"Trust is the lubrication that makes it possible for organizations to work," so said Warren Bennis, and he spoke well. Trust is also the necessary ingredient in any meaningful relationship, as the NFs will tell you. Where trust is weak, contracts and legal documents are necessary. Therefore, to trust is not a sign of weakness but an understanding of how the machinery of society operates.

Once an authority has been given power, we must trust that they will use it profitably and justly in the interests of society as a whole and not in pursuit their own interests or ideology. We are self-centered beings and sometimes selfish. Therefore, to trust others may be difficult but cannot be avoided. The SJ teen leans toward trusting authority because someone needs to lead and have the power to do so to avoid chaos. However, when authority proves to be untrustworthy or corrupt, SJs will fight the authority figure with determined attempts to restore justice and fairness.

Authority is necessary for the establishment and policing of laws. So, don't be surprised if your teen seeks to be in positions of authority in their social world. Perhaps, you should not be shocked, either, if they seek to wrestle the authority from you, the parent. It is a difficult teaching task to avoid dampening their quest to be the authority figure while, at the same time, persuading them of the wisdom to submit to authority and to the ones that have greater experience or wisdom.

As the parent, you will welcome the acceptance of your authority but be constantly challenged by your SJ teen to earn it daily. All authority figures make mistakes and this is a hard lesson for the black and white SJ teen to learn. Forgiveness is not something at which they excel. They must be persuaded to forgive the errors that are forgivable in leadership, realizing that they will need the same treatment if they rise to leadership. The bottom line is that humans are not perfect and that means leaders are not, either.

Developing this Strength — Things to Share with Your Teen

- Trust where trust is earned.
- Do not trust where trust is not being earned, unless you have no other choice but to trust (or risk).
- Model a trustworthy authority figure to your teen.
- This means a standard of right and wrong is needed if they are to make these judgments. The SJ will usually have no problem with standards of black and white, only with shades of gray. Help them see the immense importance of having reliable and good standards to fall back on. Help them develop these standards via your teaching and example.
- Develop their belief in the need for authority, its protections, services, and security as well as its betterment of society. Society will need these teens to keep it recognizing the need for responsible action and boundaries.
- Teach them that all authority must earn its right to lead and be open to their criticisms of your leadership. Teach them that some authority figures are elected and some are authority figures by virtue of their place in society such as teachers, parents, and mentors.

Supervisors — Managers — Systems — Routines

SJ teens will tend to manage the activities of themselves and others, particularly others. Their control of their environment, which includes the people in that environment, is by establishing systems, routines, rules, regulations and punishments for breaching these standards. All these rules are related to their overall beliefs which they turn into policies. In turn, these are reviewed and changed as breaches of those policies and rules take place. It is a structured mind that you will find in your SJ teen, one that wants stability. What is true today should be true tomorrow.

Order is essential to all systems, and the policies that guide the systems give overall direction and keep the goals firmly in mind. All of this is to keep that feared status, mayhem, at bay. Achieving productivity and desirable results justifies their actions in the mind of the SJ. Although this is not totally true of all SJs, it is at least an underlying mindset that shapes their thinking.

Your teen has been developing some of these behaviors since childhood. However, now that they are teenagers, they are becoming more serious in shaping their world with these actions and with this mindset. Friends are chosen with an eye to their being cooperative. Foes are those who want to create a world that is not ordered, managed, and conducted according to their plans. Everything runs to the demands of orderliness — their perception of order. If something is not on their radar, it may escape any semblance of order. Watch how your SJ teen develops their standards for order in their world and everyone else's.

In all of these routines is, once again, a need for security. An SJ needs to know what will happen and what has happened. Little is left to chance. Impulse and spontaneity only disrupt the system and the results of an impulsive act are not under control. The door that opens to chance opens to the unexpected.

So, let's see how to help and manage this teen's development. Manage is the right word only if the attempts to help appear as though they will successfully ensure the outcome of what needs to be managed. Only then will the SJ teen accept them.

Not every SJ teen will be happy with routine and management. The teenage years are often pictured as the time when the teen sows their wild oats, bucks the expectations, and thumbs their nose at the law. They will not face adult justice until they are 18 and, therefore, it is a time of greater freedom to act as they will. Experiences are facing them one after another, inviting them to try this and try that. The SJ teen who does not have a set of convictions to keep them on the path of developing as they are designed will wander and pay many a consequence.

The more the parent can and has developed the teen's core strengths and set the teen on a path of success, the easier the teenage journey will be for both. Keep the routines in place that you can. Partner with the teen in developing other routines needed to successfully get homework done and chores completed. But understand that a free ride with no home responsibilities is going to raise an adult who thinks the world should place no demands on them.

This is the time to teach and improve existing systems for saving money. Opportunities and rules for earning money and for becoming creative in the world of business are great aids in developing the SJ teen. Helping them form a business of their own for self-discipline and a taste of success cannot be bettered as a self-development project. Such simple things as babysitting and lawn-mowing will develop this teen.

Experience and guidance in managing others in a mutual project will teach many a lesson in personnel management and "business" relationships. Success in business can be instilled at this early age. If they are bent on a profession, such as nursing or teaching, preparing as early as possible is also good training.

A part-time job in a field of their choice is also helpful to the SJ's development, but don't forget to have them make time for their social life as well. Although sports will teach discipline, or should, the SJ teen does not need to be limited to a sport as a productive use of their time. Inspire them with a little help to get them going on some project. The routine tasks of keeping the books for their small business, paying the bills, managing their savings, or keeping a bank account are all basic duties that the SJ teen can profitably learn. You can teach them to manage their small business, such as babysitting, with the records of a regular business to develop a business mind. Help them where necessary.

Developing this Strength — Things to Share with Your Teen

- The practical use of these strengths is the only way to really develop them.
- Help in making their business efforts succeed, marking their progress, and celebrating when they reach their goals is great parenting for an SJ.
- Show lots of interest in the development of whatever they show an interest in that uses their core strengths.
- Help them in securing a job and setting up a bank account.
- Give opportunity to develop supportive strengths, such as planning, attention to detail, etc.
- Let them exercise their penchant for organizing some aspects of the home.
- However, give guidance in handling people and using power wisely, since a position of authority in a small group may come their way.
- Help develop their people skills.
- Teach them the way to make money is to provide a needed service better than others do.

Stoical

A stoical attitude asks us to steel ourselves against trouble and bear it with a stolid acceptance and without complaint. Do you think a teen can do that? Not many. The basic principle of Stoicism was to learn how we can be indifferent to everything that happens to us and, therefore, be unruffled by it. A few SJs exhibit this, but an SJ teen is not likely to be able to be indifferent to the many changes that take place in their lives. They need to find a way to walk calmly through the troubles though. Don't over-stress this in the teenage years. Besides, to over-stress for the adult is also a mistake. Its proper use is to learn to be able to live above the troubles of life.

It is helpful for the SJ teen to learn to delay reacting to troubling circumstances. They need to give them careful

189

thought or not react when harassed. They will want to show a "You can't get to me" attitude. It is helpful to remind an SJ of this response and if they learn to exhibit it, the teens will be robbed of a lot of its painful experiences.

Another way of viewing this trait is to let the hurts of others roll off "like water off a duck's back." To walk the gauntlet of a teenage mob that is teasing them and be unscathed is a mental achievement of no small importance. Parent, help your teen when this courageous attitude is the best reaction, but don't try to make their lives into one of total indifference to what is going on around them. Indifference is not always helpful.

Developing this Strength — Things to Share with Your Teen

- Teach your teen to stay positive. It is a better way to handle the troubles of life than to be indifferent.
- Fight off the feelings of pessimism that can weaken all the strengths of the SJ.
- Face all loss with the belief that even in the worst of times there is some good being worked out that can help us step up to the next level.
- Worry, pessimism, and loss are all things that can cause us to lose hope. Help your teen to avoid them at all cost. When you see these things setting in like bad weather in a teen's life, find out the cause of the sadness and aim at helping them remove or mitigate it.
- This strength sails close to the winds of despair and should be watched for its possible overuse and misuse.

Logistical in Work and Play (and Relationships)

An SJ's intelligence functions in a linear fashion. Each temperament has its own intelligence style. Linear thinking proceeds in an orderly fashion from one step to the next. Get the steps out of order and the process breaks down momentarily. Linear thinking is the opposite of global thinking, which is directed by leaps of imagination and intuition and the skill of reading developing patterns. (This is particularly the NF's way of thinking).

SJ intelligence is perfect for all logistical tasks. The Greek word from which the word logistics comes is *logisticos* and means something that can be calculated. The French derivative is the word for a calculator, and *logitheque* is a French software library. You get the connections. So the calculating aspect of logic is the chief function of an SJ's mind. Calculators and computers run on linear principles and are great tools for the SJ. Remember this when you think of your SJ teen's needs.

SJs are perfect for the detailed organization and operation of a campaign or the relocation of things and people, such as the movement of an army with all of its supplies and needs, to a given location on a given day. Reorganizing the pantry or a filing system in a computer or any complex assortment of items can be a satisfying task. Offer the teen a reward for completing such an enterprise and they are not only benefitting the home but developing their skills by using a core strength.

They often settle for jobs and careers that require an orderly and detailed mental exercise. Approve all logistical tasks that are well done. Planning, managing, administration, organization, and the execution of these tasks are some of their specialties.

You will notice that this penchant for order is seen in their study, work, and play. Something that is out of order is mentally jarring. If you are an NF parent, for example, this need for order and association in conversation can be tiring, but it is essential for effective communication with an SJ teen. Many misunderstandings are the clash of different intelligences.

A vacation or outing is not well done if it is not well planned. The parent can come in for criticism of the way they do things and the criticism is not necessarily ill meant. It is the drive of an orderly mind. You will need to be reminded of this often if you have an SJ teen.

If you have both an SP and SJ teen, you will notice that the SP pays attention to detail for tactical purposes and the SJ for logistical reasons. Don't play down the making of lists, the need to keep records, and the filing of those records if your SJ does this. I am not an SJ and the difference between an SJ and me in my life can be seen in the way things are stored on our personal computers. If left to themselves, the way a room is kept will also display to varying degrees this difference. Business is where order reigns supreme and it is the world of the SJ. The SJ is logistical, also, because it keeps chaos at bay.

When faced with relationships, which most of the time do not follow the principles of order or logic but are directed by the world of emotion, the SJ can have difficulty. Help them understand that emotion has a logic all its own and it is not the way they think at times. Therefore, relationships can be puzzling and simply beyond their understanding at times.

With a strong drive in the SJ to come to closure, emotions that won't stop surging cause them to be at a loss to know what's happening. "Let's make a decision and get it over with" is the SJ's stance, while emotions bark back at the inadequacy of this approach. Emotions need time to be resolved. The Fs among the SJs are more prepared for the emotional world. Once the SJs feel the reward of emotion, they will tend to want more of its meaning in their lives.

Developing this Strength — Things to Share with Your Teen

- If you don't understand logistics, learn more about it and how it affects our lives and you will be more in tune with your SJ teen.
- If they are interested in business and its systematic way of reaching success, then, again, become more familiar

yourself with this pattern of thinking and you will be more of a help to your teen.

- When talking with your teen, focus on the details, keep the conversation orderly, and explain things step-by-step. You will avoid much misunderstanding.
- Have the teen explain to you why having things in order is so important to them.
- Keep focusing on results and pointing them out to your teen because a system that is not producing the desired results needs to undergo changes.
- Remember, everything in life does not need to be regimented. Try inserting some impulsive actions to keep your SJ teen appreciating fluidity.
- Teach your teen the logic of love that lives on the richness of emotion and wants the constant refreshment of romance and the spice of life.
- Study people skills with your teen.

Communicates with the Details

We have already introduced the importance of details in an SJ teen's thinking. Now let's discover its overall importance in their lives and some of the issues surrounding communication.

Life is in the details for an SJ. All our interactions with others fall under the category of communication and its detailed expressions. Spoken communication is what we tend to think of most, but body language, the language of action or non-action, and the language of silence are also important. All actions communicate something. The arguments that often occur are not just misunderstandings of spoken communication but misunderstanding of any of the other forms of communication. Teach your teen to communicate successfully with all their actions and non-actions.

Most powerful at times are the non-verbal communications. All temperaments will use non-verbal forms of communicating pleasure and non-pleasure. Because these actions are left to the recipient to interpret, they are the most often misunderstood. For the SJ teen, a lack of approval is a major communication that can be interpreted very differently by the parent and the teen. If the parent does not approve the teen and their actions, the teen can take it as disapproval. A glance can be meaningless to the giver and profoundly disturbing to the recipient. What stands in your favor with an SJ teen is that they are not focused all the time on the intricacies of glances and moods. Most subtle non-verbal communications will go right over their heads. But watch for the changes in attitudes that signal misunderstandings.

When an SJ is in a disagreeable mood, you will not miss the communication. Their non-verbal communications that are meant to be received are usually quite obvious to you and to their friends. They want to be clear. Anger as a communication can be an outburst or a sullen mood. The sullen mood will continue at least until they are certain its message has been received.

Expressions of pleasure are usually clearly stated with the reason for their pleasure, except for the introverts who are more likely to not even respond when they are pleased. Overall the introverts express less and the ISTJ is the most non-communicative of all the sixteen types. Don't expect too much communication from them unless they are socially engaged and loving it.

Mental activity and speech for the SJ is always with the details. They think, always conscious of the details. If you want to know how an evening went, be prepared for a detailed blow-by-blow recounting and any sign of impatience on your part that they pick up will be cause for disgust or anger.

Here is a distinct benefit. If you want to know what is going on in your teen's life and you ask in a moment of openness between the two of you, you will get all the details. It is far easier to know what is happening in the life of the SJ teen than the NF teen. Use such moments to create a closer bond with them.

Developing this Strength — Things to Share with Your Teen

- Help your teen with their people skills and their understanding of undetected communications in their close relationships. The introverts will need more help than the extroverts.
- As the parent, sharpen your observational skills to detect the details in your teen's life and non-verbal communications.
- Help the teen use their skill at details effectively by focusing on the details and not glossing over them with a general observation.
- Remembering the details should also come with an understanding of them.
- By asking them for the details, you are getting them to practice the skill of remembering all the details.
- Ask them for an account of the details in the order in which they happened to keep order and the remembrance of the details working together in a true logistical fashion.
- Remind them that good communication requires they make certain the other person understood them correctly. Teach them to ask for feedback when appropriate.
- Teach them the differences between the temperaments in the way their minds work and emphasize that many relationship troubles start with misunderstandings of this nature.
- Slow to speak and slow to anger is a great discipline since it develops respect and patience.

Good Samaritans — Helpmates

Margaret Thatcher made a great observation when she said, "No one would remember the Good Samaritan if he only had good intentions." The SJ is rooted in the real world, the world of deeds and actions that can be seen. The way they typically express their love is in actions, doing things for those they care about. Therefore, the SJ is the true Good Samaritan who is not relying on good intentions to convey their messages.

There is a caring about the SJ teen that is refreshing and very rewarding to those in their lives. The teenage years are a time when changes are taking place right and left and the SJ teen can be so absorbed that they seem to care only about themselves. Then all of a sudden, they will come out of this fog and do something considerate and nice without being asked. It is likely to deeply touch you.

Along with this caring attitude is a sympathy that is more practical than it is empathetic. Embedded in their care is a sense that caring for others is also doing their duty as responsible and reliable humans. Thatcher, who was herself a classic SJ, would no doubt agree that good intentions are a form of kindness yet unborn, an immature deed, and as the expression goes, "The road to hell is paved with good intentions." Intentions need to be born in the form of actions as the SJ is wont to do.

SJs are full of determination and when they decide to do a good deed, they will follow through even in the face of difficulty. The follow-through is also marked with attention to the details. You may have noted that they will sacrifice of their own treasures to help. This is the SJ that makes society feel kindness in their incarnate actions.

The one thing you, as a parent, must not miss doing is showing your thanks and appreciation for all your teen's kind deeds to you and to others in the expanding social world of the SJ. It's not that the SJ teen is being kind to get approval. This drive in your SJ teen to care must not go unnoticed because it can be so easily devalued in our world that seems, at times, to pay little respect to kind acts. "Who are you trying to please," or "You don't need to help; let them take care of their own business," are responses that seek to degrade the very thing these skeptics of kindness want you to do for them. The person wounded on the road is passed by, by a public that is scared of the legal implications if they do help. It's a sad commentary on our culture. The SJ is to be encouraged to teach us all the need for basic human care and love.

Developing this Strength — Things to Share with Your Teen

- Approve every attempt of your teen to care for others.
- Model the same practical love for them to see how you value this strength, too.
- Stay positive and help them remain positive because a negative SJ is not likely to help others.
- Your SJ teen is a social animal and, therefore, needs to nurture the society they value. Teach them the value and importance of creating a society of worth.
- Care and love have eyes that see the needs of others. Encourage looking for opportunities to help.
- Involve them in caring for others.
- We influence all those around us. Praise your SJ for being such a gift to society and take care to honor their significant loving acts with some kind or memorial moment.

12: The Core Strengths that Shape and Fulfill the NT Temperament

You can call me Jancie. You'll have to wait a moment, though. I'm in the middle of this project. Oh, you don't have much time? What time is it? Well, just a minute and I'll be finished.

If you really want to know, I spend most of my time either reading or playing on my computer. My friend thinks I'm unsocial, but I like people as much as they do. At least, I think I do. Most of them just talk about nothing that interests me. Kind of light stuff, you know, like what others are doing and who's dating who, which doesn't interest me much. I'm really keen on this neuroscience project — how the brain works —and I'm trying to understand why neuro chemicals came to be involved in the transmission of a message from one side of a synapse to the other. Fascinating isn't it? I hope one day to be able to learn how to change the chemicals by pure mental force. It could make a huge difference to people's health.

It's true, I guess. I'm all in my mind and forget appointments and chores. But I don't care. They are not the most important things. I'm afraid most of my class is rather slow and I can't understand why they don't get good grades. I do. Sports are okay, but I'd rather be calling the plays and making up the strategy for the game. I guess I'll have to go now. Mom's calling me to dinner for the third time and if I don't go, she'll get all emotional-like. Why does she do that? Bye!

The path for teenage development is written in the NT teen's core strengths. A parent may also choose to develop any of the gifts, talents, and skills in which the teen displays or shows an interest. However, if preparation for adulthood is to focus on the core strengths, they must be developed so as to not damage the teen or damage others and give the teen an understanding of where their fulfillment in life will be. This will aid greatly in their making good choices.

Try this exercise: Ask the teen to list each of the core strengths of the NT in order of their importance to *them*. As they go through their teenage years, get them to re-list these core strengths in order of importance to them. Do it every year or two and let them see how they are developing and appreciating their core strengths and what changes in their preferences are taking place. Further self-understanding can be achieved by asking them the reasons for any changes in their listings. We want to achieve both awareness of their core strengths and a growing appreciation and understanding of them. The parent is not the judge of which core strength is more important than the other. The teen must verify for themselves.

If this is done the parent can watch the growth of their teen and the teen's self-understanding will be a tremendous help in this final rush to adulthood.

Learn your teen...

A Convenient List of the NT Temperament's Strengths

Time is relevant to the task

Strong will, determined

Strategic, theoretical systems

Intense curiosity

Questioning, skeptical

Independent, self-reliant

Calm, cool, collected

Logical, reasonable, must make sense

Ingenious

Efficient, effective, competent, achiever

Abstract in speech

Time Is Relevant to the Task

The clock can be an NT's enemy, a bear to deal with. If they must watch the clock while they work, it is nothing but a distraction and a ruination of their focus. Intense focus is one of their strengths and having to be conscious of time divides the focus, even destroys it at times.

Therefore, certain situations in their teenage years will call for careful parenting. When doing their homework, ideally, there should be no distraction. Giving them that undistracted time should not be too hard. Schedule the time they typically need and let them focus on the requirements placed on them by the teacher. But if the homework does not have their full concentration and interest, they will, themselves, entertain distractions to while away a boring time and a distasteful task. What does the parent do about this?

First, a lot of what an NT teen studies in high school is not of interest to them. Science could be an interest and maybe math, but social studies may not be. An NT will not do what does not make sense to them and this is the issue the parent faces. The parent has to make it make sense to the teen to do what the teacher has asked, and the teacher needs to make it make sense, too. Lengthy discussions are sometimes necessary to show the teen that they have to do these things in order to get good grades, which leads to scholarships when entering college. Bad grades may not get them into the school of their choice. The motivation to finish the required work needs to be the goal of the parent, and the beliefs of the NT teen have to support getting the job done, too, or motivation will not be there. Influencing those beliefs should be a primary focus of the parent.

An NT teen is influenced when the parent reasons with them. To influence their decision-making abilities, give them alternatives that force them to make a choice between a good alternative and an undesirable one. For example, "Get this homework done and we will go exploring or do something that you love. However, if the homework is not completed, you lose a privilege that completion of the homework would have made possible." Say to them, "You are smart and intelligent. Make the right choice." "Abuse a privilege and lose the privilege" is the message.

Emotion is usually never a positive influence. The reason for this is that emotion is despised by most NTs and the person who displays it is also despised. Speak calmly and without fuss or emotional display. Volume is not needed to firmly state the parent's case.

Train an NT to plan their time and make the most of their moments. Create an incentive by giving them the opportunity to earn something they want. Not all these ideas will work with all NTs all the time, so find the one that works currently.

Homework is not the only thing that the NT has trouble focusing on. Chores are another. For the parent, the solution is in creating situations and incentives that work for them. Incentives can be a reward for doing something around the house and for the parent, it is the relief of getting things done around the house. Anything that relieves the parent's load and gives the opportunity for the teen to earn something is a double benefit.

Developing this Strength — Things to Share with Your Teen

- Essential in creating motivation for the teen is keeping a positive goal in front of them. Once they can see the direction of their life and what it will take to get there, NTs can become very motivated and move with determination toward their goal.
- An NT teen thinks highly of themselves and helping them be successful in their pursuits usually increases their desire to succeed at other things.
- Keep a positive mental attitude because worry, pessimism, and negativity are not the mental context that the NT enjoys or responds to.
- Competing with the teen to increase the length of time they can focus can be a great tool that develops their strengths.
- Help the teen find constructive ways to deal with the stress of others interrupting them. They will need these skills.
- If your teen gets emotional about interruptions, show them it is not their best method. The best is to calmly ask for their space and time.
- Teach them that non-response to others can be a form of disrespect, which others do not appreciate.
- Reason with them that time is an inevitable reality and they must learn to make it their friend, not their foe.

Strong Will — Determined

All teens can be determined and so can all temperaments. Then, why is this a special issue with the NT teen? Because three forces are coming together: the natural determination of all people to be individuals and stand up for their own needs; the strong desire of a teen to be independent, make their own decisions and choose their own way; plus, for the NT teen, a powerful, quiet urge to do only what they think makes sense in the moment. If they don't do what makes sense to them, the

NT feels foolish. Whatever common sense tells them is right, they firmly believe is right and must be done.

More than other motivations that we find in the other temperaments, this is a powerful urge to act according to their cerebral analysis. NTs take pride in what they sometimes feel is their superior intelligence. That feeling of being mentally more capable than others is beginning to be felt in their teens, if it has not surfaced strongly already in your NT. We live in a world that supports the power and efficiency of the mind, and who has not been overly influenced by the belief that we are rational creatures? So, the NT teen is feeling the power of the mind and of reason.

But more is entailed. They are very often mentally bright and their ability with abstract problems supports their feelings of superiority. If their grades are high, we can expect this determination to also be bolstered by their feelings of personal brilliance and they feel amply justified at feeling this way. As parents, we should be happy. A high self-image is essential for the mental health of an NT teen. An over-estimation of one's worth is an obnoxious pride and this can hurt the NT.

However, strong determination can be a matter of "I want my own way and I will do what I can to get it." This has nothing to do with intelligence. In fact, it can often show a lack of intelligence in choosing poorly what they want. Any strength can be misused and this would be a prime example. Especially in the case of the NT parent attacking the teen, the better way to proceed is to calmly point out that there is a better choice. After time, the teen will realize that there was a better choice.

Resisting their strong will with strong and volatile emotions can earn the parent the disrespect of this teen. Sound reason and quiet, calm, unbending responses is the parenting model that the NT teen will respect.

Napoleon Bonaparte's statement, "Victory belongs to the most persevering," could be written on the foreheads of many an NT teen. Add to this determination the love of debate and you have a teen who can be formidable and stir the ire of any parent. Their mental force can be increased by the urge they feel to turn neither to the right hand or the left. But please remember that the goal is to raise a teen who will use their strengths in a wise and effective way, making their world a better place. Don't deny the development of this determination, but bend your efforts to guiding it with a core of goodness to be effective. The result will be their making increasingly good choices.

Developing this Strength — Things to Share with Your Teen

- Develop their powers of concentration and you will develop their strength of will. This is best done by competition and mental games. Encourage their intense use of focus, but don't neglect teaching the need to respect others, which means not to ignore them when they have a need.
- Sustained focus builds determination, so also encourage them to plan no interruptions or distractions.
- Determination should not be an emotional explosion for the NT teen. If it does happen, insist it is not the true NT you know and they should resort to their more effective and powerful means — a calm and cool approach.
- In order to have a calm attitude, teach them the power of first being mentally calm.
- Emotion, for the NT teen, does not have to be strongly felt. Their emotional state in which they succeed best is a steady force of will. A deep river whose current flows smooth and irresistible is the image of a mature NT's state of mind when determined.
- Teach the NT, however, that they can show too much determination at inappropriate times!
- Determination, if it is going to be a life strength, will need to respect the will of others. If it doesn't, relationships will be negatively impacted. You will have to teach good social skills to go along with tempering their determination.

- Develop this strength by modeling a determination to honor the needs of others in all your relationships as parents.
- Determination should not be the same as putting on blinders and charging ahead with tunnel vision. Determination should be a mental force linked to an open mind. As I write, I am looking out the window and I see the clouds that have swept over the Continental Divide being carried along by some powerful unseen jet stream. As they move irresistibly on their determined path, they alter shape, fading and building, shaping and reshaping, ever-changing and yet set in their strong-willed resolute path. Determination is not the same as a fixed and stubborn mind.

Strategic — Theoretical Systems

Two more things are developing in your NT teen, a superior ability to map strategy and a dependence and love of theory. The teen has observed how other people lead their lives and have decided not to settle for an unstructured life. So many people around them give little thought to how they are living or even want to live. They just live. Life is more of a happening than a well thought-out path for most. The NT disparages any thoughtless way. The mind is supreme.

Therefore, thought needs to be channelled and controlled by something, and what better than the restraints of logic and what we often, for want of a better word, call reason. Logic starts with an assumption, either commonly held or proposed, and proceeds to examine its legitimacy. One thought must "logically" follow another, all built on the assumption, and this is how we should build our arguments. The ancient Greek philosophers saw the need of sound logic to guide their mental wanderings, so they spent a good deal of their time fashioning the framework of logic. The NT teen is developing her understanding of logic and structured thought. They take pride in feeling they are the only really logical ones.

In developing their logical framework, the NT teen (like all of us) often wanders down some dead end paths. Since the NT teen is all about being reasonable, the parent will need a calm spirit while teaching them how to reason well and avoid these missteps.

Strategy is a name given to a form of reasoning that is dominant in the NT temperament. It simply takes note of any and all contingencies that can be imagined on the path to whatever goal the thinker is pursuing. We also call such happenings "what ifs." "What will we do if this unplanned event interrupts our plan?" they ask. Believing that they have thought out what can happen at every contingency gives the NT greater confidence that they can arrive at their goal.

Chess is a game of strategy. The goal is to remove as many pieces from the board as is needed to win or create checkmate. Since the chess player can only take one step at a time (a very good analogy of life), they must think ahead and see the effects of their moves on future moves. The more they are able to plan ahead and envision the effects of their moves, the more certain they are of the next move being the right one. An NT must feel confident and right. This strategic thinking is one of the ways they achieve confidence. Help them develop this mental ability. The behavior and choices the teen makes will improve with the development of their strategic mind.

But strategy is not all they need. They need the ability to think and create their steps in their head. The more they can theorize, the better their thinking processes become. Thinking theoretically is thinking abstractly and picturing the development of ideas in their mind. As children, they played with Legos and building blocks, creating things with their hands and seeing things develop before their eyes. Now they need to perfect the ability to create their projects in their mind without any visual support. This is the beginning of developing effective theoretical thinking skills.

A theory is a mental path that explains why something happens the way it does or should happen that way. All academic disciplines are involved with some form of theory. Theory is becoming the world of the teen NT.

What the parent needs to know is that they live in their heads and this virtual world is their world. It is normal for them to be creating theories or explanations about almost everything. Encourage this mental skill. They will eventually offer the world a better way of doing things and create a better place to live as they develop the theories that lead to the ingenious discoveries like those that have already changed our world.

Developing this Strength — Things to Share with Your Teen

- Give your teen encouragement and opportunity to strategize and theorize.
- Use is what develops our strengths and our inner drives. Use it and keep it. If you don't use it, you lose it.
- When they figure out how something works or how it might be able to work better, show support for their thinking.
- They will not only strategize and theorize, they will imagine how things could be created or changed. This, too, is to be encouraged. Logic does not see everything and, in particular, does not lead us to unimagined discoveries on its own. Imagination is needed. All temperaments can create, but this temperament is particularly skilled at being ingenious.
- Help them come to a better understanding of logic and how to think theoretically.
- As they develop their plans and ideas in their minds, help them to not forget the effect of human emotions on all their ideas. This way they will learn to perform more understandably in their social encounters, as well.
- Emotions are contingencies that will trip them up if they don't factor them into their thinking. Remind them by asking, "Have you taken emotions into account?"
- Help them remember, life is more than a game of strategy. Life is, above all, an encounter with emotions and people and an emotional response to all things.
- Keep them conscious that winning in an argument is less important than loving and giving.

Intense Curiosity

"Curiosity has its own reason for existing," said Albert Einstein. Everyone is curious, but the NT takes the quest to another level. You might say, curiosity exists for them. They seem to always be asking why? Or what for? Or, simply, what and how?

Learning and curiosity exist for each other and the NT is all about learning. I've found that when the NT teen is not about learning, it is because of a dislike for the subject or the method of learning. A teacher who does not want to depart from the lesson and explain why will soon be marked down as a teacher that does not know anything, at least anything that satisfies the NT student. I'm very sympathetic with high school teachers who have large classes and can't attend to everyone's needs at once, but the fact remains that some students can be turned off by inadequate attention to their inquisitiveness. Probably the difficulty that faces the teacher will never be totally solved, but it remains a need for the NT teen.

Many NT teens appear as know-it-alls and reject subjects that are required because, in their judgment, the subjects are of no benefit to them and their future. They then inadvisably shut down and even refuse to do the assignments at times. Remember, what makes no sense to them they will refuse to do. The real solution to this problem is to persuade them to do what is required for reasons that will affect their future.

But also remember that the refusal is not only rationally directed. There is a lot of emotion coming from boredom and resistance that drives their stubbornness. Ask them why they are feeling the way they feel. Tell them you are turning the tables on them and want a really satisfactory answer as to why they refuse — an answer that explains and justifies their emotions.

Seeking to arouse curiosity in the subjects they are not interested in is another approach. A positive approach always works best with an NT teen. "Only the curious will learn," said Eugene S. Wilson, so do all you can to arouse and sustain curiosity.

Words that have similar meanings to curiosity flesh out what curiosity means to an NT — words such as intrigued, interested, inquisitive, and words like unexpected, queer, unusual, astonishing. Don't forget the motivational power of their mental adventures. All these motivational emotions are thought provokers for the parent seeking an answer to an NT teen's reluctance to learn. But whatever you do, seek to spark their curiosity. Not to know can be embarrassing to them, so seek to ignite their pride in knowing things and it may be an avenue to more motivation.

Developing this Strength — Things to Share with Your Teen

- Join the curiosity of your teen. Remember, all people can be curious and benefit from it. The teen will expand your horizons, perhaps.
- When you are with your teen, ask questions of people and don't settle for lame answers. This positive modeling will create a temporary bond with your teen.
- Follow your urges and your teen's urges to discover.
- Build your knowledge further and model a desire to learn more.
- Curiosity is not just filing away facts; it is understanding them and that requires questions asked of yourself and, perhaps, others.
- Link this pursuit of knowledge to the teen's other strengths of skepticism and ingenuity.
- Never forget the cat! It was curiosity that killed the cat and curiosity, like all things, has a limit that is not wise to pass.
- Curiosity and knowledge seeking is not everything there is to life. Relationships and emotions, for your NT teen, are fields that typically need more cultivation.
- Knowledge seeking can lead to burnout, so spice up your lives with "discovery trips."

Questioning — Skeptical

Curiosity leads to questions, so we should expect them, lots of them from this teen. Because it is an intense curiosity about whatever puzzles or interests the teen, it can lead to lots of deep and puzzling questions. Both parents should attempt to answer them. If parents don't answer, the answers this NT teen will get may not be healthy or true and it may set the course of their teenage lives.

Try to be the source for their knowledge about life in particular. When they talk about friends or influential people they have encountered, try to guide them to the ones you know or whom you trust will give them balanced and wise answers. There is so much in a teen's expanding view of life to be queried. Find someone outside of the family you can depend on to help them with life's issues and cultivate connections to which they respond well. When they find someone they look up to and you are comfortable with, you have found the greatest support for their teen years and for your parenting.

Remember this about your NT teen: they are skeptical and that makes them require everyone to pass their test of making sense in order to be believed. Reason is the name of the game and they do not trust authorities that make no sense to them. Information is everywhere about drugs, sex, and other cultural and life issues. They do not have to search for it. Much of it is partial or biased information, peddled by salespeople and, let's face it, damaging. You will want to be a reliable source or find one. Like all teens, what is written carries a promise of truth, but what is personally imparted has the benefit of emotional connections and provides greater motivation.

Skepticism refuses to believe something just because someone said so. For those who trust easily, this seems harsh and critical. It is critical, but in the sense that it is a strength and not a negative weakness, this criticism is a good thing. Truth should be verified somehow. That verification is what the proper exercise of skepticism in an NT is all about. They must be mentally convinced of the reality and truth of all they hear and read.

The distrust of what they see, hear, and read goes so far as to question the veracity of experts, professors, and especially authority figures, including parents. I have spoken to some NT teens who refused to stay in college simply because they questioned the professor's veracity. What is it that impresses an NT? Degrees? No, not really. Experience and being trusted by others? No! For the NT, the information has to pass their sense of being believable and, therefore, the use of sound reason and logic has the greatest chance of convincing them.

As we have said, they need to understand logic and how all arguments are based on assumptions. Even when logic is based on accepted facts, the interpretation of those facts and the way they are perceived can destroy the most carefully presented logical argument.

Being skeptical makes sense to the NT. However, if the skepticism of your teen is bent on tearing down and destroying ideas, it has become a weakness, a negative pursuit. The strength of the NT that we refer to here as skepticism is a questioning with the goal of discovery and finding the truth. In this sense, it is not destructive. Likewise, if verification is its goal, it is a positive endeavor.

Of course, answering an NT teen with "Because I said so" is a sure way to be distrusted. You will also be despised because what NT can respect a person who trots out that sort of weak answer? You are likely not to be asked for information again unless there is no other way to get the information they want.

The NT teen is not to be feared or criticized but simply understood and directed with sound reason.

Developing this Strength — Things to Share with Your Teen

- To develop this strength or any core strength, use it; question!
- Understand that all people don't know the answer to questions that seem fundamental to the teen.

- Many times the teen is asking in order to compare your answer with others. Let them. It's their way of learning.
- Sometimes they are questioning to find confirmation of something they think you will confirm.
- Questioning is a means to an end. It's the end they are trying to find. Don't make questioning your goal. Knowledge, understanding, and wise application of understood knowledge is your goal.
- Do all you can to answer honestly and if you don't know, then tell them you will find the answer and get back to them.
- Better still, say to them, "Let's find the answer together," and do so, perhaps, on the internet (be careful about internet information, though), or the library, or from knowledgeable people.
- When they question an authority, don't show shock or disapproval. It's the authority's task to answer and convince.
- Questions open up conversations and possibilities. Statements close conversation and discovery down. With an NT, always favor questions.
- If questions turn to negative skepticism, help the teen use this strength constructively, not negatively. Help them see the difference and the different results they produce.
- We only seek to destroy what we can do without. Therefore, don't use skepticism to ruin what is good and needed.
- Remember, we are limited human beings and our knowledge is never complete. Therefore, don't assume a position of knowing everything. No one does.

Independent — Self Reliant

The coolness you often see in an NT teen comes from a very strong urge in their temperament to be independent and self-reliant. If you want to be independent, running around being warm and friendly with others is not the first thought that comes to mind. Independence suggests you keep to yourself and create an emotional and mental distance from others. So, the coolness is often not a rudeness, but an attempt to obey the urge for independence. However, it can come across as rude with a feeling of being superior and even stuck-up. Your teen should understand how they are presenting themselves and learn they must accept the consequences of their actions, whether intended or not.

But it is hard for an NT teen to feel consequences are just at times. Justice may not be able to be found. A deep urge for independence surges inside them and they feel they are being a person with integrity toward themselves. Of course, they will use this independence at times to test or punish others with their coldness and, therefore, they need to be directed to use it with a clear understanding of what it can and does do to their relationships.

A teen who is seeking independence needs to be taught to always keep their goal in mind. If the goal is to be independent, then nothing more than a desire to be independent must be revealed by the cool approach. This means an explanation is at times in order. If it has some other less acceptable goals, they must be made aware of the consequences to them and others of such actions.

This goal training is very important because it is within the logical mental pathways of the NT mind. For example: If my goal is to convey that I am favorably impressed with someone, then an unexplained coldness will not take me to my goal. If I run the risk of being seen as rude or overly confident, even proud, I am acting in a way that does not lead me to my goal. Logic says, if my actions do not lead me toward my goal I am acting illogically. That makes a strong point for the NT. Be logical, not foolishly illogical. Seen this way, the NT teen is being effectively impressed with the need to change their actions to achieve their goal.

Here is the maxim in brief: never act in such a way as to move away from your goal.

Independence has its limits. No one can be absolutely independent of others, at least not in our culture. We are all dependent on the people that grow, package, transport, stock, and sell our food, to begin with. And think of all the other dependencies in regard to power, trash, water, housing, work, learning, and more. Independence, for the NT, is limited and they are more interested in the independence of the mind than they are of physical independence.

The independence of the mind is seen in their skeptical approach to all the information out there. It is also a withdrawal from all the over-trusting behavior and loose thinking that they find in others. When it comes to social matters, it affects their ability to smoothly blend into the lives of others. They are misunderstood as a result, but it is due to mismanagement of their strengths, not to the strengths themselves. Teenage will begin the serious casting of the mold for all their social interactions.

When the time comes for a serious choice of a life partner, this independence will have to give way to a dependency on another that makes true love and mutual life possible. The NT makes the change, but not without a struggle.

Parenting is influencing by modeling first, and by logical reasoning second, to help the teen use this strength wisely and, certainly, not to overuse it.

Developing this Strength — Things to Share with Your Teen

- If we are to be independent, we need to pay great attention to knowing more, understanding what we know, and strengthening our abilities.
- Independence is not absolute, so look for the ability to also be happily dependent where it is needed.
- Help them negotiate for greater independence in ways that teach them responsibility and diplomacy.
- Plan the increased independence of your teenager and get them to earn each step with behavior that increases trust.
- Teach them that independence carries with it great personal responsibility and help them toward the development of responsible behavior.

Calm — Cool — Collected

An emotion drives all the strengths of the NT: calm. It is an emotion! Most of us, including the NT, do not think of calm as an emotion, rather the absence of an emotion. This misunderstanding causes us to misinterpret the NT and their seeming disparagement of emotion. Their calm is a necessary state of mind. Emotions that disturb cloud the NT's mind and they know they can't think as clearly. Besides, they soon discover that being calm rattles some people and it is to their advantage in confrontations.

What is calm? It comes into our language from the Greek word *kaurma*, meaning of all things heat (of the day).

Strangely, a calm attitude can cause some people to get very heated. A mother reported to me that what angered her most about her NT son was his calm. When she was mad with him and vented her displeasure, he would just stand there without so much as a twitch, and it made her really mad that she couldn't get a response out of him. When a mother's or father's anger is emotionally displayed and out of control, they have truly lost their NT teen's respect.

Calm, cool, and collected describes a state that is much desired by the NT teen. St Francis de Sales said, "Never be in a hurry; do everything in a quiet, calm spirit." That is a noble aim, but often we are not in control of ourselves or our circumstances sufficiently to be able to achieve it. When your NT teen loses it and falls into an emotional state, we must help. Argue a return to his strong point: a calm and controlled state of mind. This is the neural pathway we want for our NT teen.

"Cool" is fine when it means not heated, but if it feels like the NT teen has ice in their veins, it can be detrimental to all their relationships. People want warmth. This cool emotion needs to be kept in control as much as the heated emotions of anger and fight. A pleasant cool is what is required.

"Collected" is keeping your wits about you. This is the part of this strength that makes it so effective in discussion and debate, in confrontation, and discoveries. Encourage this all you can.

Developing this Strength — Things to Share with Your Teen

- Since there is so much benefit in being calm and collected, this trait should receive lots of enthusiastic approval and positive reinforcement, but keep the approval calm!
- We develop our strengths when we savor their benefits. The teen should feel pleased with this strength and inwardly enjoy the emotions it brings. Appreciation of a strength builds its sense of value to us.
- The NT teen shows, on the surface, mastery of their emotions when they are calm, cool, and collected. The real secret is a calm mind.
- Try not to spark the emotions of your NT because this is a neural pathway you do not want them to develop. Deliver all messages that they will not like in a calm manner.
- Because of their control over their emotions, you do not want them to take matters too far and despise emotions altogether. Teach them the value of emotions. Show them that they are using emotions all the time, just different emotions and ones that do not trouble the waters.
- Help them understand that overuse of coolness can disturb their relationships and make some of them impossible.
- Wrong use and overuse can lead to other people disrespecting them.

Logical — Reasonable — Must Make Sense

We have discussed this trilogy to some extent already. Let's take a deeper look at it. Why does the NT do only what makes sense to them?

Their emphasis is on the analytical brain and its clear functioning. It is not that they are the only ones who use the analytical part of their brains, nor are they always the most effective in its use, only that they favor it over any emotional response. Emotions don't seem to make sense to them.

Reason follows a clear structured path. Logic is controlled by accepted rules and what makes sense is firmly grounded in accepted conclusions, given a particular set of circumstances. It is comforting to be in control of your thoughts and this, too, is what logic offers. The Greeks were the ones who introduced us to the forms of thinking that they called logic. It is based on a foundation that consists of assumptions, which are usually interpreted facts, and flows via understood principles to logical conclusions.

Logic comes from *logos*, a Greek word for "word" or "reason," and is consistent in its meaning all the way through Latin, French, and into English. Even if we can't define it, we understand what it means and at least its general meaning. This is one reason why making sense is seen as being logical to the teen. It is understood. Thoughts are expressed in words either spoken or not. Logic is all about words and how we make sense, or not, when we formulate them and choose them.

Being logical is being safe. Emotions are not safe. They can fly off in any direction and create chaos if not controlled. They disturb a person to the point that they cannot think and they do this because of their speed and forcefulness. Feeling unsafe is as though you are crossing rough seas with waves coming at you from unexpected directions. Feelings are the hardest of mental happenings to get hold of and control. To change the analogy, they are a rolling sea, difficult to calm.

Being logical gives structure and a sense of safety because we can control our reason and we can easily change what we are thinking and make it make sense. Therefore, such complicated thinking as strategy is possible. Behind the NT teen's efforts at trying to make sense of their world is this demand to think by the rules. Logic is developing and becoming the mind of the NT teen. They naturally follow structures of thought that they have discerned in others. Their logical thinking is refined as they expand their reading and mental adventures.

Parenting the NT well is a matter of the parents always being reasonable and consistent thinkers. Inconsistencies are glaring departures from the normal and the NT teen will detect them. They want to hold all others to their logical way of thinking and they tend to look down on those who don't show concern for logic and reason. More and more they will change what makes sense to them as the facts of this wider teenage world forces them to reconsider. However, the NT's emphasis on reason can unnerve some parents. But if you are consistent in what you think and do, you will be impressing them with or without the strict structure of logic.

Developing this Strength — Things to Share with Your Teen

- The teen should understand that mathematics is an exercise in logic. Use math to practice your appreciation and grasp of logic.
- NTs are good at debating and, therefore, need to become good thinkers. Learning the structure of logical thinking is a real benefit to their mental development.
- Analysis is the skill of pulling an argument apart to understand whether the basic flow of language makes sense, and this is another practice from which the teen can benefit.
- Taking any statement to its logical conclusion is a way of determining its accuracy.
- Public speaking and debate are also good exercises.
- For games, the classic game that demands the operation of logic with the use of strategy is chess.
- Remember that in all our reasoning, emotions must be given their rightful place. Emotions have a logic all their own and the NT needs to understand this as they develop.

- Every thought we have contains some emotion. We cannot avoid its influence on what we say, do, and think. NTs need to grasp this.
- Learn how to use probability, presumption, and burden of proof in debate and in real life.
- Remember the limitations of logic. Life is more than reason, logic, forming arguments, and even what makes sense. There are many things logic cannot discover or explain. This knowledge is a powerful driving factor in the NF temperament as well.
- Settle for what is likely and probable in most human matters.
- Always choose to act so that it moves you toward your goal.
- Live life with more than logic

Ingenious

Because of all this thinking we could have an ingenious teen on our hands. My observations are that, for the NT, ingenuity comes from hours of study and thought. The truly conscientious teen is a candidate for this kind of discovery.

Edgar Allen Poe has a statement well worth our thought when considering the behavior of NT and NF teens. It is what blends these two temperaments and makes them siblings. He says, "It will be found, in fact, that the ingenious are always fanciful, and the truly imaginative never otherwise than analytical."

Several thoughts emerge from his words: fanciful, imaginative, and analytical all live within the compass of ingenuity. The NF is the fanciful and imaginative one who lives in these worlds and when analyzing their meanings, returns to the real world to impart the wisdom they have gathered. The NT is also imaginative, but hardly fanciful. With their intuition structured within the bounds of logic, they can become very ingenious, if by ingenuity we mean the ability to devise things that are useful and things that have never been thought of before. They are inventive, creative, and original in a pragmatic sense.

Strategies, planning, and theorizing with their sharply tuned analytical minds directs the NT to find answers that surprise. Out of this comes the urge to make all things new — to find another way of doing things. In order to be ingenious, they must generate ideas, so don't scoff at your NT teen's ideas that may seem way outside of reality. They must organize and codify their ideas and new knowledge in insightful and clever ways. Teenage NTs have astounded the world with some of their inventions and new ideas. Ingenuity is the world of the NT and the sooner they feel its powers surging in them, the better. This is one reason why the NT teen is attracted to engineering, whether it be in structural creations or in the world of chemicals or technology.

Ingenuity is one of those strengths that can hardly be overused or misused and benefits us all. Their ingenious journey begins, usually, with Legos and the creations that astounded us when they were still so young.

Developing this Strength — Things to Share with Your Teen

- To be ingenious, we must think outside the box. Encourage innovative thinking.
- Most ingenuity is the bringing together of ideas that have never been associated before.
- Time spent organizing and reorganizing ideas can be very productive. Whatever class they have a great interest in is a subject for their ingenuity.
- We have a virtual world: our mind. In this world, ideas are shuffled, sorted, and tested. Work with your teen on developing these skills.
- Let them pursue the intuitions they have, the hunches, and the insights.
- Develop all related strengths to best develop ingenuity.
- They must not race to conclusions too quickly because then their focus narrows and excludes other pregnant ideas and combinations of ideas.

- Perspiration sometimes surpasses inspiration.

Efficient — Effective — Competent — Achiever

The teen is on the quest for these and already should have shown his/her ability at reaching toward these goals. For the NT, life is despair if these cannot be realized. For the teen NT, they are the shining peaks that call them to persist.

Charles William Eliot (1834-1926) is remembered for many accomplishments in the field of education in the United States. As editor of the *Harvard Classics*, a highly acclaimed "five foot shelf of books" that avowed to give a complete education, he was obviously a seminal industrious thinker. When he said, "The efficient man is the man that thinks for himself," he nailed the attitude of the NT that leads them to their many successes.

The NT teen will, at times, show they don't think their teacher knows as much as they do and they will forever be following the call to find new and better ways of doing things. If this drive for notable achievement and mental discoveries is strong, they need the confidence and the energy that a powerful belief in themselves will bring. Along with that, they need to feel the effectiveness of their brains and the creativity of their minds. Their relaxing moments are spent in tech games or other mental pursuits, even debate about anything, seeking the thrill of competency.

Efficiency for the NT is more than being well organized (they often are not). It is being competent, which is the skill and the knowledge to do whatever they focus on successfully and in a better way than it has been done before. Therefore, efficiency, effectiveness, and competence are for them the same drive. The NT teen feels a loss of confidence when they are not competent and effective. When they enter a new sport, they have already seen where they might excel. This mental effort helps them enter with at least a belief that they can be effective. It is hard for them to attempt something if they feel they will not be effective.

Knowing they will be effective creates self-confidence and anything short of this feels unacceptable, not up-to-par for them. A mediocre performance is embarrassing and they do not want to talk about it. The thin air of an elated self-image is the air they breathe. It seems like obnoxious pride to some more humble minded parents, but these parents are faced with a challenge. If they seek to deflate their NT, they will either cause a rift in the bond of parent and teen or they will be taking away the teen's confidence. On the other hand, if they praise the teen and encourage this inflating ego they may be the cause of an offensive pride. The best path for the parent is to keep their balance and walk the tightrope between a high self-image and the slippery slope of a nasty pride. Again, the teen NT needs confidence or they won't achieve and then they will fall into the apathetic attitude of simply accepting failure and mediocrity.

All of the words that describe this drive in an NT teen are the opposite of mediocrity. Along with the loss of this drive goes the loss of their goals. No goals? A troubled, apathetic NT is being formed. They become disinterested, dispassionate, and unmoved by the challenges of achievement. Motivation, which is the natural state of an NT, has departed.

This troubled teen will turn to do almost anything to socially gain the acceptance of others. They can also build strategies to fail and be a nobody. Classwork will degrade and they will spend their time trying to climb in stature in the world of those who do not do well.

There's a drive in them to be well thought of. As I mentioned in *INNERKINETICS*, the word "chief" means a leader. Placing the letter "a" in front of the word chief is the way we got our word achieve. This is the teen who is the "chief achiever" and anything less than that signals an acceptance of failure. To accept failure is to head downhill, not up into the thin air of a high self-image's towering summits.

Developing this Strength — Things to Share with Your Teen

- In order to achieve, we must reach the goal we have chosen — be it a grade level or our own yardstick of success. In order to do that, we have to be motivated for success. Watch carefully for signs of motivation in your teen.
- Get your teen to be able to express their strategy for reaching their goal. It will add structure to desire.
- If their methodology to succeed is lacking essential pieces of knowledge, help them find the missing pieces. The NT needs to find them rather than be handed an answer. Guide them to the discovery of successful methods. A strong will and determination will help any NT teen develop this strength.
- An NT teen should be results-oriented. If the results are not there, get them to change their method. Knowing that repeating the same method after failure means they are depending more on "determination" in order to succeed and that is usually not a good decision. Find a better method, and then apply determination.
- Make sure the teen does not have an emotional block. Emotions cloud their performance.
- Encourage them to obtain and accept feedback. "Feedback is the breakfast of champions."
- Two minds are better than one. Using other people's minds is the same as gathering more information. Help them see that.
- If they fail, lift their spirit with the reminder that they are further ahead than when they started. Realize also, an over-emphasis on success as a goal can destroy the possibility of future success. Find another way to simply try again following what we mistakenly call failure.
- The NT teen needs to feed their emotions with confidence. At all costs, seek to avoid a lack of confidence and do all you can to re-instill it if it has vanished.

13: The Core Strengths that Shape and Fulfill the NF Temperament

Call me Janet, if you will. I know I'm emotional. Sometimes I love it; sometimes I hate it. I've never figured out why I am so emotional. Yes, I want to please and, above all, I want harmony in all my relationships. When there is conflict, I am demotivated and depressed and, at times, I wish I were better — actually most of the time.

I'm affected more by what might happen than by what has happened. My spirit lifts whenever I have hope and can see a light on the horizon of my life. It's then that I become very optimistic.

Did you say sensitive? I guess you're right. At times, I'm too sensitive for my own peace of mind. They tell me it's good to be sensitive because that's what is needed to be gifted, but I don't think I'm very gifted. I'm kind, though, and I love it when I make a difference in someone's life. How are things going with you? Are you all right?

This is the teen with a finely tuned sensitivity and a drive for perfection wrapped with haste in a package filled with emotion.

The path for teenage development is written in the NF teen's core strengths. A parent may also choose to develop some gifts, talents, and skills that the teen displays or shows an interest in. However, if preparation for adulthood is the focus, the core strengths must be developed so as to not damage the teen or damage others and to give the teen an understanding of where their fulfillment in life will be. This will aid greatly in their making good choices.

Try this exercise: Ask the teen to list each of the core strengths of the NF in order of importance to them. As they go through their teenage years, get them to re-list these core strengths in order of importance to them. Do it every year or two and let them see how they are developing and appreciating their core strengths and what changes in preferences are taking place. Further self-understanding can be achieved by asking them the reasons for any changes in their listing. We want to achieve both awareness of their core strengths and a growing appreciation and understanding of them. The parent is not the judge of which core strength is more important than the other. The teen must verify for themselves.

If this is done, the parent can watch the growth of their teen and the teen's self-understanding will be a tremendous help in this final rush to adulthood.

Learn your teen...

A Convenient List of the NF Temperament's Strengths

Lives in and for the future

Idealists, dreamers

Imaginative

Passionate, enthusiastic, makes value-based decisions, eager to learn

Trusting

Personal growth, meaning, significance

Sensitive

Intuitive, insightful

Emotional, from love to hate

Empathetic, caring

Humanitarian

Seekers of harmony, haters of discord

Kindhearted

People skills, diplomatic

Real and authentic, ethical

Romantic

Introspective

Perfectionists, must do and be right

Abstract in speech

Lives In and For the Future

A glance at the strengths of the NF and it is obvious that the future is their world. Idealists, dreamers, full of imagination, personal growth enthusiasts, romantic — all these and other characteristics help shape a teen who is thinking and dreaming about the future. They live in the now while also in their virtual world where they are constantly thinking of the future.

The future for the NF teen is where hope and the excitement of possibilities and expectations are found. Therefore, they daydream and lie awake at night, fashioning their idyllic fantasies around what could, might, or may be, or may never be. The world of the future is not yet, so it provides the ideal make-believe environment. It holds possibilities far more appealing than reality most of the time. It's a place to visit and to hide from the coarseness of real life. And the NF teen finds life harsh and abrasive when people are inconsiderate and hurtful, even without intending to be so.

When the future is forecasted as being bleak or devoid of relief, it will throw your NF teen into a downward spiral. That sinking feeling will last as long as there is no hope of something better. Immersing themselves in some present activity can also bring them out of their depressed feelings. It's all about emotion and the changing of negative emotions for positive ones. Emotion is the most powerful operation in the brain and the feeling of being swamped by negative emotions is hard to reverse — in fact, impossible, unless another emotion of a more pleasant nature comes along.

This should give you a clue to how you can help. Can you provide a pleasant emotion? Acts and words of love should help, don't you think? If there is nothing else to offer and the future is dark, it is the best you can give and your best for an NF is enough. You may not see an immediate response that indicates that you were successful, but give them kindness and you will help. Pleasant emotions often act slowly when the teen is depressed, but after a short time, they will give evidence of their emotions being healed. You see, for the NF, all loss of hope is a debilitating hurt. These are not weak creatures who have to be coddled. They will find their own way out of hopelessness if they have to. NFs are sensitive and rich with emotions of all kinds and it takes time to change hurtful or negative emotional contexts. Love them and give them time.

When there is light and hope on their horizon, then they sparkle with life. "Without hope, the people perish" (Proverbs 29:18), and with hope, they shine like the sun. Hope awakens passion and passion is the emotion that drives the NF, as we will see when we examine the strength called "passionate." The NF teen just needs positive emotions. Bring them some. That's all you have to do.

So, we might say that the future is an emotional thermometer for the NF teen. A good relationship that is pending will send the mercury instantly to the top. Are you a parent who is afraid of hope in case it does not eventuate and you are thinking your teen will be so much the sadder over a dashed hope than if they had no hope at all? If you are, remember, life is not best lived in the fear of negative happenings but in the joy and refreshment of the present. The NF teen needs whatever joy the future offers and needs to experience it now. Hence they seek to live happily for the moment in the uncertainty of the future.

What lies ahead has always fascinated humans. The future will not change, but we can select our place in it and plan accordingly. This, the NF teen is doing. The future is the prospect of good things for the hopeful teen. Never take that away from them. Our vocabulary is filled with words like *success, favorable outcome, a good ending, a new beginning*, and these lie in the future as fashioned in the NF's virtual world.

When the NF lives in the past, they are ruminating and usually negatively introspective. Like others, they seek to learn the lessons of the past, but being passionately hopeful, they can at times keep doing the same thing in hope of a better outcome. The present is wonderful as long as it holds on tightly to happiness. If and when it doesn't, the NF teen escapes to the future for a reprieve. "Hope deferred makes the heart sick, but a longing fulfilled is a tree of life," (Proverbs 13:12). Wise comments for the NF teen.

Developing this Strength — Things to Share with Your Teen

- They must live in the hopeful world of the future for maximum happiness. Let them. It is something, as a parent, you can't do for them. Take care not to disparage it and make them feel as though there is something wrong with them because they seem not to live in the "real world."
- Help them always to search for the silver lining in the threatening cloud. Help them gaze at the stars in the darkness of their emotional nights.
- Teach them to cling to hope. Hope will never leave them if they remain optimistic.

229

- When they want to talk about possibilities or something that has flashed on their horizon, spend the time with them, listen and talk.
- The more they use their virtual world (their mind), the more skilled they will become at fashioning pleasures in it and shaping their goals and their lives. They are meant to live there most of the time — and they do.
- The one danger you will need to be aware of is the overuse of this focus on the future. Its overuse will be seen in the teen that cannot keep their feet on the ground of reality — the one who does not want to come out of their fantasies.
- Living in the clouds of the future can be nothing but an escape. It can also be healthy. But as with all strengths, an overuse is unhealthy.
- Teach them always to fill their world with faith, hope, and love and you will parent your NF teen well.

Idealists — Dreamers

Let's focus on idealism. It's not the same as philosophic idealism. NF idealism is that everything worth thinking about must be ideal and the NFs experience this idealism as a force in their minds, even if not in reality. The NF is full of idealistic thoughts about many things, from people they meet and admire, to dreams they fashion about what they would like to be or do.

Seeing someone or some experience as ideal has an inbuilt problem. Nothing is perfect — especially people. They can disappoint you as they fall from the pedestal on which you have placed them. "I thought I could trust him" or "I thought she was better than that" can be, for the NF, a distressing awakening. Lost trust and admiration is also, for the NF, a loss of belief in oneself because they believed in their idealistic thoughts. It is not just the loss of our mental images of someone but the more serious doubt that NFs are not competent when it comes to judging people. But people are what NFs are all about, so how can they be so naive? It's because they are so idealistic and trusting that they can be fooled. They need to temper their disappointment about themselves with the knowledge that when a "T" reads only the facts, leaving out the emotions involved, they also misread people. For the NF, it's reassurance about themselves along with comfort over their lost idol that they need.

But on the other side of the coin is a point of view that can really help us succeed in life. The NF always wants to believe in the ideal and shoot for the ideal because why would you want to do otherwise? What good is there in aiming at less? The likelihood of reaching higher is made possible by their higher aim. Your teen is faced with many attempts at excelling in which they did not reach their goal, but he does not want to aim lower. In their sensitive world, being satisfied with less than the best does not seem to make sense. How can you be satisfied with less than what is possible? NFs are possibility champions. They must come face-to-face with their failures and try again — and again. This struggle is necessary. Success in anything or the reaching of any goal is in trying again, because those who succeed do so because they never give up. "Success needs practice" is another way for them to look at failure.

When it is another person's failure that has disappointed them, they feel they must love the person anyhow or learn to love them, because the subject of their idealistic beliefs is not perfect. Help them in these struggles. The teenage years are when they are struggling with these issues.

The NF is a dreamer. They live a life of fantasy in their dreams. When those wild imaginative dreams are not fulfilled, they feel no loss, just the exhilaration of experiencing the dream. Imagination is a real world that we will talk about under the next strength. Fantasy is a refreshing world, also. Stress is, at times, too much to bear for highly sensitive persons and, therefore, the NF willingly goes to the world that they are in control of: the world of their dreams. As we will find, dreaming can strengthen the imagination or, at least, give it a field in which to play. So, don't disparage dreams.

Albert Einstein is thought of today as a genius. There's even a book out, entitled *Unlock the Einstein Inside*, and the inference is that parents can help do this for their child, helping them to be ingenious. But the astounding thing is that the emphasis Einstein placed on the mind is not a major factor in this book's suggestions. Einstein said, "When I examine myself and my methods of thought, I come to the conclusion that the gift of *fantasy* [italics mine] has meant more to me than any talent for abstract, positive thinking." A well-spoken NF insight!

Fantasy, which can be the inseparable partner of dreamers, is more important than the earth bound temperaments and even most NFs are willing to give it. We live in a world that disparages it. I think that is one reason why Einstein may have given expression to his conviction. Fantasy is not a false world or an unrealistic adventure; it is a creative and magnificent achievement of the human mind. You want to unlock the Einstein in your teen NF? Then help them develop their fantasy and dream world.

The main concern for you as a parent of an NF teen is this core strength's nonuse. Encourage their flights of fantasy and their creative geniuses, as they live in both worlds. However, keep their feet on the ground in all matters of earthly necessity.

If they daydream, let them. Of all the methods for introverts to recharge (and two of the NFs are introverts), the best is daydreaming and it is the fastest. Once again, daydreaming is an escape and escaping is not bad if done for reasons of reprieve, returning again to the real world recharged.

Developing this Strength — Things to Share with Your Teen

- Use it! Dream! But don't abuse it by trying to use it to escape from responsibility.
- Whenever your spirit needs refreshing, dream.
- Treasure your dreams and if you want to keep a private record of those that may influence your future. Keep notes of those dreams that come true.
- Encourage a firm belief that the virtual world of the mind is the greatest gift God has given us.

232

- Dreaming is seeing with your mind's eyes. Practice seeing what you can't see with your physical eyes. Your physical eyes are a marvel of creative genius and your mind's eyes surpass even their grand design.
- Your mind's eyes can see what your physical eyes cannot.
- Henry David Thoreau, in effect, said, "What we look at is not the matter of importance; it is what we see." Always try to see your world for what it can be, not just what it is.
- Develop all of your strengths that help you see things before they are and things that just might be possible.
- See the good and beautiful in everything and don't focus on the darkness.
- Let the magnet of the perfect always draw you.
- Never let the emotional downs of disappointment keep you from trusting and hoping again.
- When your images fail or crash, take the broken material and try again to build better out of the ruins.
- Dreaming is one step. When appropriate, use mental force and determination and make your dreams come true.

Imaginative

The imagination is going through a transition for the NF teen. When the teen was a child, they used it in flights of fantasy and in creating imaginative friends, and it seemed never to be far away in their play, either. But now that they are teens, the real world is opening up in front of them and they are adjusting to it. Some do not know what to do with this strange apparition: imagination in the real world of practical things and ideas. Is it of any use? Are they, now that they are teens, to be more down to earth? It seems so because most of the people around them are practical and focused on the real world of practical things and ideas.

Taking a back seat of sorts, imagination can begin to fade for lack of use in the teen years. That's what happens to all our strengths when they are not given attention and focused on.

But it won't lay dormant for long if given a chance to surface. It mainly surfaces during the night hours and in impromptu performances where imagination is encouraged. Otherwise, the concrete business of relationships, study, and extra curricular activities choke it out. Friedrich Nietzsche had it right: "The struggle of maturity is to recover the seriousness of a child at play."

What is imagination? Among the Greeks, it was thought of as a desire or an impulse. Imagination can be directed or appear at will, much like intuition. They also thought of it as a thought or a consideration. It is clear they had no precise understanding of it. Imagination has a secrecy and mystery about it. It lives in our minds and does not require that it live in the real world. It seems to be unconnected to other aspects of our mental world and drifts off unleashed at times. Children know what it is and know it doesn't need a definition. Teens must recover its magic.

The parent's task is to help their teen rediscover the beauty and creativeness of imagination. Take them to Fantasy World, explaining you want to recover the feelings of childhood and live again for a few moments in the riches of imagination. Imagination has been understandably linked to success, but seldom in the classroom or college lecture room. Let Einstein return to the classroom! Without the rediscovery of this mental gold mine, your NF teen may enter adulthood lacking one of their greatest strengths.

Imagination is the rich creator of great literary works, like J. R. R. Tolkein's *Middle Earth*, for example. Stimulate the expression of your imagination around the dinner table or as you travel in the car. The mind has no limits and great thoughts, discoveries, and master pieces are waiting to be revealed.

Imagination can be so real that you can't distinguish it from reality at times. That's the way we have been designed. Therefore, we can use imagination to practice reality in our minds as athletes do and as the NF must.

Developing this Strength — Things to Share with Your Teen

- Thoughts are racing through our minds all the time. They are waiting to be recognized for their value and captured. When we grasp and think about them and try to relate them to other thoughts, imaginative creativity can come in a flash.
- Turn your mind into Adventure Land, too. Think of thoughts as exciting journeys.
- Because your world is becoming more serious, lighten it with imagination.
- Dreams can awaken imaginative journeys, so try to understand them.
- Don't worry about reconciling the world of imagination with the world of reason. Just enjoy both and let the mind wander some more.
- What is just outside of our thoughts or just off our radar may be a life changer.
- The NF is made for the world of reality laced with fantasy. They can take the parent back to their earlier, clearer days. Help them not to abandon this mental goldmine.
- Be skeptical of all the busy static on the lines of your mind.

Passionate — Enthusiastic
Makes Value-Based Decisions — Eager to Learn

Passionate
The emotion that fuels all of the NF's strengths is passion. The passion an NF teen will show is sometimes overt and very obvious and, at other times, unseen (when the teen is calm on the outside but is bubbling with enthusiasm on the inside). Internal pressure builds faster in an NF teen because emotions are surging so strong and, therefore, the fire (passion) is hotter.

Passion is an emotion that humans have lived with from the beginning of life. Our languages are flooded with words that describe passionate emotions, such as desire, zeal, ardor, enthusiasm, tantrum, and compulsion, to name a very few. There are hundreds of them. What does that tell us? Passion is very much a part of human experience and it has many facets that can reflect its ardor.

But as we have indicated for the NF, the passion can range from a gentle simmer to a full fierce boil. NFs are known for this "heat" because, as we will see later, they are the emotional temperament as well, and that is not a bad judgment about them. It is an indication of how meaningful their lives can be. Just think of emotions and passion surging together. They create a jet fuel that powers the NF system and this is the teen we are trying to guide.

Alfred Lord Tennyson had it right when he said, "The happiness of a man [teen] in this life does not consist in the absence but in the mastery of his passions." And this is the battle in the form of a tug of war that your NF teen is engaged in. All their childhood, they experienced their emotion's powers, but now they must master them or their emotions will be their master. As a parent, if you are not an NF, triple your struggle with emotions (which, if you are like most of us, you show freely at times) and you will have some idea of the intense struggle your teen faces.

Don't condemn them for their passionate outbursts. Don't we have some of our own? Oh, yes! But our adult outbursts are justified, aren't they? Effective parents can't afford to be hypocrites. I just want us adults to remember that the NF teen needs help, not criticism and condemnation followed by judgement, because it won't work for the parent or for them. Remember, if what you are doing is not working for you, the answer is not more of the same. It is understanding and help — the kind that will make your teen want you — that is needed. Passion is a power that needs directing because it will not go away and can't be forced to shut down.

An NF teen will instinctively know that, at times, their passion is a beneficial fire. Success in anything is achieved faster when driven by the white-hot heat of passion. However, it is at times unpredictable and unstoppable and NF teens can find it turning on with a vengeance when they did not plan its ignition!

Approve passion's beneficial use.   When we burn with passion, we suffer. It is not comfortable. It demands that the nervous system be on high alert and an intense focus, like the focusing of a welder's torch, pinpoints our energies.   Our emotional fuel also burns up fast. When the NF teen burns for good causes, they are the most effective change agents in our world.

Enthusiastic

Enthusiasm without passion is not enthusiasm.   But passion does not always burn white hot. It can move the NF forward at a steady simmer.   Enthusiasm comes in varying degrees of intensity.

Enthusiasm is also accompanied by another motivating emotion: eagerness.   To be eager to do something is to be motivated.   If your NF teen is not motivated, they have no interest in whatever is confronting them.   If it is important that they get motivated, don't scold and threaten.   Know that your success in motivating your teen lies in helping the teen develop an interest.   When they are not interested in something, as the old saying goes, "You are flogging a dead horse."   No matter what you do, you won't encourage movement. Always as a last resort, appeal to their helping you and pleasing you and show them they can earn something that interests them.

Words paint pictures and this word, enthusiasm, was formed from two Greek words: *en theos*, meaning "in God."   An NF teen can plug into a belief in a higher power for enthusiasm or they can understand that enthusiasm is to rise above the flatlands of their normal expression and seek the highest expression of ourselves as in *The Man from La Mancha's* impossible dream.   Without enthusiasm, the fires of human achievement are not lit. For the NF, remember, no enthusiasm means no motivation.

Makes Value-Based Decisions

Yet another source of passion is tapped here. Whatever grabs our attention and becomes a conviction becomes our value.

Values are accepted beliefs with enough passion in them to remain burning when the focus is elsewhere. Whenever we return to them, they move us and in the NF teen, they are the basis for most of their decisions. Therefore, take great care to teach your teen that their values are what they choose to become and will become. Help them build helpful and healthy values.

Eager to Learn

All NFs want to learn. The reason is they typically have low or lower self-esteems and learning is a way to give them more confidence. To know you know is to possess a poise and courage doubters don't have. Hence, it is to gain confidence.

The introverts, INFP and INFJ, are life-long learners or if they are not, they are missing a source for their happiness. To learn is to grow and like the NT, knowledge is gained for knowledge's sake. But note this: your NF teen will not want to learn just anything. Passion and enthusiasm are essential fuel for this pleasant activity. If absent, the teen will find no energy to learn. All of them are keen to learn the humanities and if not in college, they become eager students of humans and their behavior by studying them every day.

NFs are people watchers. What are people like? What drives them? Why are they doing what they are doing? What must it feel like to be dressed like that? And thoughts like "I wouldn't do that," are questions and responses the NF constantly finds fodder for thought.

Nature and any feelings that are stirred by beauty and/or ugliness readily engage the NF's emotions, which fuel their learning. Some find their life's work as students and researchers or professors, writers and teachers. Learning is power and growth. This they firmly feel. Empower your NF for a life of richer meaning by encouraging and inspiring learning.

Developing this Strength — Things to Share with Your Teen

- The NF without a fire in their heart is half dead. Life is fire for the NF teen's spirit. Be thankful for their passions.
- They must have a passion, so the parent's task is to help them find one. That will not be needed often. They usually find their own.
- When they find a beneficial passion, fan it until the glowing embers warm not only their heart, but yours, too.
- A fire grows brighter with more oxygen. Desire is enhanced with more passion. Remember, your passion can often increase theirs.
- A single passion is more intense than several passions.
- Teach your teen that they must set themselves on fire for the betterment of the world. To do so, they need to have an optimistic, hopeful view of all that is happening around them and in them and of their part in it. Become engaged with them and they will often burst into flame, too.
- Focus is a key factor in passion and learning, so learn to focus more intensely when needed.
- Teach your teen we are forming our values every day. Do whatever it takes to help them instill the values that do no damage to them or to others and those that benefit them and others.
- Teach them to be the boss and sovereign of their passions, or their passions will rule them.

Trusting

Your NF teen will no doubt exhibit a trusting attitude toward others. They want relationships. The social world is now a major focus, especially for the extroverts. NFs know one thing instinctively: if you want a relationship you have to trust. So they become the free givers of trust, which encourages all those who want a relationship with them, including all who want to abuse their trust or abuse the NF who offers trust.

When we trust others, we can get close to them. This gives the NF greater ability to motivate and influence others. That's what an NF is all about. But it also makes them vulnerable. The advantage that trust gives has to be carefully managed. This is where the parent can be more disturbed than the teen when the teen can't see the danger that lurks in their trusting attitude. "Once bitten, twice shy" does not describe the teen NF's experience, nor in most cases the adult NF's experiences. They will trust many times after they have been bitten because trust seems so right. But bitten hard enough, they can become distant and ultra-reserved.

When the NF teen falls in love, they instantly trust. Instead of telling them not to trust, lay out an agenda of trusting over small things and increasing the trust by increments in order to truly ascertain whether they can trust the one they love. They will need help with this agenda. If on the other hand they are trusting someone who is not trustworthy, discourage the relationship. Do what has to be done to protect a teen who is blind to obvious danger. You will want a lot of credit in your bank to be accepted when you do this, so build a relationship with your NF teen based on a loving, caring trust and respect for each other. Fail to do this and your influence will not be enough when the teen has unwittingly fallen into a dangerous relationship. Start now!

To return to the thought, sometimes a very bad experience will cure them of trusting too readily, but we don't want that to happen. How much do they trust your wisdom and to what degree are they attached to you? This is your concern as a parent. You have to build this relationship with trust, not with distrust.

Developing this Strength — Things to Share with Your Teen

- "Trust where your values are honored; run when they are not" is good advice for the NF teen.
- Tell the teen to believe in others but also to believe in their own need of self-protection. One belief without the other is falsely reading the facts of life.

240

- See the good in others, but wait to see that good in action before you commit. In relationships, it is a rule of thumb to pay attention to how a person treats others more than how they treat you. You will get a better picture of whether they are good and trustworthy. Note that word: trustworthy — worthy of trust.
- In all relationships, ask yourself, "Are their values the same as mine?"
- When the evidence is clear that they do not share the values you want for your life, disconnect before it is too difficult. NFs find it hard to disconnect. Therefore, they should do so quickly in order to regroup.
- For the NF, always ask the opinion of those you know have your best interests at heart and have the experience to know what you as yet may not know.
- Remember, when you disconnect in order to evaluate, you test the relationship, and if they are not willing to be tested, run!
- Don't allow yourself to be disrespected. Disrespect is telling you the person does not see you as an equal to themselves.

Personal Growth — Meaning — Significance

An NF teen finds health and happiness in personal growth. It comes naturally to them. As children, they tried to help their siblings and parents grow up, or do the right thing, or in most cases, treat others with concern for their feelings. Now they must look with a greater concern at what is and is not happening in themselves. As yet, they do not think to answer the question, "Who am I?" They know that somehow they are different from others. Not in a simple "I am conscious of me as a separate entity from you," basic self-consciousness way, but "I am truly not like others."

The urge to understand themselves and develop their core strengths is the subtle dawning of the new day of adulthood. NF teens usually have a reasonably defined idea of who and what they are going to be when they grow up. They have dreamed about it. Some have already chosen their heroes and the modeling is under way. Personal growth is not only knowing what I want to be; it is discovering the new horizons of human development. If you know your teen's temperament, you should help them become familiar with their strengths since it will help them understand why they have challenges and it will help them find the direction in which they can safely go.

A lot of modeling is going on — the sports star, the academic success model, the champion of some cause, the music star, etc. Social models also compete for their attention. Lead them to have the courage to be themselves. Help them with a belief that they can change the world if they are truly themselves. They are a bundle of possibilities and power-packed potential. Set their aim high. When you do, you also have the effect of setting their values high.

Because they live in their minds, the developing and training of the mind is a very important item in their personal progress. I am not inferring that only the NFs need this approach, simply that they are more attuned to themselves and their inner lives and need it more.

The NF teen is becoming aware of meaning in their lives. Life without personal meaning is drab, colorless, and dreary. They can have fun with the rest, but if the fun is not meaningful, they will exit what they feel is its shallow pleasures. Meaning in life for them is personal growth. They are the personal growth temperament.

Perhaps most important is that they want to be significant in other people's lives. If you are all about making a positive difference in others and for others, you need the feedback that you are, in fact, being successful. This feeling of being significant to others is the unrequested feedback they need. When people seek them out, they know they are wanted, and wanted means "significant."

Nothing crushes feelings of self-worth more than the sensation you are somehow not significant. Don't worry about their falling to the dangers of pride. The opposite, you will discover, is the tendency. Psychologist Carl Jung made an observation that when two chemical substances come together, they change each other, and so do two people with their unseen chemistry. Sometimes they never are the same again and it is this effect that the inwardly focused NF teen wants to feel they can help others achieve.

The further they progress into their teens, the more important this becomes. Listen to how they talk about the moments of real meaning in their lives and quietly affirm their feelings of importance.

Developing this Strength — Things to Share with Your Teen

- If an NF teen tells you life's not worth living or some such expression, it is probably because they have felt the pain of not being significant. Simply remind them of their importance to others.
- Growing is the opposite of dying. Not to be growing, to the NF, can feel like dying. To keep your teen mentally healthy, keep them learning something and sharing it with others.
- They climb the mountain of personal growth just because it is there. This is a mountain that beckons.
- Every human is a masterpiece of design. Now that they are teenagers, instead of telling them that they have been made wonderfully, show them their design; discuss their core strengths with them and what they can become. NF teens love to talk to those who show them what they can become. It is a point of bonding.
- The teenage years are not too early for them to read some lighter versions of self-development books and to peruse the section in the library on self-improvement.
- Keep reminding your teen that being upset about not being perfect is damaging to their every effort to be perfect.

- Learning that failures are the opportunity and initiatives to take life to a higher level is a lesson an NF teen needs to learn badly.

Sensitive

How many times I've heard, "I hate it that I'm so sensitive. It's a curse, not a blessing!" When sensitivity is misunderstood, I can understand the feeling. One thing I know: all NFs and lots of others like being treated sensitively! So, what's the difference between a sensitive touch and being hurt because you are too sensitive? Pleasure and pain. We all hate the pain and love the pleasure.

Humans are full of sensing cells from top to toe, registering anything from pain to pleasure. Non-physical feelings — like sadness, mental anguish, ecstasy, and even plain enlightenment — are emotions registered by our systems. The more sensitive we are, the more we pick up from our external and internal worlds. Beauty is more beautiful and hopelessness is a deeper pit of despair for the super sensitive ones. We simply can't choose to register pleasure and not pain with our sensitiveness. If we want one, we have to have the other!

For the NF teen, the most common pain is hurt feelings. For some, hurt feelings are regarded as a weakness and are to be simply ignored — easily said by those who don't get their feelings hurt: the *insensitive* ones who are often called by that name. The struggle between the two sides will go on forever since one can't understand the other. Some cry easily, and those who don't criticize the crier's lack of emotional control. Both have their place in our world and both should be accepted and respected.

The world needs sensitive people. We plead for them when we need them. They create the most expressive music, the tenderest of homes, the deepest feelings of love. The toughest of men often marry the tenderest of women, declaring by their action that they need and love sensitivity. Help the NF teen accept their sensitivity and seek to get them to be pleased with what they can offer the world.

Show them that hurt feelings are because they are tender and their task is not to try to be who they are not. They are to enrich the world with their giftedness that results from their sensitive reception of all things that register even slightly differently from the norm. Gifted people have to be sensitive. The more sensitive we are, the more gifted we can become. One musician will play with perfection, resulting in applause, and the same piece played by another more sensitive performer will bring people to tears. That is the artist to whom the people return for more of their superb renditions and they call it genius.

Unfortunately, to be super sensitive, we have to be vulnerable and open to the slightest influence. But once again, let me emphasize as you will need to do for your teen: it is to the sensitive ones that people return for more of what the emotional world has to offer.

Developing this Strength — Things to Share with Your Teen

- Become aware of when you are extra-sensitive. Awareness of our state of mind or of our feelings is what sensitivity is all about.
- When aware of feelings (good or bad), seek to use them or change them so that you can become a benefit to yourself and others. This will take time and practice.
- Sensitivity sparks anger at times, and all NFs will have to learn to control their emotions. Controlling begins with selecting the right or appropriate emotion. (See under "Emotional").
- Increase your awareness of your feelings and responses to nature and to all things that impress you.
- Pause and focus on what is around you, noticing how things affect you or don't affect you. Become more aware of the impact of your surroundings on you.
- Keep in touch with what is going on in the climate of your mind. Are your feelings positive or negative?

- When you become insensitive to others, you are becoming the opposite of sensitive: harsh and uncaring.
- All strengths of all temperaments are to be developed. Develop this one wisely and selectively.

Intuitive — Insightful

NFs can be very intuitive.   It begins in early childhood, troubling them with dreams and amazing their parents with their insightful understandings. It may pause in late childhood but for most intuitives, it returns to begin its journey to full flower in the teen years.

Intuition comes in many forms and the more common insights into people's feelings does little to affect the teen's development and may even go unnoticed by the teen themselves and others.   It shouldn't.   Insight into another's feelings is a needed gift in helping people.   Intuitive dreams, premonitions, and the like are a slightly different story. If your NF's intuitions raise questions or criticism, the teen will usually keep all these happenings private and confide only in someone who they have come to trust will not ridicule them. Teen growth will go on unhindered, but creative mental activity will probably be hampered.

What might concern the parent is a noticeable withdrawal from others and a more private life, exhibiting some unexplainable periods of melancholy. If this happens to your NF, seek some help from someone the teen feels comfortable with to share what is going on in their private lives.   It will only affect the teen's development if the occurrences are of a troubling nature.

Intuition and Creativity
The insightful nature of intuition can be developed and be very useful in understanding people and their emotions. It is also an important creative strength that stirs the imagination and fuels mental and emotional discoveries.   To quote Albert Einstein again, "The only real valuable thing is intuition." He is referring to the need to go outside the box of logic and explore

the world of possibilities that exist beyond the reach of analytical thinking. Intuition is knowing what the five physical senses can't tell us. It is the sixth sense, also the extrasensory perceptions that are not controllable or traceable to their source. It happens to minds open to the influences of a world of non-physical matter and to minds driven by the wonders of an active and virile imagination.

Think like a child with fresh and unconnected thoughts to find new connections. Adopt the perspective of someone who doesn't seem to understand or who criticizes your ideas, and then look back at your own. Above all, perfect the creativity of daydreaming if you want to use your intuitive powers to their maximum. The mind is made to invent and intuition is one of its secret faculties for creativity. But you can't access its revelations without a penetrating sensitivity, and that's perhaps why NFs are the champions of unbounded intuitions. Don't forget that NTs are also intuitive, but some are limited in their thinking by the need for everything to make logical sense.

Small companies increase in creativity fast. Larger companies decline in creativity and there are many reasons. The honoring of intuition and the release of its influence is much needed if the small company is going to enter the market and find a niche. Intuition will in the future be increasingly important in finding a way to excel by exiting the main stream of a society that has become lost in the rut and needs to be creative to exist. Creative minds and free-roaming thinking will soon become the new power of the future and the way to forge ahead in the commercial world. It already has, to a large extent. Make your NF and NT teen aware of this future trend.

You want your teen to be creative, so helping them develop their intuition will drive them nearer to their potential.

Developing this Strength — Things to Share with Your Teen

- Creativity should be encouraged in teenage and then it will never leave. So the earlier we start, the more comfortable we become with the workings of our creative, intuitive mind.

- Intuition happens. It cannot be forced, but it can be nudged, and the following are some ways and conditions to prod it if it wants to awaken and flower.
  - When we pay attention to our intuitions, they seem to come with more frequency. They are strengthened by use.
  - Meditation is a way to stir the mind's creative powers. Whether it is by emptying the mind of the static caused by the bustle of life and its worries or focusing on something in a state of relaxation, meditation can help.
  - Creativity sometimes emerges from deep melancholic moods. The mood is the conditioning before the revelation. When feeling down, try to be creative. It will enhance the possibility of feeling better and may spark a new idea.
  - On the other hand, people with higher levels of dopamine (the pleasure neurotransmitter) are more imaginative. Whatever the state of mind, imagination can flourish.
  - Daydreaming provides a pleasant and relaxed state of mind and is a productive context for intuitive insights.
  - Aerobic activity is another context that nurtures intuitive creativity. After the activity, spend some time seeking to solve problems.
  - To "bisociate" is to connect two unlikely thoughts, to find a new and positive result. Therefore, thinking in the world of fantasy or the world of unusual associations can spark that intuition that sees what our physical sense cannot see. Gutenburg came up with the idea of a printing press from thinking of a coin stamp and a wine grape press — two unlikely associations.
  - NFs usually find most of their intuitions in the wee hours of the morning. This semi-wakeful state is open to subconscious influences.

248

- Stress, more often than not, will dampen any intuitive inspirations.
- Having strong goals can increase fear and dampen the intuition.
- Intuition in the form of creativity will likely occur in the thinker who is unstressed.
- Don't set goals for creativity, but reward it when your teen achieves true creative thinking and results.
- Intuitions can be encouraged by special surrounds that have been the site of previous intuitions. A location to call your own can seed the mind.
- Michelangelo is an example of someone who had flashes of intuition and yet was a perfectionist who then translated inspiration and intuition into attention to detail.
- The global mind of the NF and NT is a source of unharnessed possibilities and the awakening of creative insights.

Emotional — From Love to Hate

We have already dealt with emotion and its management under the other strengths of the NF temperament, so read all of the strengths in this chapter to get all of the comments. I have written a lot about emotions and the temperaments, so for a full treatment go to *Intelligently Emotional* and *Your Child's Emotional World, Parts One and Two*. Here, we will note significant things about the NF teen's emotional issues.

Emotional management is the most difficult task an NF teen will have to face. Hopefully, they have attained a degree of success by the time they become a teen but even so, with the expanding engagements of a growing social world, the tests will come more frequently. Social pressures and the desire to be well thought of will place their own boundaries around the teen's behavior. It will help them suppress the emotional urges and think before they allow escalation of their emotions to occur.

However, the pressures to suppress them will not be as great in the home, and this is where most of the emotional release will take place. The home where respect for each other is firmly required will be the home that has most success in helping this teen to achieve effective management of their emotions. No one can manage our emotions for us. We must learn how. Awareness of the appropriateness of our emotions is where a parent can help the teen who wants to manage their emotions. Meeting negative emotion with negative emotion is a sure way to let emotions run wild in a home. The teen can't be expected to control their emotions if the parent does not.

With all teens who are struggling with their emotions, the guidance to change inappropriate emotions for appropriate ones is key to success for the NF. The NF does not want to become unemotional because if they think for a moment, they will know they value too much their wonderful expressions of such positive emotions as love and kindness. So don't try to get your teen to not be emotional. That will distort who they are. Teach them to choose the right emotion for the occasion and to learn how to stop one emotion and activate another.

They can learn when full of hate to walk away and cool, to do something else just to be able to get a hold on their feelings and change them. They may not go from hate to love in a flash, but they can go from hate to indifference and then to being socially civil and then to walking the road to love when they understand the intentions of others are not to hurt them. They should always be faced with being accountable for an emotional outburst and say sorry when needed. Accountability helps us remember the boundaries for our behavior and helps us avoid having to apologize and embarrass ourselves.

NFs are tender and are frequently hurt, meaning negative emotions flare automatically and the faster they catch themselves and take time out to think of what is the best thing to do, the more they develop the skills of selecting the intelligent emotion.

Emotions have a logic all their own and our emotions will always select a goal and an emotion that seems to be the best emotion to achieve that goal. It is the goal that the teen needs

250

to learn to change and when the goal changes, so does the selection of a more appropriate emotion. Changing the goal of paying someone back for a hurt received to understanding their perspective and loving them instead is an example.

The following methods to teach ourselves emotional management and achieve intelligent emotions are discussed in full in *Your Child's Emotional World, Part Two.*

1. Grasping the window of opportunity fast and changing the goal their emotions are to achieve.
2. Learning to express (without receiving accusations) what is troubling us.
3. Handling the hurt of dashed expectations.
4. Dealing with out-of-control emotions.
5. Teaching ourselves delayed gratification.
6. The proper use of focus and distraction.

Developing this Strength — Things to Share with Your Teen

- The above methods are invaluable when we master them to deal with the flare of emotions.
- The development of self-control will lead to ultimate mastery.
- Show your positive, wonderful emotions at every occasion that is appropriate. The use and exercise of our positive emotions will create a habitual use of them and a feeling of self-worth at being that kind of a person.
- Make joy, passion, love, faith, and hope your key emotions.
- Seek always to express the purest positive emotions you can.
- Remember to hate conflict and love harmony. If harmony is made a stronger urge, it will make the choice of positive emotions easier.
- Practice being kind to everyone and positive emotions will become your default mechanism.

- Enjoy your positive emotions. The more you enjoy the good, the more you will love the good.
- Positive emotions will make you irresistible and welcomed wherever you go, so develop their use. We lose what we don't use.
- The more the NF uses their analytical mind to understand why others do what they do, the easier it will be to select the best emotion rather than the worst.
- Remember, damaging emotions can ruin an otherwise appealing person.
- Negative emotions, if used in angry outbursts, will destroy all the good of which an NF is capable.

Empathetic — Caring

"Love is the only sane and satisfactory answer to the problem of human existence," said Eric Fromm. He was not the first to notice this. "Love never Fails," wrote Paul, the Apostle. We could create a bumper sticker, "Love is the answer. What was the question?" Empathy is a form of love that shows we care in the most personal manner.

The NF teen can be driven by empathetic feelings to an unwise overuse of this core strength. Empathy is suffering with the other person and entering into their pain to feel it with them. It is one personality entering into another personality to share both pain and love.

Understanding the NF teen's call to share a friend's pain in the deepest way is not all we need to do as parents. We must guide them to learn the boundaries of empathy. If they become so wrapped up in their friend's pain that they cannot help them, they have overused the strength and negated their chances of being helpful. There is a need to stand to the side while hauling a person out of a hole, not jumping in and becoming part of the rescue problem. The teen needs to balance the feelings of care with a reaction that enables them to take care of the problem.

Sometimes there is no way to take care of the problem and empathy alone is then appreciated. But teach your teen to focus on solving problems, not only on empathizing with troubled people. Love is an action as well as a feeling. Therefore, to show love in action is the goal of all caring people and to save a person from pain and suffering is the goal of all true love that is being expressed in empathy.

Developing this Strength — Things to Share with Your Teen

- Empathy is a very precious gift, so don't squander it. Use it where it is needed most.
- Sympathy awakens empathy. When you are sympathetic, before you become empathetic, is the time to evaluate your tactics for the use of your gift of empathy. You need boundaries for its effective use.
- Empathy takes a lot out of you. Make sure you don't allow the stress to drain you beyond your resources.
- The NF teen should have no difficulty in generating empathy.
- When your resources are drained and you become irritable or depressed, withdraw to recharge.
- Always keep yourself healthy in order to keep helping where needed.

Humanitarian

Because they are the people-to-people persons, NFs automatically care about others. Most NFs care in a personal way about the ones closest to them and those they come across in their travels. All people they touch, they care about, but some far-off land where poverty reigns seems too distant to take front billing. To be humanitarian, one needs to care about a vast segment of the human race or, to be more exact, the human race as a whole. I think NFs care about human welfare a lot, but my experience is that they will usually rate this strength lower in terms of its importance to them than most of the others for the above reasons.

253

Teens can be stirred by the stories of human pain and suffering and decide to devote their lives to helping. A parent will not need to awaken the calling. It awakens of its own accord. It will certainly demand the focus of the teen and divert the focus from other typical teen challenges and some parents may be thankful for this.

Developing this Strength — Things to Share with Your Teen

- Knowledge or exposure to the need of humans that are ill-treated or neglected is all that is needed for an NF teen to find their heart stirred.
- When stirred, they will make their own commitment to help if the calling is strong enough.
- If they do commit, they will champion a cause and seek to get others involved. The ENFP and the INFP will especially value this strength.
- A cause requires a vision and this, too, they can provide naturally.

Seekers of Harmony — Haters of Discord

Do you want to know what lies at the center of most of your NF teen's disturbances? A lack of, or loss of, harmony! Yes, an NF wants, and needs harmony and, at times, can't function when disharmony reigns. This in no way excuses the NF teen for behavior that causes disharmony. It simply directs our attention to the method of getting things back on even keel: create harmony, if you can.

A number of strengths and urges that are dominant in the NF teen indicate why they are impacted by disharmony. High sensitivity, high emotions, lost expectations, and the presence of conflict from a misuse of their strengths are some of the triggering mechanisms that stir them. A person with intense sensitivity, for example, will not only notice the presence of disharmony. Their focus will be driven to it and that means an energy center surrounding the disturbance will be formed in their minds and brain. The energy, in this case, will be a negative center and will pull negative feelings into its hungry vortex. Once the emotions have turned negative, we have a full-fledged disturbance.

So, does the parent just give in and let the teen have their way? Of course not. That's damaging to the teen, especially if in the process they learn to manipulate people with their emotional outbursts and fail to learn that it is harmful to them and others. A teen who tries to get their own way by using their emotions as a weapon will soon find in adulthood that they are punished by others and when they do this, their relationships are quickly ended.

Emotions need to be calmed and now that the child has become a teen, they are more responsible for them. They also bear more responsibility to learn to calm their own emotions because they are heading for adulthood, so this should be expected and requested of them. NFs won't have someone always near to help them calm their feelings when they are adults as their parents can do for them now. The teenage years are the final class on emotional control before they enter adulthood and are on their own. Nothing will provide more chances to practice than the occurrences of disharmony that happen in teenage relationships.

When relationships are challenged, the NF teen should view their strengths of sensitivity, strong emotions, kindheartedness, and the need for feeling they are people of integrity as strengths they should use to create harmony, not to revert and register disharmony. Their hurt feelings can be put aside in order to help others. When they do, they find their own feelings are controlled and used for good. Help the teen view themselves as the healer, the solution to any personal disturbances, and not the victim of hurt. A victim mentality causes us to become the losers and we are seen as such by others.

To become the healer of the hurts, especially when the NF teen is hurt by others, is a great opportunity to be everything they are designed to be. When we change our perspective and see ourselves in this way, it gives us a chance to learn to control our emotions in a very positive and constructive manner.

Developing this Strength — Things to Share with Your Teen

- Make sure your love of harmony is so strong that you will be definitely motivated to find it, even when hurt yourself.
- Reacting negatively and with negative emotions is not the way to save or deepen relationships.
- Always try peaceful means to resolve problems, disharmony, and hurts.
- Analyze your upsets and see where you could have become the healer.
- Don't attempt to bring harmony about with forceful means or emotional outbursts.
- Don't use anger; use loving responses. Love never fails.
- Harmony is an expression of care and love. Focus on being the most loving person you can.

Kindhearted

Kindness is a gift and an act of love. NFs, when they are not angry, love giving this gift to people. This is true of the extroverts, perhaps, more than the introverts because the introverts are (but only at times) hesitant to put themselves out there. Therefore, partner with your NF teen and spread love wherever you go. A smile can change an attitude, make a person feel important, warm up a cold heart, or lift the saddened soul. And that's all it takes to spread love. Of course, we can do more, but we can at least do this. Make kindness a family characteristic.

Rephrasing Mark Twain, kindness can be heard by the deaf and seen by the blind. When your NF teen is being kind, they are exercising their strength and making it develop more. The effect will be seen in many other moments in their lives.

Don't berate the NF when they are down and drained and are struggling with their sadness. It is then they need help, not more hurt. So, if you are seeing a lack of kindheartedness in them, encourage them to be who they are and give them a hand as you lift them back to the operation of their true selves.

When choosing a strength to develop, this is a good place to start because it is one that they feel good about and is one that is easier to do. "Just be kind because it is you" can be words that do more than just correct behavior.

The NF's kindness is best expressed in lifting someone's spirit, treating them with loving respect, and honoring them. Being kind is also not being hurtful to others. The NF does not want to be hurtful, but when hurt themselves, they can hurt with a cruel effectiveness. The negative opposite of our strengths is as possible for us as the positive expression of our strengths. The NF can love like no other and hate like no other. They can be the kindest and the cruelest, the most sensitive and the most insensitive, lovers of harmony and creators of disharmony. Whenever they are displaying the negative (opposite) of their strengths, it is not evidence that they are not NFs. Rather, they are NFs who are living or operating in their weaknesses. All weaknesses that we develop or sink into are the reverse of our strengths.

Understanding this helps us realize that the path back to their strengths, for an NF (or any temperament), is the positive use of their strengths. We can usually recognize the negative or positive use of a strength if we remember that a negative use of a strength does not help, it hurts. Put it this way, a negative use of a strength will damage someone or ourselves and that definition can be the most helpful way of teaching an NF teen the difference and how to quickly discern if what they are doing is positive or negative.

Call your NF teen to kindness. Kindness is goodness and all the way the back to Jesus, Plato, and beyond, people have realized that humans live best with each other when they are being good or kind to each other. Plato believed that goodness was the highest thought for a human to have and goodness was kindness. Your NF teen will grasp the idea of kindness being goodness. As a parent, you could do far worse than encouraging your NF teen to be kind and to use kindness as a measure of their goodness.

Developing this Strength — Things to Share with Your Teen

- Actions are the easiest thing for us to control — far easier than trying to control our thoughts. When we teach our teen that kindness is an action as easy as smiling, they can incorporate kindness into their lives faster and more effectively.
- Become aware of the many opportunities in just one day of just smiling or of doing other kind deeds.
- Talk at home about what each one did that was kind. In doing so you make the awareness of kind acts accountable and, therefore, the individual more conscious of them.
- Give kindness a prominent place in your relationship with your NF teen.

People Skills — Diplomatic

NF teens don't come with perfected people skills. They come with the natural ability to develop great people skills. We see the same thing happening as we did with kindness. When they are using their skills in a positive manner to help and not to hurt others or themselves, this is a very useful and beneficial strength. When they use their people skills to damage or hurt others and themselves, it has a destructive capability.

Because it is a natural ability, it needs teaching, training, and developing. With practice, people skills can open doors that other approaches find closed. People skills are by nature considerate of others and their needs. They are respectful and tactful, as well. Because of these, the NF can be an important influencer of others and champion of causes and comes by these things naturally.

A major use of people skills is in bringing opposing parties together, so we have seen the need on the international scene of diplomats. But in a personal arena and in every family, this strength is needed and can be used with great effectiveness, saving or solving many a conflict. Wherever there is disharmony, the NF in the family will seek to act as a mediator and diplomat. Among friends, the same will happen.

When the disturbance is with others, notice how your NF will seek to patch it up and bring peace again. They are peacemakers in the interpersonal world. Because of this, fairness and justice soon come to the fore in their attempts to reconcile people. They find it hard to accept peace if justice is not also required. It also disturbs them greatly when fairness is not a part of a community's life.

Watch for the abuse of people skills to manipulate and achieve unworthy goals. The con artist uses people skills to achieve their own selfish and criminal goals. Goals are a part of people skills and diplomacy. Therefore, for the ethical use of people skills, goals must be pure and worthy.

It will be natural for a teen NF to look ahead in life for some sort of business or occupation where people skills are needed. Help them find the place in society where they can best use their unique giftedness with this core strength.

Developing this Strength — Things to Share with Your Teen

- For the best use of people skills, the NF teen should learn about people and their behavior.
- Reading and studying books that help people understand people are a great tool for gaining the knowledge that they will need to be good diplomats in any situation.
- NFs are people watchers and the simple pastime of people watching can teach them a great deal.
- Engaging with people on a daily basis and in all social situations is essential training. It is in leadership and

attempts to get people to work together that they can also learn much.

- Encourage their use of people skills with their siblings (this will test them) and with all their friends.

Real and Authentic — Ethical

Omar Bradley thought, "Ours is a world of nuclear giants and ethical infants." Our culture is becoming more a community where everyone makes up their own moral and ethical standards and all others are expected to live with them, even if inferior ethics hurt others. Conflict is then hard to avoid. At the negotiating table, having no standards of acceptable behavior or opposing standards makes negotiations impossible. A negotiator feels this pressure and the NF who is intellectually designed to consider others and find peace among people is left with little in the way of mutually acceptable standards for behavior if everyone is a law unto themselves.

But there is another side to this ethical immaturity. The NF teen is struggling with their own ethics and although they are easily influenced by others because they want to please, they feel deep guilt when they have not been kind, loving, honest and good. Whereas SJs will adhere to an accepted standard of ethics and not waver once their values are firmly in place, NFs can waver due to trying to keep everything between people on an even keel and seeking compromise and mutual respect.

It is important, if you want to teach good values to your teen NF, to do so in a loving and convincing manner, making the principle of fairness and justice for all a strong value. This value will give them reason to treat people kindly and with respect while it keeps them focused on the values greater than tolerance. As I have mentioned, in real life, tolerance seems to end up being intolerance of those the preacher of tolerance disagrees with. Love is a far greater value and all humans would want love if they experienced both in their best forms.

All true love must be nurtured in goodness or love becomes a selfish tool. Help your teen with not only a loving home and the model of a loving heart but with logic and reason, to which they will respond. Ethics that seek the good for all is reasoned goodness. Reason it.

Teach your NF teen that life is not about how smart you are; it's about your values and beliefs.

Developing this Strength — Things to Share with Your Teen

- Teach the teen "To thine own self be true," and you will save them much pain from bad choices and guilt feelings that can tear this teen apart. Personal integrity is an essential emotional state for the happiness of all NFs.
- Teach your teen that whenever they feel inner discomfort with an action, they should challenge its true value and purpose. Find the true authentic you and show the real you in your actions.
- Model personal integrity.
- If a cause is championed, help them choose it with all care and reason. The NF chooses a cause mainly based on its values and emotional appeal. Values shape lives, just like beliefs shape lives. Passions, which values create, bind us to the cause.
- Once the NF has built a value and its ethics, they will have shaped their lives.
- Once chosen, the cause will be committed to. Halfheartedness, for an NF, is weakness because passion is their driving emotion.
- Keeping our inner life real means making choices we can live with and being consistent to them.
- If in the development of this strength your NF teen is doing no damage to themselves or others and is blessing the lives of others, they have chosen well and all the other strengths will have a foundation of goodness.

261

- Remember Plato, that great philosopher, taught the idea of the good is all embracing — the highest and most dominant thought for us humans. In an even greater way, so did Jesus. Help build it into the temperament that has been called both the ethical and spiritual temperament.

Romantic

What's to love more in an NF than their quest for romantic experiences? If you are on the receiving end, you will laud this strength. Please note: romance, for the NF, is not limited to a romantic relationship. Nature is filled with romantic encounters and scenes. Romance and beauty are married in most NF minds. Wherever there is an encounter with beauty, there is romance. Give your NF teen a wide range of romantic experiences.

When life is positive and the nutrition of happiness is being felt, the teen is in a good place — unless the happiness is destructive and damaging, of course. The NF teen can find romantic feelings whenever they are in a good place. Some parents are scared of romance for a teen and everyone knows why, but the fire of romance in a teen can't be put out. It has to be guided and nurtured so that it feeds the soul and burns in the fire ring of their heart without consuming the forest of other commitments.

Romantic tendencies can be encouraged in the arts, in poetry, writing, and painting, to name just a few. Music is a ripe field for the expression of all those feelings of beauty and romance. Give your teen plenty of freedom to appropriately express their romantic feelings, and enjoy the romance of life in its larger context with them wherever you feel comfortable. The words of Henry Wadsworth Longfellow are still applicable to the romance we feel in nature today:

As I gaze upon the sea! All the old romantic legends, all my dreams, come back to me.

We are lifted and our spirits are fed.

Developing this Strength — Things to Share with Your Teen

- Teach your teen that romance is an attitude we take to whatever we experience. Model the enjoyment of life's wonders as best you can for them.
- Take them to romantic places.
- Immerse them in the arts and in the feelings that its beautiful expressions offer.
- Model looking for the good and the wonderful in everything.
- Teach them that beauty, love, and pleasure are only enjoyed to their maximum in the womb of goodness because then it develops without being malformed.
- Offer them plenty of calming for their tumultuous spirits. Those moments will quieten the troubles of life and welcome the romance.
- Romance is feelings. Your teen is emotional and romantic. Both will give the greatest meaning to life.
- Romanticism is empty without genuine love.

Introspective

This can be the most troubling of all the NF strengths if it is used negatively. Your NF teen can suffer from self-denunciation and condemnation more than any other temperament. The NF, especially the introverts, can be calm and apparently un-phased on the outside while there is a tempest of emotional pain on the inside. They will often go for days, suffering from this self-imposed state of shame and blameworthiness, tearing themselves down and growing more and more disinterested in life's pleasures. Helping the NF to use this strength as it was meant to be used can be another of your greatest gifts to your teen.

Introspection is usually understood as a thorough search for what is wrong. It is believed that this is its prime use (if we are to judge by how it is used to inflict judgment on ourselves in the hope that self-punishment will assure we don't make the same mistake again). Let's note two things that destroy the idea that this is its real purpose. First, it doesn't work; second, its true use — to discover where and why we are succeeding, not failing and worthless — does work.

First, it doesn't work to keep us from repeating the mistake. I have yet to find the NF who beats themselves up and then rises from the bruised and battered scene strengthened rather than weakened. The more we condemn ourselves the more we destroy ourselves. Unfortunately, it was, in many cases, learned to be our most common self-destructive tool when we were young. Our parents told us repeatedly how bad we were and because we are sensitive NFs, we believed them and started telling ourselves how bad we were. We kept hearing of our lack of worth and turned with more fury on beating ourselves mercilessly. We felt as though we deserved our whippings and this slide into self-hate continued. When someone told us we were good, we refused to believe such nonsense and if we felt good, we used our introspection to find those times we were told we were no good and refute the heresy. Pride was seen to be the devil in all his self-aggrandizement and we were sold the idea that humility was to think lowly (badly) of ourselves, which is the essence of the slide into ill mental health.

It is a sad story of how feelings of worth are so easily beaten out of a child who begins life with no feelings of worthlessness. Just watch that toddler and see how pleased they are with themselves and their performances until the parent criticizes them and tries to correct them.

Let's learn that self-punishment and self-talk of our worthlessness is not the way to learn how to be better. It is the way to becoming worse. It also leads in later life to having great difficulty in forgiving ourselves.

The true use of introspection is to discover where and why we are succeeding and find the joy and vigor of self-esteem. A great and noble strength has been turned into a weapon that will cut us to pieces when negatively used. Our brains can only think of one thing at a time and it is the negative use of introspection that so easily consumes us as our brain is being used against us. We will eventually and effectively destroy ourselves.

Using introspection positively is the way to right the wrongs that we have done to ourselves in its negative and self-destructive use. Yes, it's as simple as that! Use the strength positively to search for, remember, and relive all the great successes we have had. Find the times you were true to yourself, loved yourself, felt good about your kindness, your love, and your respectful treatment of others. And here's the kicker: feast on them in your mind.

Introspection is meant to be a tool to lift ourselves up, not tear ourselves down. It is the way to find lost memories and evaluate all our deeds, discarding all the less than worthy ones and serving up to our conscious minds all that is true, noble, right, pure, lovely, admirable, excellent, and praiseworthy about ourselves.

Model this and teach this to your NF teen. In fact, why not make it a constant meal of gratitude and delicious pleasure for your spirit?

Developing this Strength — Things to Share with Your Teen

- All self-examination should be positive. It does not take hours of self-beating to see what we have done wrong and the positive knowledge that positive introspection uncovers is to be used as a step up to a new level.
- Teach your teen to create a positive image of themselves.
- Teach them to create an awareness of when they fall into self-judgment.
- Avoid all negative self-talk.
- Help your teen to learn not to fear the announcements of their failure. They cannot move up in life without failing somewhere.
- Help them learn to love the times they set aside to recall all the good and wonderful things about themselves and what

they have done and to see them as healthy times of positive encouragement.
- Tell them, "You are designed in a wonderful image and your life is to show it."
- Introspection should and can result in creative ideas. Look for them.
- Treat all self-condemnation with the knee jerk justice of the Wild West and conduct the hanging of such criminal actions against ourselves.
- Let your teen know that the longer they condemn themselves, the more difficult it is to stop the damage of self-flagellation.
- Model all this yourself.

Perfectionists — Must Do and Be Right

The feeling that I should never lose is a killer. Do you believe that? Or do you and your teen believe that you should always feel that you should win? Let's suppose you do feel you should always win. You won't! And what of the feeling that you have failed again? Is it helpful?

Why is setting yourself up for feelings of failure a good thing? Do you believe that all winners believe they will win and that such a belief is to a large extent why they win? You probably do. Here's a much better way:

Your teen is about to start a race in a track meet after weeks of training. You want them to win and can see how devastated they will be if they lose. They are running against high competition and it's not a sure bet that they can win. What do you say to them? "Set your mind on having to cross the finish line before all the others. Go now and do the very best you can, straining every muscle and running as flawlessly as you have been taught. We know you are going to do great! Tell yourself, 'I'm going to win.'"

The race is on and the competition is tough. Your teen lags behind but is showing that they are doing even better than their best. Yards to go and they are coming in fourth. Instead

266

of your heart sinking you are seeing all the improvements they have made and how they are going to be a real threat next track meet. You race up to them with enthusiastic praise and bubble over with your pride, praise, and the forecast of how they are going to scare the daylights out of their next competition. You do not let them see anything but the belief that a failure is the step before a great success as long as we don't get down on ourselves by falsely using this strength called perfectionism against ourselves. Perfectionism is shooting for perfect. It is doing the best you can do. It is setting very high standards and it is knowing that no human wins all the time.

But perhaps the most important thing about perfectionist tendencies and goals is that you know you did not aim at failure. You aimed right and if you miss attaining the perfect standard, you aim again without raising or lowering the bar and whatever you hit is your best. Your best is the promise of better. Failure needs to be renamed. It is really not failure at all but a step on the way up.

We must want to succeed more than we fear failure. It's the thoughts of fear that limit us more than anything else. Perfection is a great thought if it contains no fear of failure. If failure is not an option, then think of stepping up to success even when you fail. How many steps will be needed will be told with the passage of time because all great achievements take time. Aristotle, another of the great Greek philosophers, knew that excellence is not a single act but a habit. Build in the habit.

Don't take away the goal of perfectionism from your teen. Rather, build in the refusal to sink into mediocrity. This is what the strength called perfectionism is trying to achieve.

Developing this Strength — Things to Share with Your Teen

- I wrote in *INNERKINETICS,* "Go ahead. Try to jump over the moon if you are happily related to not clearing it unaided.

Realism should not limit you. It should make you creative. Realism has to face the greater reality: optimism."

- Perfectionism is a call to be your best at whatever you choose.
- Perfectionism is not a call to live without fault or failure.
- Celebrate with your teen all efforts that show a step up.
- Don't let good achievements die. Keep them alive in your mind.
- Failure is opportunity.
- Hope is what keeps failure from being failure. Keep hope alive!
- If you keep a mental list of your cherished achievements you will keep moving upward.

14: Creating a Future for All

Last Efforts to Bond

Bonding is limited to the wishes and actions of both teenager and parent. Being realistic, some teens have been lured away from their parents by peers or other influences and to win them back means first, the dissolution of the bond with their peers. Peers, who are encouraging behavior the parents can see is damaging, will win as long as the teen maintains the relationship with those peers. Direct opposition to the influencing peers seldom works. Sometimes, all the parent can do is offer reason and encourage an alternate way of life or give up some control in order to gain the road to the teen's heart. Sometimes, the teen must learn the hard way, if and when they learn at all.

This is why seeing our parenting tasks as helping our teenagers to make good choices is placing the emphasis where it is most needed. When faced with rebellion, a parent is left with finding the best help they can to rescue the relationship.

This practice of going our own way is called free will or free choice, which is a basic element of our design. Every teen will exercise this option and many times the parent can't be held in anyway responsible for the teen's choices. At times, parents do neglect their responsibilities, but no parent is perfect, either, so casting blame is a useless game at best. Doing our best under whatever circumstance we are faced with is acting with integrity. Self-blame, too, does not help. Self-blame falsifies the facts. The parent is not in control. There are at least two people whose actions count and the one that counts most is the teen who, in the final analysis, is responsible for their actions. The teenage years are about getting more freedom and freedom does not come without responsibility.

Seeing what opportunities remain is a better sport for the skeptic. Those opportunities are to grab what remains of our parenting role in the teenage years to fuse a bond if at all possible. If your teen is seventeen, time is running out fast. Devoting all our effort to the task is the only chance and often is successful.

What Is Required to Bond with a Teenager?

The answer may be surprising because the parent may not have seen its importance: an understanding of each other that makes the teen feel comfortable and safe in the relationship. Rarely is this a mutual effort. Teens don't have the same motivation to understand their parents. Teens equally have no demand laid on them to commit to the relationship with their parents. Such a relationship has to be won, not demanded, and it certainly will never happen by force.

Nor is bonding created by gifts. If the gift stirs gratitude, then a temporary bond is created until the teen feels again that their parent does not understand them and reverts to the company of those who do. Being understood and comfortable in a relationship has a greater pull than money can generate unless the finances are seemingly unlimited. Even then, a bond with the parent is not created. Rather, a bond with the parent's money has been made and a sense of entitlement ingrained.

We all bond with those with whom we feel comfortable and understood. Likewise, we are all limited to what the teen tells us of how they feel inside unless we have completed the Temperament Key with them. Then we know what the deepest urges of their nature are and have the advantage of the knowledge of their temperament. So, complete the temperament key with your teen again — even if you admit to them that it is for you that you are asking them to do it.

Often in the late teenage years, if a bond has not been adequately established, it is necessary to admit to the teen that you don't understand them but you really want to. It is something they can do for you that will pay them back in flush dividends. A parent who understands a teen forms a much more rewarding relationship for the teen as well as themselves.

270

Let them know how beneficial it will be for them. If they ask you whether it will mean you will let them do whatever they want, smile and say, "Honey, you are smarter than that!"

Understanding is a back door to the feeling of trust, as well. If you are speaking the teen's language — the language of their temperament's drives and urges — they will certainly feel a greater degree of trust toward you and your actions. When finally as an adult, they ask you for your opinion, they feel you are factoring in an accurate knowledge of them. It will result in the kind of bonding that seeks each other out for mutual pleasure, plus assistance.

Here are some suggested steps to bond if you have not done so already.

A Short Course on Creating a Bond

- Discover your teen's temperament and type.
- Complete the Temperament Key with your teen, even if they are not fully cooperative. You should be able to assess most of what you want to know. Do all you need to do to discover how they have been designed to function and to find their happiness. You may need a session with an InnerKinetics® professional consultant in person (or on Skype or via other media) if you are having difficulty.
- Study your teen's temperament and type until you understand why they are doing what they are doing. Remove from your mind the puzzles about them. If you don't know why they feel, think, and act the way they do, they will never feel comfortable with you or want to consult you for help, unless it concerns the need for money or freedom to do as they want. (Good sources for the information you need are *INNERKINETICS* and *The InnerKinetics of Type*).

271

- Talk with them about who they are and help them understand and identify their preferences.
- You will need to know your own temperament first and be receptive of the obvious differences of theirs.
- Become deeply involved with their interests.
- Spend time eating, exercising, watching movies, or (if your teen is a reader) hanging out at the library together and searching the web for purposes of discovery and finding answers.
- Become a supporter of their developing interests and passions.
- Create opportunities for them to develop their strengths and help them discover their direction in life. Don't just ask them what they want to be.

***

Parents Will Have to Continue Risking

To even imagine a future without risk suggests our feet are not solidly on the ground. Risk is part of life and trust is not possible without risk. Trust equals risk or there is no need for trust. Of course, not wild thoughtless risk, but risk that is calculated given the temperaments and track record of parent and teen.

We never stop learning because life will not stop facing us with alternatives and their consequences. Life is one long course in the "University of Hard, Soft, and Subtle Knocks." We never graduate. We just cease to attend this university by dying. Every choice involves risk because all the facts are never known and we make our judgments based on the past or on chance, hope, or faith, any of which we all call reason. We all know the routine of justifying our actions and choices. And justification is the right word if we don't know all the facts.

Our lack of facts is compounded and more given to risk if people are involved. First, their natural core preferences have

272

to be known, which the understanding of temperament provides and then we can still be blindsided by their choosing contrary to their natural inclinations. A brain does not operate with the consistency of a computer. It is much more open to creativity. All the facts always lie outside of our perceptions.

The word risk has been with us from antiquity because we had to have a word for this everyday challenge. Risk is involved when we refuse to hear or even when we do listen. Risk is involved when we face the unknown, which is all the time for creatures who cannot know the future. We have to learn to live with it, so we must learn to trust and walk by a faith that is big enough to lend us its peace.

Anxiety is the result of facing risk without trust. Trust your teen, but hold them to responsible action. Parent by the eternal wisdom of "Do to others as you would have them do to you," and explain to your teen that, that's how they are going to be able to best create their future — both immediate and in the years to come. Human advance is a struggle to remove the uncertainties and the effort will never end. Don't ever say, "I can never trust you." If that is true, no relationship with your child is ever possible because trust is an essential element of a meaningful relationship.

Parent with this being your consistent theme: that the way you treat people is a certain forecast of how you are asking them to treat you. Trust is to be responsibly demonstrated for more trust to be offered in return, or tightened freedom when trust has been spurned.

Partner with the "University of Hard, Soft, and Subtle Knocks" and become familiar with its curriculum or your teen will walk out into a world they have not experienced before and are not prepared for.

Parents Will Become a Q&A Service
When our child was a preteen, we operated much like a correctional officer. In the teenage years, we changed to a guidance officer, and now as they are given their legal freedoms at 18, we become more like a Q&A service. Whether they will use this service will depend on their self-

confidence, the nature of the parental bond, and the parade of emotions that accompany their moment of need. You may or may not be called upon.

You are there when needed and if consulted, be a consultant — not a commanding officer. If not consulted, don't be hurt. The choice of action has nothing to do with you. Instead, read the report their life gives you from the "University of Hard, Soft, and Subtle Knocks" and evaluate the needs so that you can offer whatever you think best.

Releasing the Teen
Strange that in a society in which we are being told a brain has not completed its development on the average until around 25 years of age, teens are granted the complete legal freedom of all adults at age 18. This does not calm the anxiety of the parent, nor does it aid the parental role. But life is living with what we cannot change and having the courage to change what we can. If you deem you cannot change it, then resolve to live in serenity with what is and resolve to trust and do the best you can. Future relationships can still be forged.

Perhaps of greatest concern for the parent is: have I, as a parent, done what I should have done to instill adequate values as a bulwark against life's temptations and deceits? The introspection is not healthy. We as parents face the future and can gain encouragement that we are still in the business of trying to model what we can for our children.

We have released the teen, but they are still enrolled in life's uncompromising university. Turn arounds are common as they continue to learn as adults. We parented in the first place, not for praise or pleasure but for the giving of our love, which found its true expression in our unconditional sacrifice. And here is the future: love, true love, never fails. We have talked of discipline and boundaries and the understanding of wisdom and knowledge and the path to good choices. We have not forgotten the love that underlies all these journeys and if allowed its full emergence, it will not be denied its supreme attempt at winning even the hardest heart.

Because you have proved your dedication in reading this book and seeking help and answers for the task of parenting, make the words of the next chapter your own.

A Final Prayer

We all pray at times, when control is no longer feasible and hope seems faint. As parents, we could pray...

- That our teen will become all that they were intentioned to be.
- That our peace of mind and heart will triumph over our own concerns.
- That our experience as parents will have matured us further as it has taxed us more than we realized when our child was born.
- That our teen will make good decisions and not only good ones, but the best.
- That many of the lessons we have sought to teach will have been well learned by us, the teachers, as well.
- That the meaning of life will be discovered by our children in a more rewarding way than we have learned it.
- That we will adjust to the empty nest and find the true fulfillment of our own lives.

I salute you, concerned parent. You are the true teachers and mentors of our world and to you the world itself owes an unpayable debt.

About the Author

Ray W. Lincoln is the author of several groundbreaking books, including *INNERKINETICS and* the Amazon bestseller, *I May Frustrate You, But I'm a Keeper,* and he is the founder of Ray W. Lincoln & Associates. Ray is a professional consultant and an expert in human nature. His 40 plus years of experience in speaking, teaching, and counseling began in New Zealand and have carried him professionally to Australia and the United States. He speaks with energy and enthusiasm before large and small audiences.

It was not by accident that he became the international speaker and consultant that he is today, guiding so many to a happier, healthier, more fulfilled life. Ray has studied extensively in the fields of Philosophy, Temperament Psychology, and Personology.

A member of the National Speakers Association, his expertise has been used as a lecturer and professor, teacher and keynote speaker, seminar presenter, counselor, and consultant. He teaches and leads in staff trainings, university student retreats, and parent education classes, as well as other seminars and training events. He also trains and mentors teachers, executives , and other professionals — all with the goal of understanding and appreciating our own temperaments and those of others. His writings and other products are used world wide.

Ray lives with his wife, Mary Jo, in Littleton, Colorado where they enjoy hiking, snowshoeing, fly fishing, and all the beauty the Rocky Mountains offer. Both are highly involved in their work (which they feel is the most important and most fulfilling work of their entire career lives), each filling the role for which they were designed, as they travel to speak to groups and to present seminars and workshops throughout the US.

www.raywlincoln.com, is a great place to order additional copies of:

- **I May Frustrate You, But I'm a Keeper**
- **INNERKINETICS**
- **A Journey Through Fear to Confidence**
- **Introduction to Faith and the Temperaments**
- **The InnerKinetics of Type**
- **Intelligently Emotional**
- **Your Child's Emotional World, Parts 1 and 2**
- **Break Free!**
- **I'm STILL A Keeper!**

We also have additional FREE resources to help you. On our website you can:

- Subscribe to our FREE monthly newsletter, which entitles you to receive 15% off all purchases at www.imakeeperkid.com , and www.raywlincoln.com by completing the form on the website or by texting RWL to 22828.
- Find more helpful resources and information about our services.

OUR SERVICES INCLUDE

Professional Consulting
Educational Seminars and Training
Keynote Addresses
Educational Materials
Free Monthly Newsletter
Membership Privileges

CPSIA information can be obtained
at www.ICGtesting.com
Printed in the USA
FSOW02n0440050316
17516FS